PUBLICATIONS OF THE McMASTER UNIVERSITY
ASSOCIATION FOR 18TH-CENTURY STUDIES

VOLUME ONE
THE VARIED PATTERN:
STUDIES IN THE 18TH CENTURY

VOLUME TWO
THE TRIUMPH OF CULTURE:
18TH CENTURY PERSPECTIVES

VOLUME THREE
CITY & SOCIETY IN THE 18TH CENTURY

City & Society in the 18th Century

EDITORS
PAUL FRITZ • DAVID WILLIAMS

HAKKERT
TORONTO
1973

LIBRARY
WAYNE STATE COLLEGE
WAYNE, NEBRASKA

Copyright © 1973 by
The McMaster University Association for 18th-Century Studies
All rights reserved

Set in Aldine Roman and Caslon Antique
by Hakkert, Toronto
Printed in Canada by The Hunter Rose Company

Cover: Frontispiece from
David Hughson, *A History and Description of London,
Westminster and Southwark*, Volume I, London.

Standard Book Number
88866-536-9
Library of Congress Catalogue Card Number
73-93037

Hakkert
554 Spadina Crescent
Toronto, Canada M5S 2J9

Contents

Preface
xi

List of Contributors
xii

Rousseau's Paris
Ronald Grimsley
3

*Some Aspects of London Life
in the Mid-18th Century*
James Clifford
19

Piranesi's Impressions of Rome
Alexander G. McKay
39

*Madrid & Spain, 1560-1860:
Patterns of Social & Economic Change*
David Ringrose
59

Community & Communication
Charles F. Mullett
77

The Enlightenment & Social Structures
Roger Emerson
99

Towards a Definition of the Scottish Enlightenment
Nicholas Phillipson
125

Music & the Court in the 18th Century
Paul Henry Lang
149

*Tobias Mayer (1723-1762):
A Case Study in the Interaction between
Cartography, Astronomy, & Navigation
During the 18th Century*
Eric Forbes
165

Newton's Principia as Whig Propaganda
George Grinnell
181

*The Encapsulated Landscape:
An Aspect of Gilpin's Picturesque*
Gerald Finley
193

*The Hope for Moral Regeneration in
French Educational Thought 1750-1789*
James Leith
215

Ideological Immigrants in Revolutionary America
Arthur Sheps
231

The Shadow of Edward Gibbon
Allan Evans
247

*A Genevan Reaction
to Diderot's Pensées philosophiques:
Jacques-François de Luc*
Douglas G. Creighton
259

Varieties of Infernal Experience:
Pope's Dunciad & Dante's Inferno
William Kinsley
281

Preface

Most of the articles contained in this volume were first presented at symposia and seminars sponsored by the McMaster Association for Eighteenth-Century Studies. As with the two previous volumes that have appeared in this series, the editors have grouped those papers they have selected for publication according to certain themes that will, it is hoped, encourage further debate and discussion. The initial papers focus on certain specific aspects relating to a number of metropolitan centres in the eighteenth century. The cities of Paris, London, Rome, Madrid and Edinburgh are among those cities singled out for special attention. The remaining papers have been chosen in order to illustrate a number of related themes in the area of eighteenth-century language, music, science and literature.

The editors wish to thank once again McMaster University for the encouragement and financial support given over the past year. They also wish to thank all those members of the Association who have given so generously of their time. Once again they are particularly indebted to Alan Samuel and the staff of A. M. Hakkert for their patience and efficiency in seeing this volume through the press.

Hamilton, 1973
                                                    P. S. F.
                                                    D. W.

Editors

Paul Fritz, Department of History, McMaster University
David Williams, Department of Romance Languages, McMaster University.

Contributors

James Clifford, Professor Emeritus, Columbia University.
Douglas Creighton, Department of French, University of Western Ontario.
Roger Emerson, Department of History, University of Western Ontario.
Allan Evans, Department of History, McMaster University.
Gerald Finley, Department of Fine Arts, Queen's University.
Eric Forbes, Department of History, University of Edinburgh.
Ronald Grimsley, Department of French, University of Bristol.
George Grinnell, Department of History, McMaster University.
William Kinsley, Department of English, University of Montreal.
James Leith, Department of History, Queen's University.
Paul Henry Lang, Professor Emeritus, Columbia University.
Alexander G. McKay, Department of Classics, McMaster University.
Charles F. Mullett, Department of History, University of Missouri.
Nicholas Phillipson, Department of History, Edinburgh University.
David Ringrose, Department of History, Rutgers University.
Arthur Sheps, Department of History, University of Toronto.

City & Society
in the 18th Century

Rousseau's Paris

This essay is not concerned with a reconstruction of the actual Paris of Rousseau's day, but with an attempt to evoke the city described in his writings — a city which, though related to a definite historical situation, owed a great deal to the influence of personal factors. At the same time it has to be recognized that although Rousseau's own experience undoubtedly helped to determine his attitude towards the capital, he had no intention of recording merely subjective impressions, for he came to see Paris as a symbol of much wider significance — as the outward sign of new influences which were profoundly affecting the development of modern society.

However far-reaching the implications of his description of Paris, it obviously owed a great deal to his own experience, and especially to his first two visits in 1731 and 1742, details of which are to be found in the *Confessions*. (Unfortunately there is now extant barely any correspondence by which we can confirm or modify the accuracy of his account, so that we have to bear in mind that the *Confessions* give only a retrospective view of this period of his life and are to some extent coloured by his later experience.) The purpose of his first journey to the capital was to enter the service of a Swiss colonel named Gaudard. Still young (he was only just nineteen), Rousseau had set off in high spirits, the journey constituting in his own words, "the happiest days of his life." His feelings and imagination were stimulated by the thought of the glorious career which lay ahead of him. Hope and excitement made him leap over possible obstacles and identify himself immediately with his "sweet day-dreams" and his newly-chosen military career. "J'allais m'attacher à un militaire et devenir militaire moi-même.... Je croyais déjà me voir en habit d'officier avec un beau plumet blanc. Mon coeur s'enflait à cette

---

1. All references, indicated only by volume and page numbers, are to the *Oeuvres Complètes de Jean-Jacques Rousseau*, ed. B. Gagnebin and M. Raymond, Vols I-IV, Paris 1959-69.

noble idée" (I, p. 158.)[1] He did not hesitate to imagine himself as "le Maréchal Rousseau" directing victorious battles, "au milieu du feu et de la fumée donnant tranquillement ses ordres, la lorgnette à la main." Yet significantly enough, as he passed through the countryside on his way to the capital, he could not help letting his heart be moved by the sight of nature and feeling regret for the life he was leaving behind; in the very midst of his military glory he believed that his heart was not made for so much "din" and, had he been free to do so, he would have remained with his quiet pastoral idyll. Although these two ideals — the heroic and the sentimental — represent two persistent and in some ways contradictory aspects of his personality and go back to his earliest years when he read Plutarch and seventeenth-century pastoral novels, they set him at odds with his immediate environment, drawing him away from its sordidness and limitations towards the world of his own untrammelled imagination. The heroic ideal made him look ahead to an as yet unrealized but perfect form of fulfilment, whilst the sentimental ideal impelled him to yearn for the lost happiness of the past. Whether he looked forward or backward, however, the everyday world tended to take the form of a dark, gloomy reality that constituted a direct antithesis to the idealistic aspirations of his inner being.

It is not surprising, therefore, that he should have received a sudden shock as he entered the outskirts of Paris for the first time. "Je m'étais figuré une ville aussi belle que grande, de l'aspect le plus imposant, où l'on ne voyait que de superbes rues, des palais de marbre et d'or" (I, p. 159). Instead of all this he perceived "de petites rues sales et puantes, de vilaines maisons noires, l'air de la malpropreté, de la pauvreté, des mendiants, des charretiers, des ravaudeuses, des crieuses de tisanes et de vieux chapeaux." So overwhelming was his first impression of sordidness and filth that he was never able to forget it. "Tel est le fruit d'une imagination trop active qui exagère par-dessus l'exagération des hommes, et voit toujours plus que ce qu'on lui dit." He adds: "Il est impossible aux hommes et difficile à la nature elle-même de passer en richesse mon imagination" (I, p. 160). Instead of finding, as he expected, a replica of ancient Babylon, he discovered a mean city that was the exact opposite of his dreams.

The personal experience following this first encounter with the capital did not do a great deal to alter his initial impression. At first he received so many promises and flattering words that "he believed his fortune to be made," but then learned that fine speeches were not followed by helpful actions, so that "this great interest which people had seemed to take in me" led to no tangible benefits; he soon concluded that the French were a polite, in their own way sincere, but superficial and fickle people. This ambitious young man, so eager to succeed and yet reluctant to solicit favours, left Paris feeling that he had been "flattered but not helped." Returning eagerly to the nature he loved so much, he began to lead a wandering life far from the capital: his rapturous account of this phase of his career shows that he was filled with a great sense of exhilaration and the expansive feeling of having "the whole of nature at his disposal." He was free and happy and felt that "a new paradise" was awaiting him (I, p. 163). Delivered from the irksome obstacles of everyday existence, he was able to plunge once more into "le pays des chimères, car il ne restait que cela devant moi" (I, p. 163). His first encounter with the capital thus represented a depressing, unhappy interlude between two idyllic phases of his life: it led him to reject the mediocre, stultifying reality of city-life as incompatible with the aspirations of an individual who had discovered the idealistic possibilities of his "original" nature.

Nevertheless, the persistence of Rousseau's ambitions inevitably drew him back to the city which had disappointed him so much. Eleven years later (in 1742), with his youth behind him and his hopes still unfulfilled, he knew that Paris was the only place which offered any hope of success to a man whose idealistic dreams did not exclude a longing for worldly glory. It will be recalled that on this second occasion he went armed with (in his own words) "a great discovery" — a new system of musical notation which he was confident would make his fortune. He was invited to explain this system to the Academy of Sciences, but when it failed to arouse more than polite interest and firm criticism, he was convinced that the judgment of academicians was no more trustworthy or intelligent than that of their social counterparts. Even so, this second visit to Paris eventually proved to Jean-Jacques that there was, after all, a brilliant side to Parisian life, both socially and intellectually (I, p. 282); for a time he was certainly attracted by this new way of life and strove hard for success and recognition. However, he was easily discouraged, as he admits, and "l'extrême besoin que j'avais qu'on pensât à moi était précisément ce qui m'ôtait le courage de me montrer" (I, p. 287). One part of his personality wanted desperately to succeed, but another pulled him back. The same ambivalence was apparent in his reactions to social life. Having had little experience of sophisticated society, he soon felt ill at ease, wanting to please, and yet remaining inhibited by awkwardness and tongue-tied silence. The mere fact that he had been seduced for a time by the brilliance of the capital was later to make him protest vehemently against its insidious influence; he eventually came to feel that the atmosphere of Paris was incompatible with the promptings of his deeper self. Even though he had been "shaken" and "disturbed" by this environment, he refused to believe that he had ever been inwardly "persuaded" or "convinced" by its pernicious attractions.

So great was his uneasiness that even after attaining literary fame, he decided to abandon the capital and renounce its pleasures; he undertook a physical and moral reform which led him back to the rural life he had always preferred. When in the last years of his life, he reflected upon this decision, he believed that a "great revolution" had taken place within him and that "another moral world" had opened up before him: by leaving Paris, he was freeing himself from the "mad judgments of men" (I, p. 1019). More important than the change in physical circumstances and "external things" was the "severe examination" to which he subjected his "inner life" and the subsequent realization that the satisfaction of his true self owed nothing to the "vainglory" he had so foolishly sought in his Parisian environment. Henceforth he proposed to find fulfilment in the seclusion of the countryside.

As his sole companion he took with him Thérèse Levasseur, the simple illiterate woman who would administer to his everyday needs. Yet Thérèse could not satisfy his inner longing — especially his desire for true companionship and intimacy — and his emotional life with her had been complicated by the birth of their illegitimate children; their liaison had been partly due to the disappointment of his hopes of glory and, to some extent, he could blame his own irresponsible attitude towards his children upon the capital with its many thousands of illegitimate children abandoned to Foundlings' Homes. Yet in his heart, he knew that this was not an adequate justification of his conduct, for he did not inwardly accept those contemporary values which allowed others to treat the problem in such a lighthearted way. Without insisting here upon the more detailed psychological aspects of Rousseau's view of this particular problem, it is already clear that his reactions to Parisian life were very ambivalent, a powerful aversion finally overcoming his initial fascination, and that even when he had left the capital, he continued to be disturbed by its effect upon his inner life.

This does not mean that the views of Paris contained in Rousseau's didactic writings were due solely to his own experience and constituted no more than a mere projection of his own emotions, but his personal feelings undoubtedly gave a depth and intensity to ideas which were also derived from a more reflective appraisal of the contemporary situation. This is already apparent in his first *Discours* which had attacked Parisian society while he was still living in its midst. After a few years in Paris, he was convinced that this great city represented enslavement and servitude. "L'homme civil naît, vit et meurt dans l'esclavage" (IV, p. 253). Instead of developing his own personality, he is "shackled by the institutions of his country." Particularly harmful is the way in which Parisian education hinders the proper development of human powers: not only are children prevented from exercising their bodies as they should, so that they become "petits, faibles, mal faits, vieillissent au lieu de grandir, comme la vigne à qui l'on fait porter du fruit au printemps languit et meurt avant l'automne" (IV, p. 496), but they are also subjected to a precocious stimulation of imagination and sexual appetite which prevents any healthy mental and psychological growth. The Parisians' values are merely those of their fellow-citizens – values imposed upon them by their corrupt environment and bearing no relation to their "natural needs."

This profound moral corruption is hidden from the superficial observer by the constant restlessness and agitation of Paris, where people are obsessed by an irresistible urge to be for ever changing their situation; they are tense, ambitious, always striving for their own advantage; in this respect they are typical of "l'esprit inquiet et remuant de ce siècle qui bouleverse tout à chaque génération" (IV, p. 252). The competitive, jungle-like spirit of the capital produces an enormous inequality of fortunes; there is a glaring contrast between "the most sumptuous elegance and the most deplorable destitution" (II, p. 232); the great gap between rich and poor is typical of a city where "men devour and sell one another" (IV, p. 831). "C'est toujours dans les capitales que le sang humain se vend à meilleur marché."

Two factors — social and economic — help to perpetuate this deplorable inequality. The first is the pervasive influence of the Court and aristocracy. Although the capital is obviously made up of various social classes, it is the aristocracy which sets the tone. There is a general contempt for the ordinary and commonplace; approval is given only to those things which please a special social group. The result is a rigid uniformity of manners which helps to explain the pattern to which Parisians conform from the very moment of birth, and the subsequent impossibility of their making any serious changes in the fixed order of social life. Even those who are excluded from the aristocracy let their lives be dominated by the values and attitudes of the higher social class. (Rousseau, it is true, also foresaw the end of that particular situation, but he did not think that this would come about through any gradual modification, but only through violent change: he pointed out that "the present order of society was liable to inevitable revolutions," since Europe was approaching "a state of crisis and the age of revolutions"; but until that climacteric moment arrived, he thought that there was unlikely to be any serious modification of the existing social structure.)

The economic consequence of the predominance of Paris concerned the distribution of the national wealth. Paris was "l'abîme des richesses," for it swallowed up a disproportionate amount of the nation's resources in unproductive activities. The prosperity of a great city like Paris was mainly artificial; "ce sont les grandes villes qui épuisent un Etat et font sa faiblesse; la richesse qu'elles produisent est une richesse apparente et illusoire, c'est beaucoup d'argent et peu d'effet" (IV, p. 851). Income from the provinces is diverted into the capital and never returns. France would certainly be more powerful if Paris did not exist. The excessive concentration of a large number of people in a single place is economically harmful to the State, because it draws the population away from the fertile areas of the countryside; agriculture, not commerce, ought to be, in Rousseau's view, the source of national wealth. "Or c'est la campagne qui fait le pays et c'est le peuple de la campagne qui fait la nation" (IV, p. 852).

It is scarcely necessary to insist here upon Rousseau's constant praise of the country and his equally persistent denigration of city-life, for this is one of the best known aspects of his philosophy. City and countryside, Paris and the provinces, symbolise for Rousseau the contrast between appearance and reality, "opinion" and "nature." The *Lettre à d'Alembert*, for example, stresses the authentic "genius" of the provinces when compared with the city. In the provinces, where there is less movement and less change of fortune and condition, we find the "simplicity of true genius."[2] There men are content to be themselves and feel no need to be constantly comparing themselves with others; in small towns we find "original" people who draw their resources from their own nature and not from some external source. All capital cities, on the other hand, seem alike. In them national character is destroyed (II, p. 242); the stifling influence of a "numerous cramped society" prevents the inhabitants of a large capital from having any individuality; those who live in Paris are not true "Parisians": they are simply like any other city-dwellers. "Paris et Londres ne sont à mes yeux que la même ville; toutes les capitales se ressemblent, tous les peuples s'y mêlent, tous les moeurs s'y confondent" (IV, p. 850). People become a mere "herd" bereft of all true humanity or personal knowledge of one another, as they are crowded together instead of being "scattered over the land which they ought to cultivate." Towns are like "ant-hills"; they are the "abyss of the human species," breeding "infirmities of the body as well as vices of the soul," deadly for their atmosphere which is pestilential in both the

---

2. *Lettre à d'Alembert*, ed. M. Fuchs, Geneva, 1948, p. 80.

physical and moral sense (IV, p. 276).

The feverish activity of a confined, over-populated city is a sign of serious physical and moral debilitation. Even the elaborate clothes and ever-changing fashions of the Parisians are little more than "base adornments" hiding misshapen bodies and corrupt souls. The general effect of urban life, as Rousseau so often insists, is a disastrous weakening of body and soul, a fatal loss of vigour, which contrasts so strikingly with the strength of ancient peoples. More especially, Rousseau likes to compare the brilliance and decadence of the Parisians with the "Teutonic roughness" of ancient times, as well as with the simplicity and innocence of primitive communities.

No doubt Rousseau had the contemporary situation in mind when in one of his last major didactic works — *Du Contrat social* — he pointed out how the real strength and support of the Roman Republic was to be found in those inhabitants who "lived in the fields and cultivated the land": the "simple hard-working life of the villagers" was much more beneficial to the Republic than the "idle and unmanly life of the burghers of Rome." "Les moeurs simples des premiers Romains, leur désintéressement, leur goût pour l'agriculture, leur mépris pour le commerce et pour l'ardeur du gain" were in striking contrast to "la dévorante avidité, l'esprit inquiet, l'intrigue, les déplacements continuels, les perpétuelles révolutions des fortunes" characteristic of urban society (III, p. 448). The modern situation is different from that of antiquity in so far as the insidious influence of Paris has led people to despise such simple strength and vigour, and to reject those very qualities which, in former times, gave both physical and moral support to the nation. If true citizens exist today, they are to be found only in the provinces, but alas! they do not live there in happy prosperity but are "dispersed in our abandoned countryside where they perish, poverty-stricken and despised." "Tel est l'état où sont réduits, tels sont les sentiments qu'obtiennent de nous ceux qui nous donnent du pain, et qui donnent du lait à nos enfants" (III, p. 26).

It is in Paris that a "natural man" — a man who, like Rousseau or the fictitious Emile, has spent his early life in a totally different environment — comes to realise the cumulative effect of urban life upon his personal being. It is in the city that he will be made conscious of (in a favourite modern term) his alienation from his original being; life in the capital does not mean a mere modification of particular aspects of human life, but a radical alteration of man's essential nature. As a striking sentence of *La Nouvelle Héloïse* puts it, "c'est le premier inconvénient des grandes villes que les hommes y deviennent autres que ce qu'ils sont et que la société leur donne, pour ainsi dire, un être différent du leur" (II, p. 273). *Emile* makes the same point in a rather different way, when Rousseau affirms that "nous n'existons plus où nous sommes, nous n'existons qu'où nous ne sommes pas" (IV, p. 308). Urban life makes men live outside themselves and prevents them from being real persons.

The way in which a sensitive man will be disconcerted, and perhaps demoralised, by his first encounter with Paris is clearly brought out in *La Nouvelle Héloïse*, where Rousseau is giving – through the letters of Saint-Preux – a retrospective account of his own reactions to the capital. The sense of inner desolation and loneliness is well illustrated by the reference to Paris as a "desert." There a man does not feel that he belongs to a true community. "La société y est si générale et si mêlée qu'il ne reste plus d'asile pour la retraite et qu'on est en public jusques chez soi" (IV, p. 739). There is no personal relationship, no true intimacy. "A force de vivre avec tout le monde on n'a plus de famille, à peine connaît-on ses parents; on les voit en étrangers, et la simplicité des mœurs domestiques s'éteint avec la douce familiarité qui en faisait le charme" (ibid.). Saint-Preux experiences an acute loneliness in the "silence" of this "desert" – an inner sense of personal desolation which, paradoxically enough, is created by the noise and din of a bustling city-life.

The description of Paris in *La Nouvelle Héloïse* takes up a point that dominates all Rousseau's reflections on the subject: Saint-Preux is immediately struck by the essential contradiction between appearance and reality; what counts in the capital is outward show, not inner feeling; Saint-Preux is conscious of a merely external politeness and false demonstrations of courtesy which bear no resemblance to "the simple touching effusion of a frank soul." In Paris "a man does not dare to be himself." Rousseau illustrates his point by using the image of the mask: Paris is a city where nature is hidden, where natural feelings give way to selfish demands. Nobody says what he really thinks, for the main purpose of people's speech and actions is to produce a favourable effect upon others; secretly they seek to advance their own cause and use language and gestures as the "mask of self-interest." Urbanity is but a way of deceiving others into thinking that we are well-disposed towards them, whereas our real purpose is to take advantage of them, and to use them for our own ends. "Chacun feignant de travailler à la fortune ou à la réputation des autres, ne cherche qu'à élever la sienne au-dessus d'eux et à leur dépens" (II, p. 969).

Yet in a city where nothing is stable, this mask has constantly to be changed. Since everybody is manoeuvring to secure his own advantage, he has to be constantly adapting himself to new situations; as he moves from one social group to another, he must behave in a way calculated to obtain favour in each. It is necessary for him "to leave his soul at the door" and don and doff attitudes "as a lackey does his livery" (II, p. 234). There are no firm principles capable of guiding his conduct, because there is no moral stability, no genuine personal intercourse, only "a vain appearance of feelings which change at every moment" (II, p. 236).

Language thus becomes of paramount importance in a city like Paris, whose society is dominated by a certain "jargon" understood only by the initiates. Speech is turned into "pure verbiage" (II, p. 255). "Tout n'est ici que babil, jargon, propos sans conséquence" (II, p. 254). It is a question of saying fine things rather than of doing good actions. Once again everything is governed by appearances. Each person's object is to "shine," to dazzle others by his wit and thoughts; he does not seek to be natural but only to please. This is because the real motive behind people's behaviour is vanity: they seek only to secure the approbation of others. Inevitably language becomes the instrument of a subtlety and refinement which are made to serve unworthy ends and are cultivated at the expense of moral values. This secret and persistent self-seeking through the clever exploitation of language and reason is particularly evident in Parisian intellectuals and writers, whose sophisticated subtlety has no connection with the love of truth, but is actually opposed to it; these fine word-spinners and subtle reasoners merely encourage the spread of falsehood or ignorance. Once again Rousseau makes plain the opposition between intellect and virtue, fine speeches and good actions. Intellectual, social and linguistic brilliance all serve the cause of self-glorification; every man wants to be distinguished from others. That is why each philosopher's vanity impels him to construct a system whose main characteristic is to be different from all the rest.

These various factors are simply the outward expression of the fundamental cause of most modern evils — the reversal of natural relationships. As Saint-Preux says of Paris, "il semble que tout l'ordre des sentiments naturels soit ici renversé" (II, pp. 270-1). The same idea is also stressed in the *Lettre à d'Alembert*, which is not simply an indictment of the theatre but of the unnatural and corrupt city which has produced it. As is well known, Rousseau insists that the theatre can exert no formative influence on the citizens' life, for it simply expresses their desires and feelings; it is always an effect, never a cause, for it flatters and embellishes existing inclinations and manners and never goes against current taste; more especially, it seeks to please by encouraging emotions and passions at the expense of reason and virtue. True entertainment, on the other hand, like work itself, should be derived directly from man's authentic nature; it should be a part of his natural life, expressing the personal relationships involved in his everyday activities. The theatre, however, runs counter to this; the man who sits there with a crowd of others is merely isolating himself from them, for his whole attention is directed upon the stage; as he allows himself to be transported into the realm of fantasy and imagination, he forgets the realities of life. The theatre is a "dark cavern" which restricts a man's life, and shuts him off from communication with other people. As such, it reflects the anonymity and impersonality already seen to be typical of large capitals. Moreover, the artificiality of the French theatre is revealed by the precedence given to speeches over actions. This is what the Parisian audience, accustomed to words rather than deeds, really wants, so that Racine and Corneille, geniuses though they are, present only "talkers" on the stage. Moreover, the personal attitude of theatre-goers is also typical of Parisians, who go to the theatre in order to be seen rather than to enjoy what is presented on the stage; their interest remains peripheral to the plays themselves, for they are more concerned with the actor as an individual rather than with the character he is supposed to portray.

In a still more striking respect the theatre brings out the "reprehensible reversal of natural relations" characteristic of large cities. By attaching supreme importance to the subject of love, it thrusts forward women to prominence and power and so confirms the ascendancy they have already achieved in social life. Parisian women, for example, not only set themselves up as arbiters of literary taste, but they are also self-assertive and dogmatic. It is women, not men, who are alleged to "know everything." Rousseau was convinced that woman's most fundamental characteristic was her modesty and *pudeur*, and that she was meant by nature to lead a "retired domestic life." In large towns, on the other hand, modesty is treated as "ignoble and base"; "c'est la seule chose dont une femme bien élevée aurait honte" (*Lettre à d'Alembert*, pp. 115-6). In the *salons*, women are transformed into idols before whom men must bend an adoring knee. Yet this homage paid by men to women is not a token of genuine respect. Men, in fact, despise women while obeying them and "insult and mock them with their very compliments": women are "flattered without being loved, served without being honoured" (pp. 139-40).

Paris, like any other great city, encourages all this by the indiscriminate mingling of the sexes. Whereas the ancients, as well as the modern Genevans, believed in the separation of the sexes, allowing each to follow its appropriate mode of existence, modern Paris not only refuses to admit any distinction between the sexes, but actually tries to reverse their natural roles. To the unnatural life of the *salons* Rousseau opposes the Genevan custom of letting men and women have their own separate social life: men meet together in their *cercles* where they enjoy their own particular pleasures, whilst women take part in *sociétés* with activities more appropriate to their taste. Such pastimes have "quelque chose de simple et d'innocent qui convient à des moeurs républicaines" (p. 133).

This reversal of natural roles in Paris, though appearing to give women complete superiority, allows them no personal reality. Their behaviour is determined by what others expect of them; they do not exist in their own right but only as the objects of another person's "look." In a strikingly modern sentence, Saint-Preux observes that women "tirent des regards d'autrui la seule existence dont elles se soucient" (II, p. 273). When you meet a woman in some public place, you do not find a Parisian but "a mere semblance of fashion" — an artificial being completely moulded by her environment; she is no way different from others in gait, figure, manners, speech; "rien de tout cela n'est à elle, et si vous la voyiez dans son état naturel, vous ne pourriez la reconnaître" (ibid).

Yet another sign of this reversal of natural relationships is the precedence given to the young over the old. In Parisian social life "impudent youth" adopts "a conceited, vain air" and an unyielding, peremptory tone, while "les anciens, craintifs et modestes, ou n'osent ouvrir la bouche, ou sont à peine écoutés" (*Lettre à d'Alembert*, p. 67). So pervasive is the influence of self-assertive youth that old men are to be seen imitating the young in their pathetic efforts to obtain women's attention: they would much rather be tolerated "by the help of their absurdities" than be completely ignored. Characteristically, the theatre merely serves to reinforce this trend by giving old men subordinate, hateful or ridiculous roles.

In view of all this, it is not surprising that Emile, in spite of a brief sojourn in Paris, will not remain there any longer than necessary. When the time comes for him to seek a wife, he will certainly not look for her amongst the Parisians! The fourth book of *Emile* ends with a joyous farewell to Paris: "Ville célèbre, ville de bruit, de fumée et de boue où les femmes ne croient plus à l'honneur ni les hommes à la vertu. Adieu, Paris; nous cherchons l'amour, le bonheur, l'innocence; nous ne serons jamais assez loin de toi" (IV, p. 691). Emile will look back upon the days spent in Paris with a "disdainful eye." This city of "chatter" will never be the centre of his life, or the place where he will seek his life's companion (IV, p. 770). Too long a stay in the capital would merely serve to deprave him, and make him despise the natural values and feelings which should be the basis of his happiness.

At first sight, therefore, Rousseau's description of Paris seems to be one of unrelieved gloom and to present an extremely pessimistic view of human nature — a stark antithesis between good and evil, with the latter being an indissoluble aspect of urban life. A closer view, however, reveals that this contrast is not quite as absolute as Rousseau at first seems to suggest. It will be recalled that Jean-Jacques himself was both attracted to and repelled by Parisian life, and could never completely overcome a certain ambivalence of attitude. In spite of the severe strictures of the first *Discours*, it is worth noting that the work begins by describing the attractive aspects of social life; Rousseau speaks of the "delicate, fine taste," the urbanity of manners, the "unpedantic, philosophical tone" of the Parisians, the "natural yet prepossessing manners" of an environment which also offers the possibility of "sound studies," and gives people a chance to perfect themselves through "the intercourse of society."

Moreover, Rousseau acknowledges that Emile's education cannot be completed without some acquaintance with Paris, for it is only there that he will find the means of developing good taste. Although it is inferior to the basic impulse of genius in so far as it is "l'art de se connaître en petites choses" (IV, p. 677), taste requires intelligence and perspicacity, and "c'est l'esprit des sociétés qui développe une tête pensante ... Si vous avez une étincelle de génie, allez passer une année à Paris. Bientôt vous serez tout ce que vous pouvez être, ou vous ne serez jamais rien" (IV. p. 674). Paradoxically, it is necessary to go to the very source of bad taste in order to acquire the capacity for acquiring a good one! Whatever we may think of modern literature, Rousseau points out that all important contemporary authors have been formed by or had some contact with Paris. The reason for this is that the instrument of taste is quite different from its moral origin. The problem, therefore, is to use city-life in a way that helps us to acquire a refined taste without corrupting our morals. Even the theatre, which elsewhere Rousseau castigates so fiercely for being morally pernicious, has its role in the formation of taste, and

Emile's tutor does not hesitate to take him there. Modern man's error is to have let his taste become corrupted through excessive delicacy and refinement; he has become so "subtle" (always a pejorative term in Rousseau's vocabulary) that he has lost contact with the source of genuine beauty.

It is important to remember that, in Rousseau's view, the ultimate basis of taste cannot be acquired, for it originates in sensibility, which means that, though it exists in all men, it does so in varying degrees. Nevertheless, he also insists that the formation of a man's sensibility depends on various factors, and especially on his social environment; to develop sound judgment and sharpen his critical powers he has to know many societies and many different kinds of people. Moreover, it is only in societies with the time for amusement and leisure (in other words, in societies having a certain standard of wealth and luxury) that taste can be effectively cultivated. Admittedly, excessive luxury and extreme social inequality will merely stifle taste through "the tyranny of opinion," while the vanity of social life will also be harmful to true taste by encouraging men to distinguish themselves from others instead of persuading them to seek what is pleasing in its own right; great luxury makes them love what is "difficult and costly," so that "le prétendu beau, loin d'imiter la nature, n'est tel qu'à force de la contrarier" (IV, p. 673). Notwithstanding these grave dangers, Paris is the only place in France where a young person will find conditions that will help him to acquire good taste.

If a young man will rightly seek to develop his taste through contact with Paris, he will also have to realise that its source has been poisoned by city-life, and that the modern world is far from the simplicity of nature which "goes to the heart." Rousseau affirms that it is only in the writings of the ancients that authentic natural genius is still discernible. Valid models of taste, therefore, must be sought among the ancients and not the moderns, for in Paris we are far from "the happy simplicity of their ways," and find only "vices adorned with the fine name of talents." In the long run, any benefits conferred by Parisian life will be far outweighed by the disadvantages, and that is why Emile's sojourn there must be as brief as possible. It is only through abandoning the large towns and seeking the peaceful seclusion of the provinces that people will be able to escape from a "horrible corruption" (IV, p. 853).

Paris, then, for Rousseau, was more than a large city: since it represented some of the worst evils of modern society, it was the absolute antithesis of those natural values which, in Rousseau's opinion, provided the indispensable basis of man's true happiness. It is not surprising, therefore, to find him directing his thoughts away from the capital towards a completely different mode of existence; the image of the vast featureless "desert" of Parisian life gives way to the vision of a self-sufficient "island" – of an intimate community that relies for its survival on the moral strength and active participation of all its members. This means that, in spite of his deep aversion to Paris with its thousands of anonymous inhabitants, Rousseau did not urge his fellow-men to retire into solitude – and, in this respect, he believed his own personal existence to be exceptional – for, as he put it in one of his last works, "notre plus douce existence est relative et collective, et notre vrai moi n'est pas tout entier en nous. Enfin, telle est la constitution de l'homme en cette vie qu'on n'y parvient jamais à bien jouir de soi sans le concours d'autrui" (I, p. 813). Consequently, the evils of large towns should not drive a man into desperate isolation, but should spur him on to fashion for himself a social life closer to the needs of his original, but as yet unfulfilled, nature.

Ronald Grimsley

Some Aspects of London Life in the Mid-18th Century

Perhaps the title of this essay should be "The Other Side of the Enlightenment," for what I shall be stressing are aspects of city existence usually ignored by those who write about the eighteenth century. For the most part we tend to emphasize historical or intellectual matters — the rise of free thinking and attacks on traditional religious beliefs, the gradual shift from strict classical imitation to more free personal creativity, the empirical rise of science. Not that the *philosophes* were unaware of the practical problems of everyday living. In the *Encyclopédie* there are numerous pictures of water pumps and mechanical devices of all kinds. But concentration was chiefly on ideas and new concepts.

In contrast I shall stress various ordinary details of everyday living for an average Londoner in the mid-eighteenth century. What was it like to spend a day in the Fleet Street area? What were his personal concerns? What dangers were always hanging over his head? How did his existence compare with ours in a big city today?

Throughout, as my chief example, I shall use Samuel Johnson, who has been my major interest for many years, and particularly I will concentrate on his middle years — from 1749, where I left him in my *Young Sam Johnson*, until he met Boswell in Tom Davies' back parlor in 1763. These were the central, most productive years of Johnson's life — when he completed the *Dictionary*, wrote the *Rambler*, the *Idler*, *Rasselas*, and others of his most representative works. Boswell in the *Life* has much to say about these works, but little about Johnson's everyday existence. What was he doing most of the time? Boswell did not know. He had to rely for details about these years on what information he could draw out of other friends of Johnson who were still alive when the *Life* was being written. Consequently there are large gaps. Boswell very wisely concentrated on the later years for

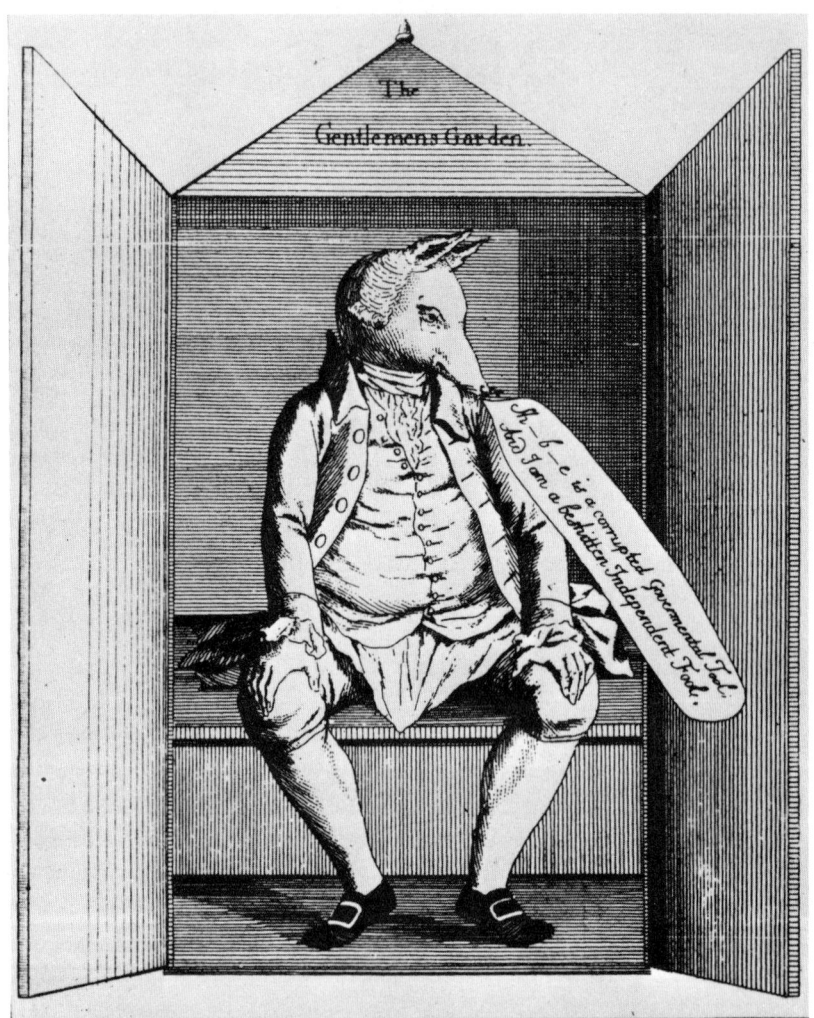

which he had much more reliable information. Some of the earlier gaps I hope to be able to fill from material not available to Boswell — newly discovered letters, public records, newspaper items, and various other sources.

In attempting to describe a person in another age the biographer must somehow try to imagine what life would have been like. He must create for the reader his version of the life-pattern of his subject. At least that is my conviction, though I realize that many great biographers in the past have ignored details of this sort, and have preferred to concentrate wholly on personal relationships and intellectual concerns. These are what made up a large part of diaries and correspondences. For example, it is almost impossible to find out where the subject washed his hands or took a bath, or evacuated — or who did the marketing for food, or how the streets were lighted near his home — or a thousand other minor details of this kind which we today take for granted, as did the men and women of other periods. Yet it is quite possible that physical details of this sort had great influence on the subject's mood when making important decisions, and on his health at all times. If, then, it is at all possible to discover the facts, they should be included in any full-length life study. To be sure, many readers may object that such matters as plumbing and lighting are really unimportant. To which I would reply that in some instances they may be more important than merely listing a person's social engagements year after year, if they follow a monotonous pattern. Many recent biographies of modern writers, such as Mark Schorer's *Sinclair Lewis*, John Unterecker's *Hart Crane*, and Carlos Baker's *Hemingway*,[1] have been severely criticised for giving too many chronological details. We would have welcomed instead more homely facts about everyday routines.

The trouble is that it is so hard to find out the facts. Nobody in the eighteenth century mentions just where he washes his hands, just as few people today would put this in a letter, or even a telephone call. When I try to find out about the plumbing facilities in Johnson's house in Gough Square off Fleet Street in

---

1. For further discussion see my *From Puzzles to Portraits: Problems of a Literary Biographer*, 1970, pp. 114-18.

1750 I am up against a blank wall. There never seem to be any references such as "Why, Sir, my water pitcher was smashed this morning and I had to borrow Tetty's from the second floor." Or "The maid hasn't emptied my chamber pot for days." Nor can I find anywhere details describing how such matters were accomplished.

As an example, when Samuel Johnson washed his face what facilities did he have? Where did the water come from, and where did the dirty water go? When he took a bath, if he ever did, where was the tub – in his bedroom, or in the basement near the large fireplace in the kitchen? Again, what happened to the dirty water? I can find no references to such matters in any surviving records. Thus all we can do is guess, using what general evidence has been assembled as to the normal customs of the day.

I might begin with the matter of plumbing. In 1750 at 17 Gough Square, where Johnson was living with his wife, Tetty, there were certainly no bathrooms, and probably no running water. No ordinary London house at that time had a separate bathroom, and hardly any nobleman's. In France there may have been more. Artists there delighted in picturing ladies in their baths, but not in England.[2] As Oliver Brackett, writing in *Johnson's England*, puts it: "On the whole there is a curious reticence on this subject in the domestic history of England in the eighteenth century. The writers of the time, whether through modesty or lack of interest, have no comments to make either on the subject of washing or the bathroom."[3]

We today are so used to bathrooms that it is difficult to imagine a fairly large house without a permanent tub of some kind, or a shower. And we assume any decent citizen would have running water in a basin. But not Samuel Johnson! When he washed it was undoubtedly in a china bowl, with water from a nearby pitcher – just as did our own forefathers until very recently. But where did the water come from? And where did it go? These are not easy questions to answer. By the mid-eighteenth century most houses on major streets did have leaden pipes

---

2. Oliver Brackett, "The Interior of the House," *Johnson's England*, ed. A. S. Turberville, 1933, II, pp. 130-31.

3. *Ibid.*

bearing water from conduits coming into the basement or kitchen, but the water was turned on for short periods only three times a week.[4] Thus the householder had to have a cistern or tank in the basement where water could be stored. For those without pipes the contents could be replenished from rain through gutters on the roof, or by bucket from a nearby parish pump. And there were water carriers in most parts of London.[5] Since Johnson did not live directly on a major street, it is unlikely that he had any pipes from the outside. In any event, water had to be carried upstairs by servants in pitchers or buckets. The difficulty of securing large amounts of water may be one obvious explanation of the infrequency of bathing and the small size of the portable tubs. Since this must have been a constant difficulty it is a bit strange that there are practically no surviving comments in letters or diaries concerning water problems, no casual remarks about being out of water and being unable to take a bath, or about the fact that the water carrier had not come and a maid had been sent out to the pump. Everyone appears to have assumed that such matters needed no comment.

What happened to the dirty water no one can tell. And even more difficult is the matter of what became of the contents of chamber pots. Those familiar with Hogarth's prints would say that they were thrown out the window.[6] This may have often occurred in poorer sections of the city, but I doubt that it was common practice in Gough Square. Trevelyan provides a colorful description of an early morning in Edinburgh in the early eighteenth century, when the contents of close stools were thrown into the street from windows four or five stories high.[7] It was good manners for those up above to cry "Gardy-loo" (Gardez l'eau) before throwing, and this may have been the origin of the term "loo" used for receptacles of this sort. (There are many other theories for the origin of the term, I might add.) Those walking

---

4. See Dorothy George, *London Life in the Eighteenth Century*, 1925, p. 103, and Lawrence Wright, *Clean and Decent: the Fascinating History of the Bathroom & the Water Closet*, 1960, pp. 62-63, 93-94.

5. Sir D'Arcy Power, "Medicine," *Johnson's England*, 1933, II, p. 277.

6. "Night" from "The Four Times of the Day," 1738.

7. G. M. Trevelyan, *English Social History*, 1942, pp. 437-38; cited in *Clean and Decent, op. cit.*, p. 76.

below would yell up "Haud yer han" with other expletives, but it was a dangerous business. All pedestrians were advised to keep in the middle of the street. The ordure thus cast out into the streets was supposed to be cleaned away by scavengers and other workers but sometimes remained for some time, increasing the stench and the difficulty of walking.

There is no doubt that this practice of throwing waste materials out the window did sometimes occur in London, and was not merely a Scottish practice. In 1721 the Grand Jury of the City of London warned constables and watchmen of the "quantities of soil cast into the streets in the night time," and in 1755 in Marylebone there was a local act forbidding "night soil" to be thrown in or near the streets.[8] But by this time it is my conviction that most decent households took care of the problem in other ways.

Swift's advice to chamber maids to empty pots out of the window was obviously meant as satire, recommending the exact opposite of what he thought proper.[9] And his suggestion that maids should never empty chamber pots until they were quite full, and should carry the utensil openly down the front stairs where all could see and smell, is similarly meant to shock.

In most houses off the main streets, in courts or side alleys, there would have been no open sewers or sewer pipes entering the houses. When a law-abiding citizen had to obey the calls of nature he did so in various ways. As we have seen, there were no water closets which could be flushed out into waste pipes. Most London houses apparently had a privy, or "place of convenience," in the back yard, sometimes called a "Jericho," or "jakes," or "house of easement," which stood apart at the bottom of the garden over a cesspit dug in the ground.[10]

Apparently Sir Joshua Reynolds at his house in Leicester Fields had an outside privy, and because he hated to waste time

---

8. Dorothy George, *op. cit.*, pp. 352-53. John Gwynn, in his *Essay on Improvements*, 1750, listed ordure lying in the streets as one of the worst nuisances of the day. See George Rudé, *Hanoverian London, 1714-1808*, 1971, p. 135.

9. "Directions to Servants," *Prose Writings of Jonathan Swift*, ed. Herbert Davis, Vol. XIII, 1959, pp. 53, 60-61.

10. Marjorie and C. B. Quennell, *A History of Everyday Things in England*, 1933, III, pp. 90-91.

going to and fro he built a private staircase at the back of the house leading from his studio to the garden. James Northcote later described to Benjamin Haydon how in the course of a day one could hear Reynolds "dart down and up again striding over 5 or 6 stairs at a time — anxious not to lose a moment."[11]

For houses with no back yards, where structures abutted each other, the cesspits were dug directly under the basement floor, and it was here that the waste products would have been thrown. Certainly there would have been a cesspit under or near almost every separate house in the city.

Pepys, who lived in a row house which shared a common wall and a common roof with others in the row, had his "house of office," where members of the family could do their business, in the cellar. Unfortunately, the basements did not always have effective walls separating one house from another, and sometimes the contents of full vaults would spill over into the neighboring cellar.[12] Conditions in many houses a century later undoubtedly were much the same.

It was customary to have the vaults, or cesspits, periodically cleaned out, and there were special workmen called "Night Men" who came with their wagons at night to do the job. Unfortunately, the contents usually had to be carried in buckets through the house, not a very sanitary or fragrant procedure! In the Guildhall Library and elsewhere there are a number of eighteenth-century business cards of "Night Men," advertising their availability and experience. Joseph Waller, for example, a chimney sweeper and Nightman from Islington, advertised that he "keeps Carts and Horses for emptying Bog-Houses, Drains and Cesspools with the utmost expedition." Henry Hastings — "Nightman & Poleman" for the city and suburbs, in a very ornate, rococo advertisement claimed that he "Decently performs what He undertakes being always at the work himself — Empties Vaults . . . Sespools, unstops

---

11. I owe this information to Professor F. W. Hilles, who has sent me a copy of Haydon's marginal comments made in Vol. I of the *Works of Sir Joshua Reynolds*, 3d ed., 1801, xcviii ff. This was Haydon's copy and is now in Hilles's collection. See Hilles, "Reynolds among the Romantics," *Literary Theory and Structure: Essays in Honor of William K. Wimsatt*, ed. F. Brady, J. Palmer and M. Price, 1973, pp. 267-83.

12. *The Diary of Samuel Pepys*, ed. Robert Latham and William Matthews, 1970–, I, p. 269 (20 Oct. 1660); p. 304 (29 Nov.).

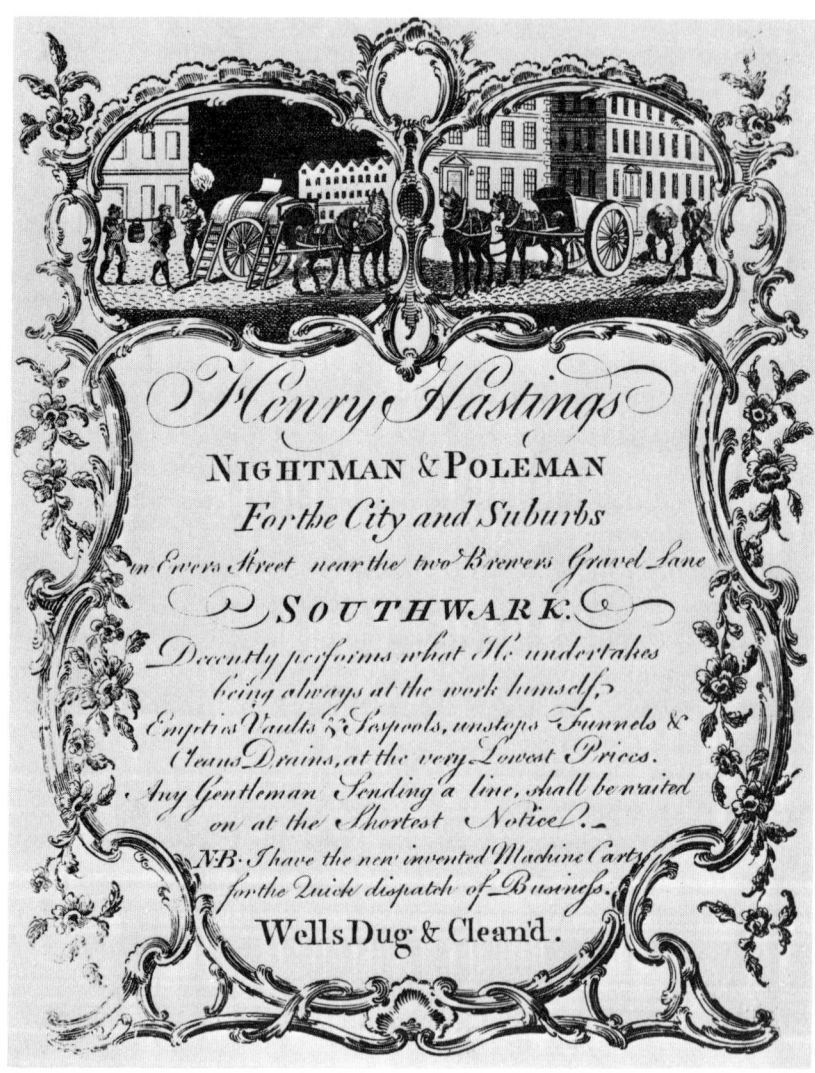

Funnels & Cleans Drains, at the very Lowest Prices." And William Woodward advertised that he "keeps Carts & Horses to Empty Privies, Drains & Cesspools, at the Shortest Notice & on the most Reasonable Terms."[13]

Being a "Night Man" must have required a particularly limited sense of smell, and the work also at times had its dangers. On Thursday, 5 July 1753, while emptying the vault of a public house in Southwark called "Tumble-down Dick," some of the workers were completely overcome. The *Gentleman's Magazine* later described what happened:

> The first man that went down, overcome by the stench, call'd out for help, and immediately fell down on his face; a second went to help him, and fell down also; then a third, and fourth went down, when these two were obliged to come up again directly: and the stench of the place being by this time greatly abated, they got out the two that went down first; but the second was dead, and the first had so little life in him, that he died in the afternoon.[14]

At first the ordure which was carried away in wagons was used by farmers as fertilizer, but as the city grew and the distance to farms became too great it was dumped into the Thames or into covered ditches.[15]

Unfortunately at Johnson's house in Gough Square, now a museum, there is no evidence to show where the privy, or close stool, or Jericho, stood, or where the cesspool was located.[16] The most one can do is speculate. The privy, or earth closet, might have been outside the house near where the present caretaker's

---

13. Wright, *op cit.*, pp. 145, 147. Also Ambrose Heal, *London Tradesmen's Cards of the XVIII Century*, 1925, No. lxvii.

14. *Gent. Mag.* 23, July 1753, p. 341.

15. In Japan during the nineteenth century privies were emptied regularly by men who had regular routes. The importance to farmers of what they collected for the enrichment of their soil was so great that if three persons occupied a room together the sewage paid the rent of one; if five occupied the same room no rent was charged. Edward S. Morse, *Japanese Homes and Their Surroundings*, 1886; reprinted 1961, pp. 231-32.

16. From a letter of Margaret Eliot, present custodian of the house, 16 August 1972, quoting Phyllis Rowell her predecessor. The suggestion made in *The Good Loo Guide; Where to Go in London*, compiled by Jonathan Routh, 1965, p. 32, that Johnson had a loo in a second-floor hallway window seat cannot be proved.

house is, or it might have been in the basement where the stairs come down from the ground floor. There may have been a seat right by the stairs, or there may have been other seats on the upper floors. There were no permanent built-in closets in the house. All they would have had would have been movable pieces of furniture, with screens to insure some degree of privacy. As a later expert described the situation, "any dark hole, corner, cupboard, place or recess next a living room or bedroom" was considered a fit place to hide a "close stool."[17] Of course, having one easily available in the main rooms of the house did on occasions result in some embarrassing moments, as when Pepys came home and surprised Lady Sandwich, who had come to see him, "doing something upon the pott" in his dining room.[18]

There must have been chamber pots easily available in all upper bedrooms, usually sitting under the bed. As readers of Smollett's *Peregrine Pickle* will remember, these were normally used during the night and were emptied the next morning by maids and footmen. Peregrine, as a joke, bored holes in his Aunt's pot with disastrous results.[19] Presumably the contents of the pots, if not thrown surreptitiously out the window, were carried down and emptied into the cesspit. In some better homes there may have been large drain pipes leading directly into the pit in the basement into which waste material could be emptied.

If for some reason, perhaps the inefficiency of the maid, there was no pot under one's bed, a person might be in real trouble. On one bitter cold morning when Pepys needed badly to urinate, and there was no receptacle in the room, he relieved himself in the fireplace.[20] Apparently the chimney was a frequent substitute. Paved with bricks, it would not have retained the odor as long as boards, and a roaring fire would soon clean out the mess.

To be sure, in most fine houses there may have been parts of upstairs rooms curtained off, or completely screened, which served as places where ladies could retire. Unfortunately, all this has disappeared. But one can still see pieces of eighteenth-century

---

17. S. Stevens Hellyer, *The Plumber and Sanitary Houses*, 1877, p. 2.
18. *Pepys Diary, op. cit.*, V, p. 129 (21 April 1664).
19. Tobias Smollett, *Peregrine Pickle*, 1st edition, ed. J. L. Clifford, 1964, p. 65.
20. *Pepys Diary*, V, p. 357 (28 Dec. 1664); VI, p. 244 (28 Sept. 1665).

furniture which show what was the usual practice. In some large dining room sideboards there are lower doors designed for pots, with additional back openings so that maids and liverymen could empty them without being seen.[21] I have often wondered whether the major reason for the separation of males and females after dinner — so accepted as part of social behaviour in the eighteenth century, and today as well — originated from physical necessity. There were no bathrooms, and the men relieved themselves in the dining room, pots being readily available from the sideboards, while the ladies went off to commodes in other parts of the house. It is unlikely that some were forced to go outside or down into the basement to privies. With traditional delicacy, hardly anyone thought fit to describe exactly what went on, but at least two foreign visitors were shocked. The Duc de la Rochefoucauld, in describing one dinner he attended in London, commented: "The sideboard too is furnished with a number of chamber pots and it is a common practice to relieve oneself whilst the rest are drinking; one has no kind of concealment and the practice strikes me as most indecent."[22]

And another French visitor, Pierre-Jean Grosley, referring to what happened after dinner in London in 1765, wrote: "the women having retired, and the room being furnished with a certain necessary utensil, they [the men] lean upon the table with their elbows, drink about, and settle the affairs of the nation."[23]

Yet one wonders whether the practice on the Continent was essentially so different. Certainly human needs were the same. Nancy Mitford describes one practice which developed at Versailles during the seventeenth century, where church services tended to be very long, and "women who were not certain of being able to hold out for the necessary hours used to arrive at the

---

21. Sometimes there were secret recesses in the walls where pots could be hidden. One was found recently when restoring a house in St. George Square, Edinburgh, built about 1740. After extensive inquiries I have not been able to locate a picture of an 18th-century sideboard, with an open door showing where the chamber pots were left.

22. *A Frenchman in England 1784*, translated by S. C. Roberts, 1933, pp. 30-31. See also W. S. Lewis, *Three Tours Through England in the Years 1748, 1776, 1797*, 1941, p. 60.

23. Pierre J. Grosley, *A Tour To London*, translated by Thomas Nugent, 1772, I, p. 151.

chapel with a small china receptacle which they concealed under their skirts and which was called a Bourdalou."[24]

In the inventory of the belongings of d'Alembert, after his death, were two chamber pots and a bidet, as well as some other crockery items, as to whose use we can only guess.[25] They are described as a chair for cleanliness on its wooden base, an armchair of convenience covered with cane, and a bucket to wash his feet. These were all found in a "cabinet servant de garderobbe." Moreover, in the bottom of d'Alembert's buffet was a chamber pot and a syringe in a case, probably used for enemas. All these in the dining room!

Naturally there was a wide variation in the decoration and arrangements for outside privies and Jerichos, and for close stools and inside commodes. When Johnson and Boswell were in the Hebrides in 1773, on the island of Coll, they talked about "little-houses" and the fact that at the new castle, just as at Raasay, there was none included in the new building, though there had been one in the old castle.[26] This led to further discussion of what happened to a person on a privy seat. Johnson said that "if ever a man thinks at all, it is there. He generally thinks then with great intentness. He sets himself down as quite alone, in the first place." When Boswell insisted that a man is "always happy" under these circumstances, Johnson refused to agree. And when Boswell described an elegant quilted seat he had seen at the Dutch Ambassador's in Paris, Johnson insisted "Sir, that is Dutch; quilted seats retain a bad smell. No, sir, there is nothing so good as the plain board." Thus I think we may assume that somewhere at Gough Square Johnson had what we used to call a "one-holer" with a plain board.

How people occupy their minds at such times obviously lies outside the scope of this essay, but it might be pointed out that

---

24. Nancy Mitford, *The Sun King*, 1966, p. 71. Louis Bourdaloue was a priest who came to the court in 1675 and whose sermons were noted for their length.

25. "Inventaire après le decès de M. J^n le Rond D'Alembert: 1er Dec. 1783" in the Minutier Central of the Archives Nationales in Paris, LXXXIII, 619, p. 5. I am indebted to Professor John Pappas for this information.

26. *Boswell's Journal of a Tour to the Hebrides with Samuel Johnson: Now First Published from the Original Manuscript*, ed. F. A. Pottle and C. H. Bennett, 1936, pp. 291-92.

Boswell argued for having books and prints easily available, and that Johnson mentioned a gentleman who always had a "set of the *Spectator* in that place." Lord Chesterfield, giving advice to his son in December 1747, mentioned a man he knew who was "so good a manager of his time, that he would not even lose that small portion of it which the calls of nature obliged him to pass in the necessary-house."[27] Chesterfield's acquaintance gradually went through all the Latin poets while on the seat. "He bought, for example, a common edition of Horace, of which he tore off gradually a couple of pages, carried them with him to that necessary place, read them first, and then sent them down as a sacrifice to Cloacina; this was so much time fairly gained; and I recommend to you to follow his example."

Perhaps too much attention has been given to matters of plumbing and chamber pots, but my reason is simply that these were part of the everyday life of any citizen, a part which has for too long been ignored. And though we keep talking in generalities about the Enlightenment and the rise of science, sanitation is one aspect of existence which was scarcely touched by the new ideas. As the Keeper of the Guildhall Library recently put it in a letter, conditions in London in the mid-eighteenth century "were not all that different from those prevailing in Medieval London."[28]

In another way, however, London had become enlightened. Indeed, the streets and squares of the British capital by the mid-century were the best lit of all the great urban areas of Europe. A visiting German prince, arriving in London at night, actually jumped to the conclusion that it must have been especially illuminated in his honor.[29] As is evident from the various Acts of Common Council, much thought had been given to street lighting. In 1736, for example, it was decided that globular glass lamps were to be set up "at the distance of Thirty yards from each other, on each side of the street, even with the posts of the foot passage in the great or High streets, and in the smaller or

---

27. *Letters of Lord Chesterfield*, ed. Bonamy Dobrée, 1932, III, pp. 1066-67 (11 Dec. 1747).
28. Letter from Donovan Dawe of the Guildhall Library, 25 Aug. 1972.
29. Charles P. Moritz, *Travels, Chiefly on Foot Through Several Parts of England in 1782* (entry for 5 June 1782). See Roland Bartel, *Johnson's London*, 1956, p. 15.

lesser streets not exceeding the distance of Thirty five yards or as the Alderman, Deputy and Common-Council men of each ward should direct."[30] By 1739, so I am told, there were probably 4,825 lamps in 26 wards, which were maintained by seventeen contractors at a cost of £9,698 14s 5d. These contractors were responsible for obtaining and repairing the lamps, for supplying wicks and oil, and for lighting and extinguishing them throughout the year — keeping them on from sunset to dawn.[31]

According to the legal agreement, one light was usually thought sufficient for five houses. Esmond de Beer, who has made a close study of this matter for the late seventeenth and early eighteenth century, tells me that Gough Square would thus have probably been entitled to two or three lamps.[32] And according to contemporary maps of the area the courts leading into Gough Square were well populated and paved, so that they, too, would have been adequately lighted. The lamps, using whale oil, may not have been as brilliant as our modern electric bulbs, but apparently they were quite effective. Proof of this comes in the ready acceptance in court trials of detailed evidence from observers of criminal acts which occurred late at night. When Johnson came home from The Club in the early hours of the morning he did not have to feel his way along in pitch darkness. Indeed, he may not have had any lighting difficulties at all.

For all this illumination Johnson had to pay his modest share. The surviving St. Bride's Lamp Ledger shows, for example, that for the period from September 1755 to March 1756 Johnson paid four shillings and four pence.[33] The next year he was assessed the same amount but apparently failed to pay. Then, alas, there follows a gap in the Guildhall records.

Johnson also paid regular fees for police protection (not very effective, as we shall see) and for "scavengers." In the "Ledger for the Watch and Scavengers" from 25 December 1755 to 25 December 1756 Johnson paid three shillings and six pence

---

30. See Esmond S. de Beer, "The Early History of London Street-Lighting," *History*, n.s. 25, March 1941, pp. 311-24. Also *Notes and Queries*, 5 July 1941, pp. 4-8.
31. *Ibid*.
32. From a letter to me of 4 Sept. 1972.
33. Guildhall Library, No. 3428.

quarterly for the "watch" and five shillings annually for scavengers.³⁴ The office of scavenger arose sometime in the fourteenth century, when he was an unpaid official responsible for seeing that the streets were kept clean and in good repair. He collected and paid the wages of the raker who removed rubbish and swept the streets. By the eighteenth century the scavenger was paid for his services and his duties were clearly defined.

In several statutes passed during the reign of George I it was stipulated that scavengers should bring their carts into the streets every day except Sunday and holidays, give notice by ringing a bell, or some other signal, stay a convenient time, and bring away all dirt and rubbish. If they did not obey these rules they were subject to a fine of 40 shillings.³⁵ In the same statutes the inhabitants were also ordered to follow definite rules — to sweep their streets every Wednesday and Saturday, not to lay ashes or dirt in the streets before their houses, and other mandates — or to pay a fine of ten shillings. In addition, householders were required to keep streets, lanes and alleys before their doors paved to the middle of the street.

From overwhelming evidence it is clear that these statutes were not generally obeyed. The scavengers certainly did not come every day, nor were they very efficient in removing filth. In the April 1742 issue of the *Gentleman's Magazine*, in one of the parliamentary debates which Johnson wrote largely from his own imagination (remember that they were ostensibly debates in the Senate of Lilliput, which were assumed to follow closely actual parliamentary debates the year before) a speaker supposed to represent Lord Tyrconnel brought forward a motion for the better cleaning and paving of the streets.³⁶ He launches forth:

> The filth, sir, of some parts of the town, and the inequality and ruggedness of others, cannot but in the eyes of foreigners disgrace our nation, and incline them to imagine us a people, not only without delicacy, but without government, a herd

---

34. Guildhall Library, No. 3430.
35. For a later summary of some of these statutes see *Gent. Mag.* 23. Oct. 1753, pp. 472-73.
36. *The Works of Samuel Johnson*, 1825, X, pp. 239-40; first published in *Gent. Mag.* 12, April 1742, p. 179 (debate of 24 Feb. 1740/41).

of barbarians, or a colony of hottentots.

The most disgusting part of the character given by travellers, of the most savage nations, is their neglect of cleanliness, of which, perhaps, no part of the world affords more proofs, than the streets of the British capital; a city famous for wealth, and commerce, and plenty, and for every other kind of civility and politeness, but which abounds with such heaps of filth, as a savage would look on with amazement.

The putrefaction and stench, the speaker continued, causes of pestilential distempers, must be corrected. There seems little doubt that part of the obvious outrage which pervades the speech echoes Johnson's own observations of the streets and alleys in his own neighborhood.

By the mid-century conditions were so bad that some citizens of London and Westminster were moved to apply to parliament for new laws which would provide better cleaning of the streets, along with other improvements. This drew a reply from someone who signed himself "W.W." in the *Daily Advertiser* for 22 October 1753 (reprinted in the *Gentleman's Magazine* for October) in which he pointed out that laws already on the books, if properly obeyed, would render new laws unnecessary.[37] What was needed was more effective enforcement of the existing statutes. But I shall not describe this argument further. Certainly by the early 1770s requirements had become a bit more realistic. In a scavenger's contract now in the Guildhall Library, sometime after 1771 it was stipulated that for one year, with his servants, horses and carts, he was to come at least twice a week into all the streets, and "sweep, take up and carry away, all the Mud, Soil, Filth, and Slop, which shall be found therein." And also twice at least in every week he was supposed to come and "carry away all such Dirt, Dust and Ashes, as shall be found, or placed, or put by the Inhabitants before their Doors, or elsewhere in proper Conveniences for that Purpose; as also all Straw laid before the Doors of such as shall be sick."[38]

37. See note 35. In the 1750s there were fifteen scavengers for the ward of Farrington Without.
38. City of London Sewer Act, Guildhall Library, No. Fo. Pam 55. See also Charles

But what about Johnson's quarterly taxes for "Watch," or we would say, police protection? One has only to browse about in the daily newspapers to see that walking on the streets of London in the mid-eighteenth century was not safe. Muggings and robbery were just as frequent then as in New York City today. In January 1749 the *Whitehall Evening Post* complained that "The Frequency of audacious Street Robberies repeated every Night in this great Metropolis, call aloud on our Magistrates to think of some Redress."[39] After remarking on the hazard of sustaining a fractured skull, the writer continued, "The Villains now go in Bodies, armed in such a Manner, that our Watchmen, who are generally of the superannuated Sort, absolutely declare they dare not oppose them." The papers were full of schemes for reducing thievery and crime.

In the *Penny London Post* there was an account of a gentleman who was coming down the Strand, when he was met "by three Fellows arm'd, who tripp'd up his Heels, one of whom pick'd his Pocket of 27s, the second took his Shoe and Knee Buckles, the third his Hat and Wigg, and all us'd him very ill because he had no Watch in his Pocket."[40] And there is the account of a man attacked by three men, "who robb'd him of six shillings, and beat him most unmercifully because he had no more for them."[41] Except for the differences of clothing, these might have come out of a New York city newspaper.

In April 1750 the celebrated sculptor Roubilliac "was robb'd of his Watch and Money in Dean-Street, Soho, by three Fellows; one presented a Pistol to him, and swore he would blow out his Brains if he made any Noise; and while he was giving him his Money, a second came behind and took out his Watch."[42] When another man was robbed also near Soho Square, "as one of the Rogues was taking the Buckles out of his Shoes, a Pistol went off which was held to his Ear, by which a Slug went thro' the Corner of his Hat" — which frightened the robbers and they fled.[43]

Pendrill, *Old Parish Life in London*, 1937, pp. 127-28.
    39. *Whitehall Evening Post*, 14-17 Jan. 1749.
    40. *Penny London Post; or Morning Advertiser*, 4-6 Jan. 1749.
    41. *Daily Advertiser*, 6 Nov. 1749.
    42. *Daily Advertiser*, 3 April 1750.
    43. *Daily Advertiser*, 6 Feb. 1750.

There are varied accounts of the ingenious devices used by robbers. One tells of a gentleman near the bottom of Gray's Inn Lane accosted by another well-dressed man who "said a gentleman had just shot himself and, calling to a boy at a distance to shew him where he lay, on which both went into the place where the boy led them, when two persons came, one of which held him while the other took his watch and money, with which they went off."[44] A man robbed of twenty-five guineas was forced to get out of his chair so that the robbers could "search under the seats to see if he had conceal'd any Thing."[45] Another had his pockets picked while watching a game of cricket in Moorfields.[46]

There is one difference from accounts in our day. Often the onlookers actively took the side of the one being robbed, and themselves punished the criminals. "Tuesday night last two Women were detected in Covent Garden, as they were endeavouring to steal the Cushion Seats out of a Gentleman's Coach which stood near the Play-house Door; for which they were dragged to the Pump in the Market Place and severely treated by the Populace before they were set at Liberty."[47]

Robbers and muggers were not the only dangers for pedestrians on London streets. Accustomed as we are to speeding automobiles, we tend to think how safe it must have been when there were only slow carts and horse-drawn vehicles. Anybody could get out of their way. But the newspapers contain numerous accounts of accidents to drivers of carts, injuries when coaches turned over, of a woman killed by a Dung-cart, children run over by wagons, and there were people gored by wild animals, and pedestrians killed by overturned wagons, or runaway coaches.[48]

To be sure, there were lighter moments for those who wandered about the streets of London in the mid-eighteenth century. In May 1749 there was an extraordinary wager settled in St. James's Park. A little girl of eighteen months was allowed thirty minutes to walk the length of the Mall, which is half of a

44. Hugh Phillips, *Mid-Georgian London*, 1964, p. 204 (quotation from *General Advertiser*).
45. *Daily Advertiser*, 15 Feb. 1750.
46. *Daily Advertiser*, 18 May 1750.
47. *Whitehall Evening Post*, 21-23 Feb. 1749.
48. See *Daily Advertiser* for 1750.

Robert Stone
NIGHTMAN & RUBBISH-CARTER,
At the Golden Pole the Upper End
of White Cross Street, near Old Street

NB. Decently Performs all he Undertakes
now carried on by his Daughter

MARY BURNET.

mile, but performed it in twenty-three minutes "to the Admiration of Thousands of Spectators."[49] And if one were interested in new inventions one could go to Mr. Cock's lower Great Room in Spring Gardens, during the third week of January 1759, to see a newly invented "Patent Machine, which goes without Horses, and will carry four Persons five or six Miles an Hour; being moved and guided by one or more of the Riders."[50] What could that have been? For those who walked the streets there were pleasures as well as dangers.

In this essay I have not touched on a number of other important aspects of everyday life, such as cooking, cleaning, ways of securing food, and doing laundry, but I hope I have at least made clear the need for more detailed research on how people in London actually existed in the 1750s. Particularly for biographers it might be as important to know where a person took a bath as to know the names of the people he dined with week after week.

James Clifford

49. *General Advertiser*, 12 May 1749.
50. *Public Advertiser*, 16 Jan. 1759.

Piranesi's Impressions of Rome

Italy's Republican destiny rested in the hands of two Triumvirates; from the standpoint of literature it rested with another three, Livy, Vergil, and Horace. Italy's most vigorous, influential illustrators formed yet another triad, Canaletto (Antonio Canale, Venetian, 1676-1729), Tiepolo (Piacenza, 1691-1765), and Giovanni Battista Piranesi (Venetian-Roman, 1720-1778). The last of these became Rome's most celebrated graphic artist, a veritable hero of the eighteenth century, complete master of the grandeur, magnitude and drama of Rome's antique past and Baroque present.

Born a Venetian in 1720, Piranesi soon succumbed to the lure of Rome's majesty and contemporary excitement, and as fantast and archivist of Rome's disintegrating glories, an obsessed historian with an engraver's burin, he captured the popular mind in every corner of Europe, England, Scotland, and later the newly-created United States.

His work as graphic artist has been called the most extraordinary monument to nostalgia in Western art. He was intrigued and thoroughly bewitched by the ruins of Imperial Rome when he arrived at the age of twenty; they were, in his words, "the most perfect that architecture had ever achieved." Schooled in the architectural tradition of Andrea Palladio (Venetian, 1508-1580) and profoundly affected by the theatrical designs of scenography of Giuseppe and Domenico Valeriani, Ferdinando Galli-Bibiena, and Juvarra, Piranesi infused new life into his medium. He brought to printmaking the genius of an architect manqué, a designer and a draughtsman, and ushered in a radiant period in the history of prints. By his efforts Rome was revived as a stage for present display and the illusion of its immensity and grandeur, past and present, was never more dramatically presented.

Eighteenth-century burghers, dilettantes and patrons of Gran Turismo, bought his prints as casually as their modern counterparts buy postcards, slides, or Alinari and Anderson photographs. Collectors vied with one another to fill their cabinets and scrapbooks with the thousand-odd Piranesi prints, above all the celebrated *Vedute* — the "Views of Rome." Today his prints command attention as a reflection of his life and times. For Piranesi worked with his sketch book and etching needle in much the way a magazine photographer works with his Leica or Hasselblad; he was an on-the-spot witness to many exciting archaeological finds, an artist capable of capturing the brilliant atmosphere of the Roman skies, veristic, never falsely picturesque, and more chauvinistic than the native Romans in his defense of Roman architecture against the Philhellenes. He recorded what he saw imaginatively, as an architectural and poetic fact.

His most admired work remains the *Carceri d'Invenzione*, the "Imaginary Prisons" which he engraved in 1745. Vast halls, galleries with no exit, a bewildering array of ramps, staircases, and stone voids provide a hallucinatory vision of an underworld with unseen viewers, an infinity of space defying reason with a proliferation of vaults, an opiate vision of awful realms and endless ineluctable space (Plate I). The same vision, a kindred enormity,

I

the grandeur of dungeons, recurs somewhat surprisingly in his haunting views both of the cistern at Castel Gandolfo and of the titanic ruins of Hadrian's Villa at Tivoli.

In W. S. Gilbert's words, "there's a fascination frantic/ in a ruin that's romantic" (Mikado) and Piranesi's visions of fallen, disintegrating grandeur excited a flood of tourists, old and young. Horace Walpole, visiting Rome in 1739-1740, confessed: "I am far gone in medals, lamps, idols, prints and all the small commodities to the purchase of which I can attain. I would buy the Colosseum if I could." But the traveller's response was not always attuned to Piranesi's images. Goethe, a visitor in 1786, at the age of thirty-seven, residing near the Piazza del Popolo end of the Via del Corso, traipsed through Rome's palaces and ruins, gardens and wastelands, triumphal arches and cathedrals with Teutonic earnestness and perseverance, but complained that Piranesi's Baths of Diocletian and Baths of Caracalla failed to meet his expectations; Flaxman found the ruins to be "on a smaller scale, and less striking, than he had been accustomed to suppose them after having seen the prints of Piranesi." Others responded more enthusiastically. Sir John Soane, a student of architecture in Rome from 1778-1780, was greatly impressed with Piranesi's prints. His biographer, Adolf Michaelis, a Victorian archaeologist, comments that "the longing to visit that wonderful city was not a little awakened by the magnificent engravings in which the Venetian Piranesi ... represented the ruins of the Eternal City with wonderful poetic feeling and artistic skill.... Men made pilgrimages to Rome to acquaint themselves with these astonishing monuments; whether their exalted expectations were fulfilled or disappointed, depended on the degree of enthusiasm which they brought with them." Sir John was only one in a host of connoisseurs and scholars passing through Rome in Piranesi's lifetime, Winckelmann, the archaeologist-adventurers Gavin Hamilton and Thomas Jenkins, Robert Adam, Panini and Robert, Alessandro Magnasco, Salvator Rosa, Claude Lorrain, Sir William Hamilton, and countless others. But for the young Soane, Rome belonged to Piranesi.

The artist's association with Rome after 1744 was constant, and although he was terribly poor during his entire career, he never renounced his love for his adopted city. Most of his adult life he spent in a workshop first assigned to him by his liberal patron, Giuseppe Wagner, a Venetian engraver and publisher, who enabled the promising young artist to establish himself permanently in Rome. Opposite the French Academy, stronghold of the picturesque school of Claude Lorrain and Hubert Robert, at that time housed in the Palazzo Salviati, in a likely locale for the art trade, Piranesi found a most congenial environment for his work as etcher, writer, publisher, shopkeeper and restorations expert.

His veneration for ancient ruins and Baroque splendour was matched frequently by the literary giants of the age, by poets like Alexander Pope, who provides an almost photographic profile of the ruined city in the first fifty lines of his Fifth Epistle in the *Moral Essays*, by John Dyer, whose *Ruins of Rome* (1740) in 545 thoroughly declamatory verses provides a fairly comprehensive picture of the city and its history, a work which, in Samuel Johnson's verdict, raised "greater expectations than the performance gratified." More engaging are the statements of travellers and visitors with no axe to grind, no servitude to Calliope to blunt their honest reaction. Piranesi might exclaim that "the sewers, the filling of the valleys, the walls of Rome, the aqueducts, (Plate II),

II

the paved roads" were the true magnificence, but the conditions of living, particularly in the environs of these vast remnants of past glories, were often appalling. *Botteghe oscure* opened off malodorous alleys, dark and musty even in mid-summer and with creaking overhangs which would have inspired Juvenal (or Johnston) to justifiable terror. Rome was then a city of some 100,000 souls, all entitled to enter the marvelous piazzas, sculptured spaces of human and divine scale but their elegance, old and new, was impaired by gruesome hovels, tumble-down huts and despairing bundles of humanity who found rest and retreat in these once elegant quarters. Rome was a welter of contrasts, of aspiring Renaissance palaces, converted ruins, and outright squalor. Cowboys tended their cattle on the mounded meadow of the Campo Vaccino, Rome's hallowed Forum. Washerwomen strung their threadbare laundry beside the columns of ancient shrines; blacksmiths plied their trade in disintegrating temple precincts; lean-tos rotted against the walls of the Forum Boarium and the Arch of Titus. Vergil's wistful recollection of an Arcadian Rome, site of Evander's Pallanteum, found ironic echo in eighteenth-century Rome where the pastoral dream was realised in the countrified aspect of the metropolis. Tobias Smollett, the English novelist, took up residence in the Piazza di Spagna in 1765. Though a keen admirer of Piranesi's plates, he was not blind to the depressing aspects of the city: "a great plenty of water has not induced the Romans to be cleanly. Their streets, and even their palaces, are disgraced with filth. The noble Piazza Navona is adorned with three or four fountains, and all of them discharge vast streams of water; but, notwithstanding this provision, the piazza is almost as dirty as West Smithfield, where the cattle are sold in London. The corridores, arcades, and even staircases of their most elegant palaces, are depositories of nastiness, and indeed in summer smell as strong as spirit of hartshorne. I have a great notion that their ancestors were not much more cleanly."

Squalor aligned with opulence did not impair Piranesi's vision or affection for the city. Rome commanded his allegiance from the very outset: "When I saw in Rome how most of the remains of the ancient buildings lay scattered through gardens and ploughed fields where they dwindled day by day, either withering away, or being quarried into to steal fragments for new buildings, I resolved to preserve them by means of engravings, I have therefore drawn all these ruins with all possible exquisiteness." But while Piranesi sketched and engraved his near idolatrous views, the luminous skies, those infinite backdrops for his brilliant effects of light and shade, were suddenly darkened by the publication of Johann Joachim Winckelmann's *Gedanken über die Nachahmung der Griechen in der Malerei und Bildhauerkunst* in 1755. Like a bolt of lightning Winckelmann appeared in Rome with his eulogy of everything Greek. Convinced that Greece was an Earthly Paradise where it is always springtime and where men have time to think beautiful thoughts, Winckelmann and his corps of Romantics acclaimed the Greeks as neglected supermen. The adoration of Greek art had become a religion and the champions wrote with evangelistic fervour. The only competitor with the "glorious Greek" was the "noble savage," preferably the North American version. When Benjamin West, fresh from Pennsylvania, first confronted the Belvedere Apollo in 1760 he registered his astonishment by exclaiming "My God, how like he is to a young Mohawk warrior," almost as inane, perhaps less derogatory, than Stendhal's account of the English milord who visited the Colosseum where he caught sight of papal convicts at work among the ruins. "Finest thing I've seen in Rome," he exclaimed. "It will be magnificent when they have finished it." (Plate III).

At any rate, Winkelmann's extravagant eulogies of the noble simplicity and calm grandeur of Greek art and architecture brought Piranesi to the point of distraction and to Ciceronian polemics. To add insult to injustice, Piranesi's Scottish companion, Allan Ramsay, published (anonymously) a violent attack on Roman art and architecture in a work entitled *The Investigator*. J. D. Leroy's study, *Les Ruines des plus beaux monuments de la Grèce*, published in 1758, coupled with Winckelmann's appointment as Librarian to the Maecenas of the age, Cardinal Alessandro Albani, brought Piranesi to fever pitch against the avant-garde philhellenists. His counter-manifesto of Romanità challenged the Greek faction with a scenario on behalf of the Etruscans as the indigenous and determining influence in Italy. For Piranesi the splendours of Rome's functional architecture, the aqueducts,

PIRANESI'S IMPRESSIONS OF ROME • 45

III

IV

roads, drains and the like, were the heritage not of Greece but of ancient Tuscany. These were the true incarnations of Roman magnificence and there was no Greek admixture. He disparaged Greek architecture for its fussiness, its ornate character, its tendency to frivolity and caprice, strange argument for such a master of Roman ornament throughout his artistic career. With Quixotic bravura he challenged the Vitruvian thesis of dependence upon Greece and included in his Etruscan repertoire not only Attic vases but even the Doric temples of Magna Graecia. When Stuart and Revett published their *Antiquities of Athens* in 1762, the issue was settled once and for all. Nevertheless Piranesi's counterblast and advocacy of Etruscan engineering as decisive in Rome's architectural eminence was not entirely inaccurate; the British School in Rome, and others, have repeatedly provided evidence for Etruscan influence and direction in Roman engineering. It is therefore imperative that modern research be directed to Piranesi's Philippic — *Della Magnificenza ed Architettura de' Romani* (1761) in order to elucidate the artist's sources and to evaluate his place in the mainstream of Enlightenment aesthetics. His systematic, scientific exploration of Roman remains unquestionably provided him with an enviable experience and substantial background for his interest in aesthetic theory and the history of Roman civilization. His failure to distinguish between Etruscan, Italic, and Greek colonial or Hellenistic forms should not blind scholars to the importance of his statement and the partial veracity of his position.

Throughout his architectural and topographical studies, Piranesi never lost sight of contemporary humanity, ephemeral, frenetic, discerning or oblivious in the midst of past grandeur. Influenced undoubtedly by the example of Stefano della Bella, whose seventeenth-century gypsies often bear striking resemblance to his tatterdemalion beggars, and to Neapolitan Salvator Rosa, who left behind a medley of soldiers in fanciful antique armour, striking proud attitudes with their halberds and engaged in whispered asides, Piranesi's conversation groups among the ruins seem more hectic, certainly more extreme in their condition of wealth or poverty (Plate IV). Bianconi, his first biographer, commented scathingly on Piranesi's addiction: "Instead of studying the nude

V

or beautiful Greek statues which are the only good models (shades of Winckelmann's mania), he set himself to drawing the most gangrenous cripples and hunchbacks in all Rome. He loved to sketch twisted legs, broken arms, and sprung hips, and whenever he found one of these horrors by a church door, he thought that he had discovered a new Apollo Belvedere or a Laocoon, and ran home to draw it." But Bianconi's myopic view could never cope with the imaginative vigour and audacity of the Venetian. Critics have gratefully catalogued a veritable encyclopaedia of the multiple trades and occupations of eighteenth-century Rome from his passing parade: princely aristocrats parleying with vegetable hawkers; convulsive connoisseurs of antiquities bargaining with grave-robbers; supercilious English *milordi* and animated *ciceroni*; prelates, monks, and shambling beggars; soldiers, elegant ladies and harassed housewives; sausage salesmen and shepherds; furniture craftsmen, fishmongers and farriers, richly caparisoned horses with proud rococo carriages; and tubercular wrecks sprawled amid the shadowy overgrown ruins (Plate V).

Trained as an architect, a profession which he repeatedly signals in his frontispieces and signatures, Piranesi found few

VI

VII

opportunities outside of his prints to show his talents. Two major commissions came his way however, a sanctuary to complete the Borromini Church of San Giovanni in Laterano, and the restoration and redecoration of the Church of Santa Maria del Priorato and the Piazza dei Cavalieri di Malta (1764-1766). Erected originally in 1568, the Church of the Knights of Malta, perched proudly on the Aventine, high above the Tiber, was sorely in need of a new vault and façade and general overhaul. Piranesi produced a splendid monument for his patron Cardinal Rezzonico, nephew of Pope Clement XIII. Tourists have looked through the bronze keyhole of the garden door to catch sight of the dome of St Peter's framed in an avenue of trees in the distance, but few have had the good fortune to enter the Church to admire Piranesi's inventive use of exuberant decoration, the bold reliefs which impart a restlessness and tension to the white interior, exemplary use of the ancient motifs which he advocated so strenuously for contemporary architects. The other commission, the favour of Clement XIII, was never executed. The drawings disappeared soon after their completion in 1767 but were luckily recovered in a European family collection as recently as 1968. The twenty-three drawings were exhibited in the Low Memorial Library of Columbia University in 1972; the papal altar and *baldachino*, masterpieces of Venetian lightness and *trompe l'oeil*, won a host of new followers for Piranesi.

Piranesi's most durable monument derives not so much from his role as architect but from his labours as recorder of ancient constructions. His output of Roman views is contained within three collections of plates, many of them of extraordinary size: the *Varie Vedute*, the *Antichità Romane de' Tempi della Repubblica*, and the *Vedute di Roma*. The four volumes of *Le Antichità Romane* (1756) constitute his masterpiece, a labour of love which turned sour with the failure of patronage (Plate VI). Piranesi had enlisted the financial guarantees of a young Irish visitor, James Caulfield, Lord Charlemont, and so undertook to dedicate the collection to his young *praesidium et dulce decus*. But the promise miscarried and with justifiable ire Piranesi excised Lord Charlemont's name with the zeal of Octavian-Augustus consigning Marc Antony or Cornelius Gallus to *damnatio memor-*

iae. A letter accompanied the defamation, as indignant and resentful as Dr. Johnson's notorious letter to Lord Chesterfield only two years earlier.

The *Vedute* have been maligned for their fanatical nature, their resort to stock formulae, their outrageous extravagance, and yet this artistic interpretation of ancient Rome somehow still conditions our ideas of the essential character of Roman architecture: emphatic, abiding, and solid; enormous in size and mass; gigantic structures with near infinite space within; exuberant in ornament and richly complex in its outward show.

The Theatre of Marcellus, Augustus' memorial to his deceased son-in-law and heir, has an almost Cyclopean massiveness; the Appian Way, truly Regina Viarum, is a marvel of meticulous superhuman engineering, with paving blocks of incredible scale; the half-buried Temple of Vespasian, wrongly identified as the Temple of Jupiter Tonans, is huge in comparison with its setting; still unexcavated, Piranesi has depicted a colossal corner of the temple with his characteristic *Commedia dell'Arte* players congregating near the mouldering entablature. The Colosseum he presented in seven views from different vantage points and in several panoramic views of the sector. Most startling is the bird's-eye view of the interior, where the volcanic aspect evokes somber reflection on its ghastly service to the populace. The pyramidal tomb of Gaius Cestius on the Via Ostiensis, product of the early Principate of Augustus, later incorporated within the wall of Aurelian, was a romantic attraction then and now. Towards the close of the century the Papacy conceded the first burial ground for non-Catholics beside the pyramid to which Piranesi assigns a scale to match the Pharaoh's monuments. The Republican Round Temple by the Tiber, sometimes called the Temple of "Vesta," shares its Ionic elegance with the present-day depression. Hadrian's Tomb, a repeated subject, emerges as a dark and awesome monument, tomb become fortress, less Papal than Mycenaean in its irresistible scale, as terrible as the Bastille. Aqueducts, bridges (a favourite subject) (Plate VII), tombs, come with astonishing rapidity and diversity from coppers of ambitious size. All have the same colossal scale and massive monumentality, an epic dimension, a cross between accurate archaeological statement and surrealist vision.

Accused of hysterical fancy and monumental confusion, Piranesi's archaeological interest in the topography and architecture of the ancient city was no passing fancy. By 1760 he had become a force in European archaeology, widely respected as a serious student of the problems of construction and aesthetics with which the ancient architects grappled. He prided himself on his election as an Honorary Fellow of the Society of Antiquaries (London) in 1757, and his dedication of his Campus Martius volume (1762) to the Scottish architect, Robert Adam, along with plates for Sir William Hamilton, Jenkins, Gavin Hamilton and others, serve notice of his pretensions to the status of artist and archaeologist alike (Plate VIII). Relying on various literary sources and earlier records, on the extant remains, and on the fragmentary marble plan of Rome dating from Severan times, Piranesi was inspired and instructed in his fanciful restorations of the buildings of the Campus Martius for his one-time friend and colleague, Robert Adam. But he could equally well provide accurate drawings of monuments now lost or hopelessly dilapidated, superb studies of the Emissarium, the drainage channel, of Lago Albano (1762?), the spacious complexities of the Cistern at Castel Gandolfo (1764), and the remains of Hadrian's Villa at Tivoli. Measured plans, cross-sections, and elevations were burnt indelibly into his plates. When Gavin Hamilton drained the Pantanello, a swampy area northwest of the Villa of Hadrian in 1769, Piranesi assisted in the recovery of many fine pieces of marble sculpture and other antiquities which he later offered for sale at his shop on the Corso. His plan of the villa, ten feet long and distributed over six plates, was published posthumously by his son Francesco in 1780 and served as the standard and generally reliable plan of the Villa for several generations. One must be cautious in consigning eighteenth-century excavators and archaeological draughtsmen to the ranks of treasure-seekers and charlatans. They often kept exceedingly careful records of high quality and on the whole were superior to the excavators of the early nineteenth century. To be sure, Piranesi's elaborations in the Campus Martius volume are highly imaginative, even comical to our eyes, but they do prefigure some of the modern restorations and, almost without exception, Piranesi's elevations are accurate reflections of the ground plan which appeared in his volume.

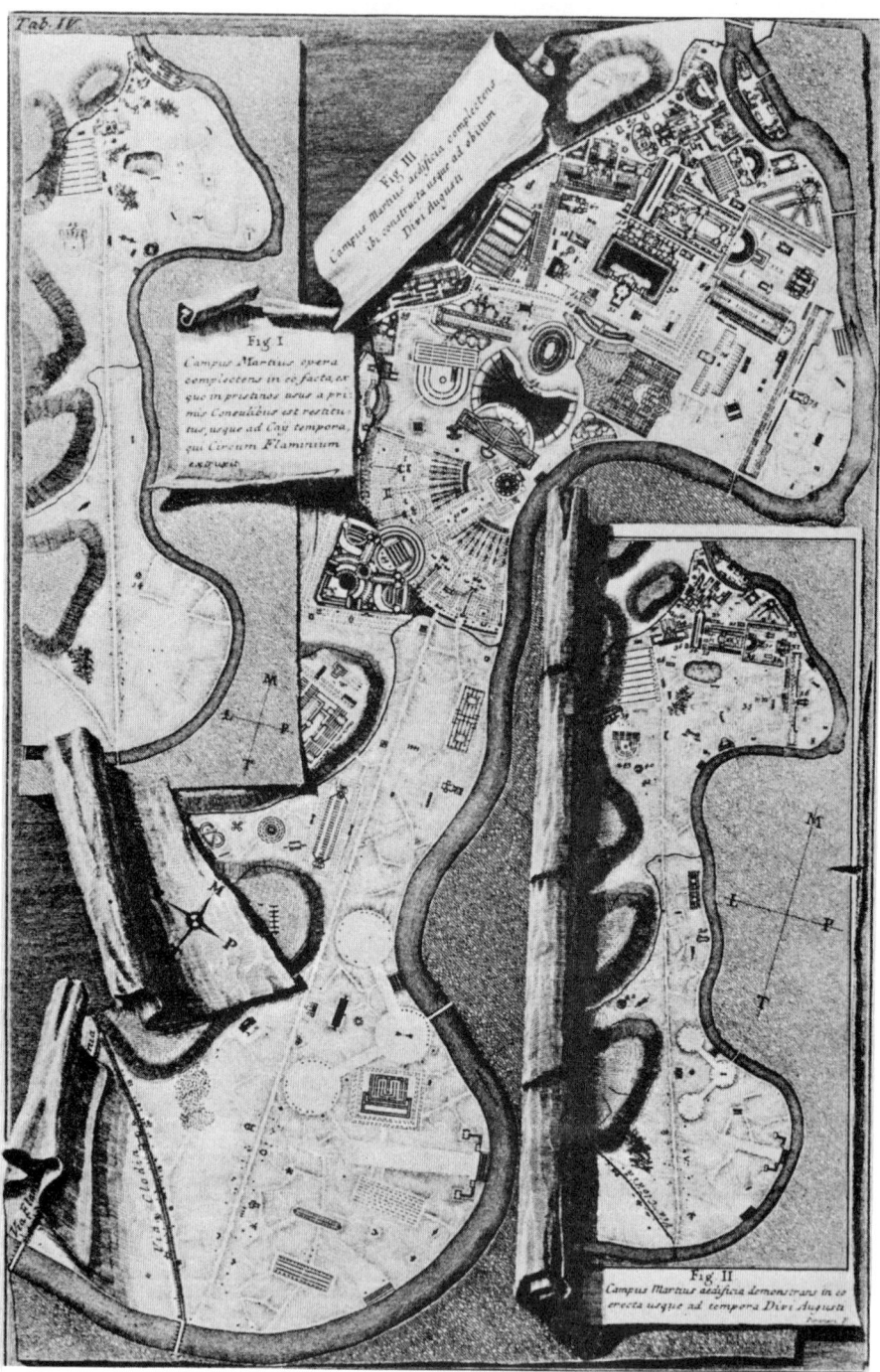

IX

His systematic representation of orders, capitals, and other architectural elements was stupendous in its variety and accuracy (Plate IX). His transcription of the *Lapides Capitolini sive Fasti Consulares triumphalesque Romanorum* (1762), excavated originally during the sixteenth century at the expense of Alessandro Farnese (later Pope Paul III), were compiled in a new edition which aimed at providing a correct transcription, an exercise which Piranesi found endlessly boring but challenging nonetheless and worthy of completion.

Scholars have noticed that Piranesi attacked his ruins, broken columns, entablatures, reliefs, and foundations with the curiosity of an anatomist, stripping, sectioning, sawing, in order to discover the structure in all its layers and functions. Columns buried until then in the slums of Rome, he exhumed and recorded. John

Adams once passed judgment on Thomas Jefferson, another enthusiast for Rome, as "the best brusher-off of dust" he had ever known; in the presence of Piranesi's industry he would have been aghast (Plate X). The architectural sectionings in Piranesi's works are sadly and unworthily neglected on several grounds. Not only are they evidence of his feeling for abstract design, for they are beautiful plates of composition and draughtsmanship, they also have an importance beyond the artistic. Piranesi obviously subscribed to what we proudly term the methodology of scientific archaeology; but he goes beyond the factual reproduction to abstract design and so surpasses his original material (Plate XI). Once we have accommodated to the artist's conventions the drawings become intelligible and useful.

England and France, particularly during the Napoleonic era, divined their future by looking backward into the mirror of classical antiquity. Robert Wood's *Ruins of Palmyra* (1753), Stuart and Revett's *Antiquities of Athens* (1762), and Gibbon's *Decline and Fall of the Roman Empire* (Vol. I, 1776), are vivid testimony to the retrospective attitude among the English. But there was genuine aesthetic enthusiasm there as well. Piranesi, who always found the English his best customers and staunchest advocates, remarked shortly before his death that Venice was passé and that he would much prefer to reside in London because the English were the only people who really were concerned about the arts. Their enthusiasm as collectors of antiquities and their taste for his etchings are manifest in the fifty-odd dedications to Englishmen of recently acquired marble urns, sarcophagi, tripods, lamps and other household items excavated from the Villa of Hadrian and elsewhere, often by the artist himself. His predilection for Egyptian ornament, always somewhat exotic in the Roman context, appears in his specially designed mantlepieces and in a rather bizarre coffee house for the English trade in the Piazza di Spagna, a design unfortunately lost, designed to compete with the still extant Caffè Greco on the Via Condotti. The Egyptian vogue languished somewhat until Napoleon's Egyptian campaign in 1799 when a mélange of hieroglyphics and a pride of sphinxes invaded Europe's squares and drawing rooms. Piranesi's imperial Roman style was directly inspirational to the French Empire style,

PIRANESI'S IMPRESSIONS OF ROME • 55

X

XI

XII

tailor-made for the self-made Emperor, and integral to the design of England's master furniture craftsmen, Adams, Chippendale, and Sheraton.

During the final year of his life Piranesi revisited Naples and Campania where he had earlier thrilled to the excavations at Herculaneum and Pompeii, both begun during his youth, and the antiquities of Pozzuoli, particularly the submerged Macellum (market-building) of Trajan, the so-called Serapeum. The Doric temples of Paestum proved equally impressive and his last project was measuring and sketching the monuments of colonial Greeks, once despised and ill-defined, in the malarial flatlands of ancient Poseidonia-Paestum (Plate XII). He died on November 11, 1778, and lies today in the Church which he redesigned, Santa Maria del Priorato on the Aventine.

Bianconi, for all his aversion to the human actors in the etchings, nonetheless called Piranesi "the Rembrandt of antique ruins." Horace Walpole, in his *Anecdotes of Painting in England* (1771) hailed his visions of Rome as works "savage as Salvator Rosa, fierce as Michelangelo, and exuberant as Rubens."

One may fairly argue that there are four Romes of potent,

durable imagery: ancient, rennaissance, and modern, and, not least, the Rome of Piranesi's impressions. His vision of eternal grandeur and decay remains etched in the mind of the viewer forever. Horace's epilogue — *exegi monumentum aere perennius* — "I have completed a memorial more durable than bronze, loftier than the decaying pyramids of Kings" (*Odes* III, 30, 1-2) finds its peer in the preface to Piranesi's *Diverse Maniere* (1769):

> Someone will perhaps accuse my works of extravagance, but whoever he may be I desire he will show me where they are wanting with regard to the laws and rules of good design, or proportion, of character, and of form. If he be not able to shew me these defects, I shall be very easy by what names my works shall be characterised by such as think every thing extravagant which deviates from the old monotonous style. I hope the public will do justice to my labours, and will discover in these designs, and in those which I shall hereafter publish, an ardent zeal for the fine arts, but chiefly for architecture.

Alexander G. McKay

Plates

I. Prison Interior. From *Invenzione capric di carceri* (1760)
II. View of the Water Tower of the Acqua Giulia. From *Trofei di Ottaviano Augusto* (1753).
III. Colosseum (Flavian Amphitheater), exterior. From *Vedute di Roma* (1776).
IV. Temple of the Deified Trajan (Dogana di Terra). From *Vedute di Roma* (1770).
V. View of the pedestal of the Column of Antoninus Pius. From *Trofeo o sia magnifica colonna* (1775-76).
VI. The Arch of Constantine. From *Antichità Romane* (1760).
VII. The Mulvian Bridge. From *Vedute di Roma* (1770).
VIII. Plan of the Campus Martius. From *Campus Martius* (1762).
IX. The Column of Trajan. From *Vedute di Roma* (1758).

X. Architectural elements. From *Vasi, candelabri, cippi, etc.* (1778).

XI. The Arch of Constantine and Colosseum. From *Vedute di Roma* (1776).

XII. The "Basilica" and the Temple of "Neptune," Paestum. From *Différentes vues . . . de Pesto* (1778).

Madrid & Spain, 1560-1860: Patterns of Social & Economic Change

Madrid did not experience the fairly constant, unbroken growth of most cities of Western Europe after 1500. Rather. the city expanded rapidly from 1560 to 1630, contracted substantially from 1630 to 1685, then stabilized until about 1730, after which it grew steadily to a new peak in 1800. Thereafter it experienced another contraction which lasted into the 1830s, followed by renewed growth in the 1840s and after. Since cities consume what rural areas produce, this pattern of urban growth had important implications for the region in which Madrid was located.[1]

Prior to the nineteenth century there are virtually no signs that Madrid performed any important mercantile functions for the region around it. Of over 800 specific commodity transfers documented for the middle and later eighteenth century in Castile, about half involved Madrid as a destination and exactly two involved Madrid as a center of distribution or manufacture.[2] Economically, Madrid was a consumer of domestic agricultural commodities and imported manufactures. The city produced political services in the form of policy making and administration, and social services in the form of a context within which the notables of Spain sought after prestige, position, and power. The city's erratic growth and political nature played an important role in the development of a conservative elite which long dominated the interior portions of Spain into the twentieth century.

---

1. David R. Ringrose, "Madrid y Castilla, 1560-1850. Una capital nacional en una economía regional," *Moneda y Crédito* 111, 1969, pp. 65-122.

2. David R. Ringrose, *Transportation and Economic Stagnation in Spain, 1750-1850*, Durham, N. C., 1970, Maps 3-13. Details on movements of goods are now available in the Spanish edition, *Los transportes y el estancamiento económico de España (1750-1850)*, Madrid, 1972. Appendix.

In the middle decades of the sixteenth century the interior of Spain had developed a fairly active urban life, a considerable range of craft industries, and a relatively dense population. Later in the century, however, the interior towns began to lose their industrial markets and with them their commerce and population. Castile was being de-urbanized. The international differences in prices and labor costs generated by the impact of a large new money supply and by intense demands for basic foodstuffs first allowed non-Spanish manufactures to capture Spain's overseas markets and then to penetrate those of Spain proper. After about 1610 increasing economic stagnation throughout Europe and Spanish America finished the destruction of Spanish industry, while the commerce and banking which survived came under control of Italian and German interests. This was reinforced by soil exhaustion and vulnerability to disease on the part of the population as rural resources were stretched beyond their limits, and demographic decline set in during the 1590s.[3]

Paralleling these trends was a process which we can call the institutionalization of empire. A vast military and political system had to be governed and the numerous positions it offered provided an obvious alternative outlet for the nobility. In the fifteenth and early sixteenth centuries this group had a tradition of military service and a great interest in building up its social and economic position. Much of the nobility had been far from finiky about the sources of its wealth and had been active in commerce and even commercial fishing.[4] As the range of options was narrowed by economic stagnation, it became necessary to look for other sources of income and prestige. Under Philip II these opportunities were principally available outside of Spain proper, but under Philip III this changed considerably.

---

3. Bartolomé Bennassar, *Recherches sur les grandes épidémies dans le nord de l'Espagne a la fin du XVIe siècle*, Paris, 1969; Antonio Domínguez Ortiz, *La sociedad española en el siglo XVII*, Tomo I, Madrid, 1963, pp. 53-160; José Gentil da Silva, *En Espagne, développement économique, subsistance, déclin*, Paris, 1965, pp. 97-189; Noël Salomon, *La campagne de Nouvelle Castille à la fin du XVIe siècle, d'après les Relaciones Topográficas*, Paris, 1964, pp. 303-304; Vicens Vives, *Historia económica*, pp. 373-93.

4. Ruth Pike, *Enterprise and Adventure; the Genoese in Seville and the Opening of the New World*, Ithaca, N.Y., 1966; Ruth Pike, *Aristocrats and Traders; Sevillian society in the 16th Century*, Ithaca, N.Y., 1972; Charles Verlinden, "Italian Influence in Iberian Colonization," *Hispanic American Historical Review* 33, 1953, pp. 199-211.

A second aspect of the institutionalization of empire was the need for a permanent administrative center. In 1561 Philip II named Madrid as capital and gradually the lawyers, clerks, and officials congregated there. Until Philip II's death, however, Madrid's development was relatively slow, and in forty years the city expanded from around 35,000 inhabitants to approximately 65,000. Its primary function remained political, and the real center of the economic and social life of the elite continued to be in the nearby city of Toledo.[5]

With the accession of Philip III, government and courtly life altered radically. The Court became an extravagant and active place where favors, offices, and pensions were available if one had connections. The center of the aristocracy's social life shifted rapidly to Madrid and altered that city with amazing speed. The population exploded from 65,000 to possibly 170,000 between 1600 and 1630. The *Plaza Mayor*, the royal palace, and the water system were all begun about 1608 and represent heavy governmental investment in the city's infrastructure.[6]

This rapid growth posed serious problems for the Crown and the solutions had unfortunate effects on the Spanish interior.[7] Adequate food supply was imperative for the stability of the city and safety of the government. The fundamental problem was the inelasticity of the agricultural system upon which the city depended. During the sixteenth century the provinces of Madrid and Toledo had experienced relatively rapid population growth and developed specialized agriculture oriented to the expanding urban market. But Madrid's explosive growth after 1600 could not hope to find a correspondingly rapid increase in agrarian output. In fact, the resources of the area were stretched to their limits by 1600. The alternative for the Crown was to expand, in the frequent years of poor harvest, the area which Madrid monopo-

---

5. Domínguez Ortiz, *Siglo XVII*, pp. 129-39; Ringrose, "Madrid y Castilla," Appendix I; Michael Weisser, "Les marchands de Tolède dans l'économie castillane, 1565-1635," *Melanges de la Casa de Velazquez*, Vol. VII, 1971, pp. 223-36.

6. Ringrose, "Madrid y Castilla," pp. 100-1.

7. Some aspects of this are to be inferred from Michael Weisser, "Crime and Subsistence: The Peasants of the *Tierra* of Toledo, 1550-1700," unpublished Ph. D. dissertation, Northwestern University, 1972. The specific problem will be documented in a forthcoming article by David R. Ringrose, "Madrid and Toledo, 1560-1650: Competition for Supply."

lized. The result was the progressive embargo of more and more supply zones, including the customary supply sources of Toledo, the principle commercial and industrial center of the interior. The act of redirecting flows of supplies away from Toledo undermined that city's economy.

The situation did more than undermine Toledo. The most intensely felt demand was for wheat. The governmental controls included embargoes on shipments of grain to destinations other than Madrid, differential pricing of bread to attract it to Madrid, and elaborate quota systems imposing bread delivery schedules on towns up to forty miles away. At the same time, the government imposed ceiling prices on grain as it left the farms. It has long been considered doubtful that such controls were very effective, but recent work suggests that they were taken seriously.[8] The effect of such controls was to preclude the small producer from benefiting from high wheat prices in bad years when he faced high prices himself. In years of plentiful harvest, on the other hand, low grain prices made it impossible for the small farmer to recoup. The same situation benefitted the individuals and institutions in a position to store surpluses from good years and contract for their delivery in short years on favorable terms. The result was a heavy pressure on the small grain farmer and a tendency towards consolidation of cereal lands into larger holdings.

At the same time, the intense demand for cereals generated by Madrid created a deteriorating market for wine. As wheat became expensive, buying power shifted to the more vital foodstuff and per capita use of wine declined.[9] As a result, while average wheat prices rose nearly 60 per cent from 1590 to 1610 (based on five-year averages), wine prices declined about 25 per cent. The

---

8. Earl J. Hamilton, *American Treasure and the Price Revolution in Spain, 1501-1650*, Cambridge, 1934, and *War and Prices in Spain, 1651-1800*, Cambridge, 1947, p. 98, maintains they had little effect. Carmelo Viñas Mey, *El problema de la tierra en la España del siglo XVI*, Madrid, 1941, assumes they had considerable impact. If Segovia was typical, the *tasa* governed large sales fairly far into the seventeenth century: see Gonzalo Anes and Jean Paul le Flem, "Las crisis del siglo XVII: producción agrícola, precios e ingresos en tierras de Segovia," *Moneda y Crédito* 93, 1965, pp. 22-23.

9. This is a clear case of the effects of relative elasticities of demand in a society at the margin of subsistence. It follows the formulation of Ernest Labrousse regarding the pre-revolutionary decades in France very closely. Ernest Labrousse, *Fluctuaciones económicas e historia social*, Madrid, 1962, pp. 371-79.

great wine producing centers of the provinces of Toledo and La Mancha were badly hit and their vital statistics suggest steadily declining population after 1590.[10]

In sum, up to 1630 the development of Madrid turned the normal cycle of varying harvest yields into a self-reinforcing pattern of recurrent food shortage and high prices, rural distress and dislocation, migration to the capital, and with each new crisis the need for stronger efforts to divert supplies to the city, undermining further the economies of neighbouring towns. As of 1630 Madrid remained not only a huge market for agricultural surpluses, but was literally the only one in the interior following the collapse of Toledo between 1610 and 1630.[11]

After 1630 the imperial system which supported Madrid began to break down.[12] The American silver mines had become a mainstay of government credit, but by the 1630s Spanish America was in the midst of a depression of its own and bullion production was but a fraction of the late sixteenth-century totals. At the same time, with the Thirty Years War, military costs reached staggering proportions. In 1640 the situation became bleaker still when Catalonia and Portugal revolted, followed by another rebellion in Naples in 1646. The government was pressed for revenue and during the 1630s and 1640s taxes in Madrid rose rapidly, largely in the form of excise duties (*sisas*) on the sale of basic necessities. The first such taxes had been imposed in 1583, and others were added in 1607 and 1618. But these early *sisas* had been specifically dedicated to the food supply system and public works — the revenue was invested in the city itself. But the new taxes in the 1630s were specifically dedicated to servicing loans raised for various campaigns in Germany, the Low Countries, and Catalonia. The new taxes extracted capital from the economy of the city. Economically unstable at best, the city had no productive capacity

10. Based on vital statistics drawn from parish registers in several towns of New Castile by Michael Weisser of CCNY and generously made available to me.
11. Toledo declined from over 60,000 inhabitants in 1608 to around 15,000 in 1631. Michael Weisser, "El Greco's Toledo: The Crisis of Urban Society in the Golden Age," presented to the Third Annual Conference of the Society for Spanish and Portuguese Historical Studies, Rutgers University, April, 1972.
12. The details of the following paragraph are documented in Ringrose, "Madrid y Castilla."

of its own and lived from the peculiar set of political and social institutions which channeled public and private flows of wealth to it. Now these flows were being reversed.

The effect on the city quickly became evident, and in the mid-1630s annual consumption of wheat, wine, meat, and olive oil began to decline. Simultaneously the government sought to tax the nobility and revive its obligations to perform military services while reducing the possibilities of patronage at Court. The Nobles shifted their attention back to their own jurisdictions and estates. In the process, they, too, ceased to channel flows of wealth to the economy of the capital. The Crown actually encouraged this since, in its need for cash, it sold off wastelands and jurisdictional and tax collection rights over hundreds of towns and villages across Castile, thereby acquiescing in a long-run decentralization of authority.[13]

By the end of the seventeenth century, the interior of Spain had undergone a fundamental reconstruction.[14] Excepting Madrid, the cities had shrunk to small dimensions, rarely exceeding 15,000 inhabitants, and many regions had been almost depopulated. The provinces around Madrid were left lightly populated with soil deteriorating through neglect. The remaining agricultural activity was confined to the best cereal land and vineyards, with the major emphasis being placed on cereals with lower labor requirements such as rye.[15] There was increased emphasis on livestock and the olive appeared as a cash crop in New Castile.[16] Land was more heavily concentrated in the hands of the aristocracy and church, and it is likely that share-cropping and day labor were much more prevalent than a hundred years before. The total regional output

---

13. Antonio Dominguez Ortiz, "Ventas y exenciones de lugares durante el reinado de Felipe IV," *Anuario de Historia del Derecho Español* 34, 1964, pp. 163-207; Charles J. Jago, "Aristocracy, War, and Finance in Castile, 1621-1665; The Titled Nobility and the House of Bejar During the Reign of Philip IV," unpublished Ph. D. dissertation, Cambridge University, 1969, pp. 150-51.

14. Gentil da Silva, *En Espagne*, pp. 161-79; Domínguez Ortiz, *El siglo XVII*, pp. 115-60; Jaime Vicens Vives, *Manual de historia ecónomica de España*, Barcelona, 1967, pp. 375-93.

15. Anes and le Flem, "Las crisis del siglo XVII," pp. 16-17.

16. While olive oil was an important crop in the eighteenth century, there is little evidence of it in the sixteenth. Salomon, *Nouvelle Castille*, pp. 86-87; Carmelo Viñas y Mey and Ramón Paz, *Relaciones de los pueblos de España ordenadas por Felipe II, Pro Vincia de Madrid*, Madrid, 1949; *Provincia de Toledo*, 3 vols, Madrid, 1951, 1963.

probably declined considerably while the distribution of wealth shifted in favor of the elite. Thus we see already the basic lines of Spain's rural society for the next 200 years and more: sharply unequal distribution of wealth with economic and political power concentrated in the hands of local lords. These changes removed any stimulus to spark the growth of the rural population or to promote better techniques of agricultural production.

If in the seventeenth century Madrid contributed to the long-term restructuring of rural society in Castile, in the eighteenth century the capital played an equally important role in attracting the attention of the aristocracy back to Court and began the process of turning wealthy men, both rural and urban, into the agro-commercial oligarchy associated with the nineteenth century.

As in the early seventeenth century, there was a close correlation between the eighteenth-century recovery of the Spanish Empire and the size of its capital. Prior to 1715 imperial reforms were tentative,[17] but after the War of the Spanish Succession relations with France were regularized and the upper levels of administration reorganized. In the late 1720s serious efforts began to rebuild the Spanish Navy and by the 1730s smuggling and privateering in the Caribbean by other powers became risky. The economy of the Empire improved as silver production began to increase, providing Spain with vital foreign exchange for her European trade. By the 1730s the results were being reflected in the capital. Population and consumption began to rise, and the social and cultural life of the capital started to develop.

During the seventeenth-century crisis the population of the city fell to between 100,000 and 110,000 inhabitants in the 1680s and remained at about that level until after the War of Succession. Subsequently, there was a steady growth and official figures suggest about 130,000 inhabitants in the 1750s, 160,000 in 1787, and 170,000 in 1797. These figures are probably low, and the total was probably around 200,000 in 1800. This estimate is based on impressions of a sizeable floating population and, more

[17]. There were some attempts at stimulating commerce and the center of the Indies trade was shifted to Cadiz. The monetary system remained relatively stable after 1680 according to Hamilton, *War and Prices*, pp. 53-54.

concretely, on a comparison of total annual consumption of wheat, wine, and meat in the late eighteenth century with similar data for the 1840s when the evidence for a population of around 200,000 is fairly secure.[18] Assuming that the higher estimate is accurate, it represents an 80 per cent increase in the size of the Madrid market between 1720 and 1800. Even with allowances for error, by the end of the eighteenth century the subsistence requirements of Madrid matched or exceeded those of Madrid and Toledo combined in the first years of the seventeenth century.

The importance of this development in the Spanish economy is supported by evidence that Madrid not only dominated the interior but compared favorably as a market with the great port cities. (This renewed prosperity seems to have been confined to the capital.) Taxes on commercial activity in other interior towns such as Toledo, Albacete, León, Benavente, Ávila, Segovia show virtual stagnation until after 1770 with only moderate and usually temporary increases thereafter. In Madrid alone do the indicators show strong and substantial growth in commercial activity.[19] Apparently the new quantities of produce being sold into Madrid did little to generate rural buying power and thus stimulate local market activity. This lack of alternative markets left Madrid as the only outlet for agricultural surpluses in the interior.

In terms of commercial activity, setting aside manufactures and luxuries, the market value of the basic food, drink, and fuel used by Madrid was about 400,000,000 *reales* per year around 1790,[20] a figure somewhat less than the estimated value of commerce at Cádiz, but considerably above the 250,000,000 *reales* which Pierre Vilar gives for the commerce of Barcelona in the same period.[21] The figure for Madrid, in fact, is over one-fifth

---

18. This is based on the analysis comparing levels of wheat consumption in Ringrose, "Madrid y Castilla," pp. 93-97.

19. The serial data to support this will appear in David R. Ringrose, "Perspectives on the Economy of Eighteenth Century Spain," *Historia Ibérica* 1, 1972, now in press.

20. Based on consumption figures found in Antonio Matilla Tascon, "El primer catastro de la villa de Madrid," *Revista de Archivos, Bibliotecas y Museos*, LXIX, 1961, pp. 463-530; Pascual Madoz, *Diccionario estadístico-historico de España*, Madrid, 1849, Vol. X, pp. 993-1036. The prices are taken from Hamilton, *War and Prices*, Appendix I. Since the latter probably reflect wholesale prices, they are probably low and thus tend to deflate the total.

21. Pierre Vilar, *Catalunya dins l'España moderna*, 4 vols., Barcelona, 1963, IV, p. 129.

of the estimated value of all of Spain's European and American commerce in the late eighteenth century. This economic weight, plus the stagnation of the rest of the interior, makes clear the important commercial relationship developing between Madrid and the agricultural society of the interior.

Further evidence is provided by the evolution of the mechanisms by which wheat, wine, olive oil, meat, and fuel were attracted to the city. Between the early seventeenth century and the late eighteenth century important changes took place in the capital's supply system, in its patterns of consumption, and in the areas of the interior from which commodities were drawn. These changes indicate both increased commercialization of agricultural products and the rigidity of the rural structures which developed in the seventeenth century.

The most suggestive change is the degree to which the government had come to rely on market mechanisms and on intermediaries with capital and commercial skills to provide supplies. For example, in the early seventeenth century the city relied heavily on direct control of wheat and bread movements, price controls on wheat, discriminatory price fixing on bread, and elaborate quotas and delivery schedules for bread from towns around Madrid. Supplementing this was a municipal grain depot which supervised the flow of wheat into Madrid and its distribution to the bakers.[22] By the later eighteenth century this had changed considerably. There is little evidence of differential retail prices, although the price of bread in the city was regulated, and there are no references to embargoes directing the movement of wheat. There was still a pro forma attempt to control wheat prices at harvest times, but even religious suppliers ceased to acknowledge it in the eighteenth century. The principal agency of intervention was the wheat depot in Madrid. Most of the grain entering the city came through market operations at prevailing prices. In the background, those managing the wheat depot followed prices and the volume of shipments carefully and arranged their own activities so as to supplement the market and dampen upward price movements. They obtained supplemental supplies for the

---

22. *Archivo Histórico Nacional, Alcaldes y Corte, año*, 1609, f. 406; *año* 1610, f. 570-72; *año* 1614, f. 22.

city from relatively distant sources such as La Mancha to the South and Old Castile to the North. By the 1780s there was a permanent system of government purchasing agents and grain depots in the latter region. This system of purchasing wheat and contracting for its delivery by professional carters, provided a sizeable portion of the city's annual requirements.[23] The important thing to note is the large share of the wheat which the government simply oversaw rather than directly administered. Even where administration was active, the initial purchases were done with reference to market prices in the supplying regions.

Similar changes affected wine and fuel. Earlier, wine producers were often forbidden to ship anywhere but Madrid and faced a dictated ceiling price. The *taverneros* of Madrid then sent out agents to buy at wholesale for retailing in the licensed *bodegas* at regulated prices.[24] In the eighteenth century there is little mention of control of destination or price ceilings. Instead, the city contracted with *taverneros* or larger brokerage consortiums such as the *Cinco Gremios Mayores*,[25] for delivery of stipulated quantities at negotiated wholesale prices, payable by the retailers in the city. The charcoal supply evolved in a similar fashion, with the *Cinco Gremios Mayores*, the Five Great Guilds of Madrid, which dominated the wholesale trade of manufactured articles within the city, at times contracting for deliveries of quantities which represent a considerable fraction of the annual supply.[26]

In general, although there was still government regulation of basic supplies, the process was increasingly related to market behavior and commercial middlemen. This suggests a situation in which the price signals generated by long-term market growth in Madrid could be read with reasonable clarity by rural producers and recipients of rents and tithes.

---

23. Anes and le Flem, "Las crisis del siglo XVII," p. 24; Ringrose, *Transportation*, pp. 37-41.

24. *Archivo Histórico Nacional, Alcaldes y Corte, año* 1598, fols. 160, 169-70; *año* 1625, fols. 49, 73.

25. The *Cinco Gremios Mayores* originated as the five leading merchant guilds of Madrid in the seventeenth century. By the eighteenth they controlled the wholesale commerce in imports and manufactures in Madrid and were increasingly involved in long-distance trade and urban supply. See: Miguel Capella and Antonio Matilla Tascón, *Los Cinco Gremios Mayores de Madrid. Estudio crítico-histórico*, Madrid, 1957.

26. Ringrose, *Transportation*, p. 38.

The degree to which this trend was under way may be reflected in the abortive and little studied experiment with free trade in grain in the 1760s. We know little about the pressures which brought about the experiment, and it is generally treated as a fiasco resulting from doctrinaire reformers applying inappropriate physiocratic ideas.[27] But even so, free trade in grain, given the inelasticities of supply imposed by poor transport and the irregularity of the climate, clearly would have benefited the *señores*, clerics, or middlemen able to accumulate and store grain from year to year. If the minor nobility of eighteenth-century Toulouse could see this clearly and espouse physiocratic free trade doctrines, it is not startling to see landed elements in Castile reacting in the same way.[28]

In sum, one can infer that, underlying whatever political maneuverings were going on between nobility and enlightened reformers during the eighteenth century, the landed proprietors were developing an underlying dependence upon the Madrid market. Their need to turn rural produce into other forms of wealth, and the need of the government to keep the city adequately supplied, combined as the basis for a pattern of urban-rural market-conscious associations which were among the principle components of the basis of the agro-commercial oligarchy of the mid-nineteenth century.

The countryside responded to Madrid's growth apparently by concentrating largely on expanding the production of established types of crops by traditional methods. A certain amount of enclosure was going on, but it is not clear how much of it involved introduction of more labor intensive agriculture. Professor Anes has uncovered a list of 142 authorized enclosures for agriculture during 1755-1773, 37 per cent of which are in the six provinces readily identified as Madrid's hinterland. The types of cultivation are not specified, but the change in exploitation could only be a response to the Madrid market. Similarly, throughout the eighteenth century the carters' associations were complaining of the enclosure of their reserved pastures near Madrid for sedentary

27. Vicens Vives, *Historia económica*, pp. 467-70.
28. Robert Forster, *The Nobility of Toulouse in the Eighteenth Century: A social and Economic Study*, New York, 1971, pp. 70-72.

sheep raising, tree planting, and occasionally for agriculture. Moreover, where the area under a particular crop did expand, there is little evidence of improved technique. On the royal estates around Aranjuez, the area planted in cereals expanded considerably between 1770 and 1795, but the seed/yield ratios fell from 1:10 to 1:7.5. Such diminishing returns suggest the expansion of traditional modes of exploitation onto less fertile land.[29]

Underlying patterns of rigidity are also suggested by the pattern of consumption in eighteenth-century Madrid. In the sixteenth century New Castile had been a region of cereals and vines, but with the loss of internal markets and population, both went out of production on a large scale. At the same time, livestock increased in importance in the rural economy and the olive appeared in New Castile as a labor-saving cash crop. When Madrid began to expand in the eighteenth century, the region responded, but only within the patterns of production established in the seventeenth century. New Castile provided rapidly increasing quantities of olive oil — to the extent that per capita use in the city doubled and trebled that of the early seventeenth century. At the same time, meat consumption rose steadily and, although the data does not permit comparison with the early seventeenth century, it is clear that Madrid consumed more meat per capita than any large city in eighteenth-century Europe.

Conversely, wine consumption rose only moderately during the century, and on a per capita basis fell to half what it had been in the early seventeenth century. Moreover, to provide for a much smaller annual consumption it was necessary to extend the supply region far south into La Mancha, an area only marginally important a century before. The districts in New Castile which had once produced tremendous quantities of wine for Toledo and Madrid simply did not respond to renewed demand. Nor did the region respond well to the stronger demand for cereals. Important quantities did come from all over New Castile, but the scanty evidence at hand actually shows declines in production in many areas around Madrid and Toledo between the 1730s and the 1780s. The government, which in the seventeenth century had

29. Gonzaol Anes, *Las crisis agrarias en la España moderna*, Madrid, 1970, pp. 151-57; Ringrose, *Transportation*, p. 112.

depended on La Mancha and Guadalajara, with occasional recourse to Old Castile and Andalucía, was now forced to develop an elaborate procurement system in Old Castile in order to fill out the city's needs.[30]

Apparently the types of exploitation based on plentiful land and scarce labor which developed in the seventeenth century were the ones which responded to Madrid's renewed growth. Logically, renewed urban demand should have shifted the region back towards cereals and vines. The failure of New Castile to respond in this manner is undoubtedly associated with the apparent prevalence of short-term rental contracts and frequent rent increases recently documented for at least some seventeenth-century estates,[31] and the increased control of rural administration, justice, and tax collection by the *señores* resulting from the sale of such rights by the Crown during the Thirty Years' War. These powerful local interest groups enforced a very uneven distribution of rural wealth and this limited population by keeping the peasants at the edge of subsistence. These conditions made the peasants highly susceptible to recurrent subsistence crises and encouraged them to emigrate from the villages. This limited the supply of labor, the crucial factor of production in intensive agriculture.[32] Yet this organization of production was so bound up with rural power that the risks to the elite inherent in changing the organization and providing direct incentives to the peasant outweighed the long-term benefits of increased total production.

The landlord, while maintaining traditional arrangements in the fields, behaved in a more "modern" fashion in dealing with the produce he was able to extract from his lands. Given the rising demand of Madrid, the impossibility of export out of the region, and the lack of alternative markets, Madrid was the only focus for the commercialization of agrarian products. As this dependence grew, a powerful agro-commercial interest group appeared. Its emergence is suggested in part by a certain ambiguity in the attitudes of many elite elements around the government. On the

---

30. Ringrose, "Madrid y Castilla," pp. 80-82, 85, 106.
31. Jago, "Aristocracy, War, and Finance," pp. 209-11.
32. Ester Boserup, *The Conditions of Agricultural Growth: The Economics of Agrarian Change under Population Pressure*, Chicago, 1965, chapters 4 and 5.

one hand they gave considerable support to certain "liberal" reforms, such as freeing the internal grain trade, improving roads, stimulating rural industry, devising new credit facilities, and modernizing maritime commerce and imperial administration. On the other hand, they resisted serious land reforms and their conservatism in this area eroded the possibilities of agricultural improvement. Conservative policies of social control made it pointless for the peasant to improve yields because the results would quickly be lost as rent.[33]

The inflexibility of rural institutions was probably reinforced by the nature of Madrid as a market. In many countries the peasantry has responded to new market opportunities, but usually because the market offered incentives in the form of better manufactures. In this case, Madrid had hastened the destruction of the industrial craft towns of the sixteenth century and in the eighteenth did little to provide such goods herself.[34] Production for the market thus offered no incentives to the peasant, even though sale of surpluses to the market did for the elite.[35] The elite, after all, wanted luxury imports, manufactures, and, above all, the services of the capital — position and prestige.

As a political capital, Madrid worked fairly well. But its inability to operate as a manufacturing or distribution center, and the inability of any such center to operate while competing with Madrid for supplies, removed many of the important urban to rural connections which in England allowed the two to develop simultaneously.[36] In the case of Madrid the capital offered primarily economic and political opportunities to the landed elite. Once this urban-rural relationship was established, espousal of certain liberal doctrines only masked the underlying ties of what eventually was identified as the oligarchy of the interior.

This general hypothesis is supported by a number of other

---

33. Vicens Vives, *Historia económica*, pp. 472-74.

34. Some indication of Madrid's failure to operate as an entrepot can be seen in the maps of transport activity in Ringrose, *Transportation*.

35. The situation may have resembled that discussed by Alfred Cobban for France, where feudal dues and rent collection were commercialized, rather than the actual exploitation of the land. Alfred Cobban, *The Social Interpretation of the French Revolution*, Cambridge, 1965, pp. 25-35.

36. Wrigley, "A Simple Model of London's Importance."

indications of an urban-rural commercial nexus in the eighteenth century. The middle of the century saw experiments with a number of joint-stock trading companies intended to revive Spanish commerce and industry. Among these were companies based on Zaragoza, Toledo, Granada, and Estremadura.[37] No analysis of their membership or of stockholder lists has been made, but some of the most prestigious noble families of the country participated.[38] Most of these companies soon foundered, but at least one, the Caracas Company, functioned successfully for sixty years.[39] The hints of noble participation suggest that commerce was not an alien concept for the second estate. Furthermore, the *Cinco Gremios Mayores*, which dominated several categories of wholesale and retail trade in manufactures in Madrid, was involved in these joint-stock companies. Through their *Compañía General de Comercio*, founded in the 1760s, they managed royal factories all over Spain, farmed several important taxes, traded with America and the Philippines, and contracted to supply both the military and the capital. In the 1780s the company had accumulated nearly 400,000,000 *reales* in deposits, which were used to extend credit to public and private customers.[40] Clearly there were numerous economic relationships between the wealthy elements of the interior. By the 1780s the *Banco de San Carlos*, predecessor of the Bank of Spain, was functioning, and it may well be interesting to learn just who actually participated in it.[41] The Bank in turn was involved in a grandiose *Real Compañía de Filipinas*, which incorporated the Caracas Company and included capital from the *Cinco Gremios*

37. For an account of the Toledo Company, with some references to others, see: Eugenio Larruga, *Memorias políticas y económicas sobre los frutos, comercio, fábricas y minas de España*, 45 vols., Madrid, 1785-1800, VII, pp. 59-418, VIII, pp. 1-94.
38. William J. Callahan, "Crown, Nobility, and Industry in Eighteenth-century Spain," *International Review of Social History*, Vol. XI, 1966, pp. 444-64.
39. Roland Dennis Hussey, *The Caracas Company, 1728-1784*, Cambridge, 1934.
40. Vicens Vives, *Historia económica*, pp. 522-24.
41. Earl J. Hamilton, "Plans for a National Bank in Spain, 1701-1783," "Foundation of the Bank of Spain," and "The First Twenty Years of the Bank of Spain," Parts I and II, in the *Journal of Political Economy* 57, 1949, pp. 315-36; 53, 1945, pp. 97-114; and 54, 1946, pp. 17-37 and 116-40, respectively. Also, Earl J. Hamilton, "El Banco Nacional de San Carlos (1782-1829)," in *El Banco de España, una historia económica*, edited by Pedro Schwartz Giron and Rafael Anes Alvarez, Madrid, 1970, pp. 197-231.

Mayores, and which was to undertake overseas trade, supply credit to the Crown, and construct interior canals.[42] Here too there is evidence of simultaneous involvement by commercial and aristocratic elements.

The same period saw the economic societies movement in Spain, and here again one finds quite an amalgam of landed and urban interests, espousing proposals for technical innovations and the imporvement of interior commerce and transport.[43] To be sure, the societies were active largely because they were fashionable, but there was considerable noble participation and it would be interesting to cross check some of the membership lists with those of the trading companies and with names of suppliers of agricultural produce to the city. Certainly some aspects of the economic reforms recommended by the societies were not so at variance with the interests of the landed element.

It is against this perception of Madrid and Castile in the eighteenth century that we must place the generally accepted picture of Spain in the nineteenth century. In this view the social and economic oligarchy which dominated the country changed significantly, incorporating elements of the landed nobility, "bourgeois" landowners who had purchased the disamortized church and municipal lands, developers and speculators in railroads and urban real estate, upper echelons of the army, and the wealthy commercial elements of the coastal areas.[44] This agro-commercial oligarchy crystalized quickly after domestic peace in 1839 and was the basis of the dominant *Moderado* party of the middle decades of the nineteenth century — a political force similar to the Orleonists in France.[45] Yet this oligarchy emerged

---

42. Maria Lourdes Díaz-Trechuelo Spinola, *La Real Compañía de Filipinas*, Seville, 1965.

43. Robert Jones Shafer, *The Economic Societies in the Spanish World, 1763-1821*, Syracuse, 1958.

44. Juan Beneyto Pérez, *Historia social de España y de Hispanoamérica*, Madrid, 1961, pp. 351-56, 368-93; Raymond Carr, *Spain: 1808-1939*, Oxford, 1966, pp. 196-209, 281-86; José Luis Comellas García-Llera, *Los moderados en el poder, 1844-54*, Madrid, 1970, pp. 60-80; Richard Herr, *Spain*, Englewood Cliffs, N. J., 1971, pp. 87-98; Antoni Jutglar, *Ideologias y clases en la España Contemporanea*, Tomo I, Madrid, 1968, pp. 15-20, 76-87, 101-24; Vicens Vives, *Historia Económica*, pp. 553-57, 560-83.

45. Comellas, *Los moderados*, pp. 66-69; Charles Moraze, *The Triumph of the Middle Classes*, Garden City, 1968, Chapter 5.

not within the context of the nineteenth century, but within that of the eighteenth century and the growth of Madrid.

Given the persistence of pre-industrial economic structures, this continuity of social development is much easier to accept than the idea that the aristocratic and bourgeois elements of the interior were perforce drawn into a "new" oligarchy in the course of twenty or thirty years after 1840.[46] There is little doubt that there was a considerable renewal of personnel through mobility into (and probably out of) the elite of the interior, but the bases of the oligarchy were laid down in he seventeenth and eighteenth centuries and were associated with the development of Madrid as capital of the Empire and as dominant market for the agriculture of the Spanish interior. The collapse of imperial and foreign trade, the value of which fell by two-thirds between 1792 and 1827,[47] simply weakened the great port cities, leaving the commercial nexus focused on Madrid in a position of relatively greater importance economically, socially, and politically. The nineteenth century in Spain thus becomes a continuation of the eighteenth century, rather than, as is often assumed, representing a break with previous patterns.

David Ringrose

46. This is particularly true if one uses the perspective suggested by Peter Laslett, *The World We Have Lost*, New York, 1965, Chapters 1, 2, and 9.

47. Josep Fontana has outlined with great effectiveness the collapse of agriculture and commerce in the periphery, but refuses to admit any degree of commercialization oriented to Madrid and therefore insulated from the collapse of the Empire. Josep Fontana Lázaro, "Colapso y transformacion del comercio exterior español entre 1792 y 1827. Un aspecto de la crisis de la economía del Antiguo Régimen en España," *Moneda y Crédito* 115, 1970, pp. 3-23; and his *La quiebra de la monarquía absoluta (1814-1820). La crisis del Antiguo Régimen en España*, Barcelona, 1971, pp. 39, 48, 52.

Community & Communication

That in the eighteenth century men differed no less sharply over rural and urban values than they do in the twentieth is quickly attested by Josiah Tucker, Dean of Gloucester, and Samuel Johnson. Although these two illustrious and dogmatic spokesmen agreed on politics and doubtless many other subjects, including Americans, they were clearly far apart as regards cities. In 1781 Tucker, whose trade was religion but whose religion was trade, published a refutation of Locke wherein he also forcibly registered his hostility to cities, especially overgrown ones. His blast is quickly summarized.[1] Such cities, he said, "ought not to be encouraged by new privileges, to grow still more dangerous; for they are, and ever were, the seats of faction and sedition, and the nurseries of anarchy and confusion ... where nothing is held sacred." "If," he continued, "a man has any sense of rectitude and good morals, or has a spark of goodness and humanity remaining he cannot wish to entice men into great cities by allurements. Such places are already the bane of mankind in every sense, in their healths, their fortunes, their morals, religion, etc., etc., etc." What, the historian must ask, would publicists do without the ubiquitous etc.?

To turn from this threnody, which has had many repeats in the past two centuries, to the rhapsody of Dr. Johnson, is to get a far more informing introduction to the town's role in eighteenth-century England.[2] "The happiness of London," he pronounced, "is not to be conceived but by those who have been in it;" there was "more learning and science within the circumference of ten miles ... than in all the rest of the kingdom." A great city was the "school for studying life; and 'the proper study of mankind is

---

1. *Josiah Tucker: A Selection from his Economic and Political Writings with an Introduction*, by Robert Livingston Schuyler, New York, 1931, pp. 536-37. Tucker voiced these opinions in *A Treatise concerning Civil Government, in Three Parts*, 1781. Could he, one must ask, have published his works in a village?
2. *Boswell's Life of Johnson*, 2 vols, Oxford, 1924, I, pp. 213, 281-82, 383-84, 415; II, pp. 14-15, 137, 193, 284; and *passim*.

man.'" Yes indeed, the town, as he said in the last year of his life, was his element.

Although both men were motivated by London, each phrased his opinion in terms that could apply to towns *per se*; and Tucker must have been aware that towns grow without encouragement. Admitting the validity of some of his disgust and the extravagance of Johnson's eulogy, it is the great lexicographer, not the gloomy dean, who has set the tone of what follows, yet the two complement one another in revealing how large the town bulked in contemporary consciousness and to what extent it was decisive in eighteenth-century culture. To put it so is to think not in terms of 10,000, 50,000, or 1,000,000 inhabitants but of the town as value. Throughout the century many forces were proclaiming the kingdom of man, the town most of all. William Penn saw in the country the works of God, but he conceded more than he knew when he found in cities "little else but the works of man."[3] When John Pomfret, Pope, Goldsmith, Wordsworth lauded rustic peace it was not at Walden Pond but near some fair town they'd have a private seat; what made the rural retreat seductive was the proximity of urban civilization.[4] Although the pastoralists proscribed "ten thousand baneful arts combined to pamper luxury and thin mankind" and insisted that the accumulation of men in cities, where the uniformity of their occupations produced a craving for extraordinary incident which the rapid communication of intelligence hourly gratified, blunted the "discriminating powers of the mind," most of them wanted *rus in urbe* and *urbs in rure*. After all, Pope wrote his "Ode in Solitude" at Twickenham and Josiah Tucker anticipated Adam Smith *because* the seats of sedition were

---

3. "Some Fruits of Solitude," no. 220, *The Peace of Europe: The Fruits of Solitude and Other Writings*, Everyman ed., p. 46.

4. John Pomfret, "The Choice" (1700); Alexander Pope, "Ode on Solitude" (1700); Oliver Goldsmith, "The Deserted Village" (1770); William Wordsworth, "Preface to Lyrical Ballads" (1800). From an earlier day comes a pertinent reflection in Giovanni Botero, *Treatise concerning the causes of the magnificence and greatness of cities*, c. 1700, trans. by Robert Peterson, London, 1606, pp. 43, 44: "It is necessarie that the Citie wherein you will found an Academy, be of an wholesome ayre, and of a pleasant and delightful situation, where there may be both rivers, fountains, springs, and woods. For these things of themselves without any other help are apt to delight and chere up the spirits and mindes of students. Such were in times past, Athens and Rhodes, where all goods arts and learning flourished most above all other."

also the seats of trade.

The concern here, however, is not the dichotomy of rural *versus* urban, whether expressed in the fable of the country mouse and the city mouse or in a dissertation on the machine in the garden, rich though that theme be, but the impact of urbanism in one area, the area of language, as manifest chiefly in one man, Dr. James Anderson, a Scot for all seasons.[5] But before considering his particular significance and its relation to our general theme, a quick review of the socio-intellectual environment is valuable.

As critics and eulogists alike made clear, no phase of English life remained untouched. The problem, then, is less to avoid overstatement than to integrate some particulars with contemporary culture, even to underscoring the obvious. If one were to list the characteristics commonly cited of eighteenth-century culture, how many would reflect the power of the town? Nearly all, even the sentimental revolt against civilization which sent beaus and tits back to nature in a coach and four with hampers of delicacies. The civilized man was played off against the noble savage, not the village rustic, and the bourgeois replaced the landed aristocrat as the pillar of society. For all the publicized frivolity, what the historian lights upon are curiosity, improvement, lust for learning and its communication through periodicals, circulating libraries, societies, and clubs. The pervasive ideal is intellectual progress, doubting and seeking, tearing down and building up. It consists, said Cassirer, "less in individual doctrines than in the form and manner of intellectual activity in general."[6] Could one, for instance, put the age of improvement in a period dominated by rural values? Could such campaigns as law reform and anti-slavery exist except where the works of men flourished? Could periodicals and societies multiply without towns? Is the eighteenth-century MS., the "blue-stocking," conceivable in a rustic setting? The

---

5. For a summary of Anderson's life and achievements see the present writer's "A Village Aristotle and the Harmony of Interests: James Anderson (1739-1808) of Monks Hill," *Journal of British Studies* 8, 1968, pp. 94-118, and "The *Bee* (1790-1794): A Tour of Crotchet Castle," *The South Atlantic Quarterly* 66, 1967, pp. 70-86.

6. Ernst Cassirer, *The Philosophy of the Enlightenment*, trans. by Fritz C. A. Koelln and James P. Pettegrove, Boston, 1955, pp. ix, 5. See also Paul Hazard, *The European Mind, 1680-1715*, and *European Thought in the Eighteenth Century from Montesquieu to Lessing*, Cleveland, 1963, *passim*.

intellectual creeds — all the isms — are urban-oriented, for ideas ferment in *community* where communication is easy.

Articulation and communication of those creeds required words, and some men quickly appreciated that old words and, even more, old meanings, did not meet new needs. Simultaneously they apprehended, without fully comprehending, that traditional social, political, and economic theories could no longer determine conduct in an increasingly industrial society. Out of the nursery of chaos, induced in part by the survival of rural values and traditions, came proposals for cure, strikingly manifest in efforts to fit the medium to the circumstances.

The major expression of *these* efforts was a steadily mounting harvest of English grammars and lexicons to the extent that during the last third of the century twice as many "grammars" were published as in the preceding hundred years, these in addition to those published before 1765, which continued to circulate and to appear in new editions.[7] Moreover, Greek and Latin grammars, though widely criticized as irrelevant to contemporary needs, were still in use, providing the sandy foundations on which many English grammars were built. The concern was not new, as every student of the preceding centuries well knows, but the focus had changed from that dominant before Bacon and indeed continuing long after. Whereas at first the stress was on transforming a vernacular into a language, freeing it from crudities and extravagances, countering the charge that the English had become eloquent before they became grammatical, the emphasis during the seventeenth century turned to making English a fit vehicle for the expression of ideas, an emphasis increasingly voiced and broadened throughout the eighteenth century as men appreciated the need for precise, clear, and concise communication in areas other than science. The growth of professions, their increasing specialism, the complexity of an industrial society, and proliferation of periodicals variously exposed linguistic inadequacies.

To be sure, educators had since the mid-seventeenth century been insisting that to neglect the study of English caused mischief

---

7. See the very informing work by Ian Michael, *English Grammatical Categories and the Tradition to 1800*, Cambridge University Press, 1970, especially appendixes VI, VII, VIII.

to the commonwealth: the true end of grammar was to speak and write well in a language already known, hence the inappropriateness of Latin grammar. That such gospel, however sensible, was slow to affect practice is clearly attested. There are many persons, said Daniel Turner in 1739, who "have had seven or eight years' education in our common schools that are not able to write twenty lines together with any tolerable propriety." Similarly in 1766 Henry McNab inquired, "Do we not every day meet with scholars who, having finished an English course of instruction, can neither spell, pronounce, read, speak, nor write their own language without violating ... its principles of expression or grammatical instruction?" To this question the *Critical Review* supplied an answer in 1771: "We have at present an infinite number of English grammars; but few are worth reading. They are filled with beggarly elements, mere technical terms and phrases, dry definitions, scholastic subtleties and rules attended with innumerable exceptions. The authors seem to have had no idea of applying their directions to any valuable purpose." As the *Monthly Review* neatly put it a year later, "a good English Grammar will not appear until ingenious men turn their thoughts to their native language."[8]

Actually several "ingenious" men were turning their thoughts to the subject, among them men whose major activity lay outside the grammarian's fold. Such a one was John Horne Tooke, whose public career prompted Thomas Arnold to exclaim, "God forbid I should ever be such a clergyman as Horne Tooke." Having been, as he saw it, the victim of the deceptive language of the courts, he was the quicker to insist that if men wished to avoid important error they must seek the meaning of important words, words of the greatest consequence to mankind. He knew that there was a good deal of pretense in grammars which in some instances should be sub-titled "an Exemplar of the subtle art of saving appearances, and of discoursing deeply and learnedly on a subject with which we are totally unacquainted"[9]: this recalls Goldsmith's earlier opinion that the paucity of good essays on language in England

---

8. Michael, *English Grammatical Categories*, pp. 1, 147, 201, 281-82, 490, 495-97.

9. John Horne Tooke, *Diversions of Purley*, 2 vols, London, 1786, I, p. 8 n.

illustrated Scaliger's intent to assign "the man he would have completely miserable no other employment than that of composing grammars and compiling dictionaries." Goldsmith himself was convinced that whatever grammarians said about the use of language its true use was to conceal thought. Nevertheless, in a more serious vein, he did maintain that the "language of the natives of every country should be also the language of its polite learning."[10]

Nowhere was the effort to fit the medium to the message, to improve its character, and to relate it to the total culture more explicit than in Scotland. Among Scotsmen the most assiduous in these pursuits was the aforementioned James Anderson whose concern embraced grammar, lexicography, and universal language, all pointed to intellectual ends and persisting throughout his adult life. What is significant about that concern is its existence. However commonplace his opinions — they were not entirely so — however pedestrian his exposition, that a Scottish farm boy, self-educated though of broad, important and original insights in several areas of knowledge, recognized the inadequacies of the English tongue for communicating ideas, and sought to repair the deficiencies, is worth attention. That he had company among fellow-Scots, some far more famous than he, also deserves attention. Adam Smith, Adam Ferguson, Sir James Stewart, David Hume, Lord Kames, Lord Monboddo, Thomas Reid, *not one a grammarian*, all rated language the most fundamental institution for man's community life. Many of them, be it observed, were, like Anderson, political economists, a significant item in an increasingly industrial society.

Smith, tracing the progress of language, warned against ambiguity, criticized translations as "languid and tedious," and exalted the style that expressed in the most concise, proper, and precise manner an author's thoughts.[11] Ferguson, concerned with the signification of such terms as *natural, welfare, interest,* warned

---

10. *The Collected Works of Oliver Goldsmith*, ed. by Arthur Friedman, 5 vols, Oxford, 1966, I, pp. 125, 281, 394.

11. *Lectures on Rhetoric and Belles Lettres delivered in the University of Glasgow by Adam Smith reported by a student in 1762-63*, ed. with an Introduction and Notes by John M. Lothian, Edinburgh, 1963, pp. 16-17, 38, and *passim*.

against mistaking a "mere innovation in language for a discovery in science" and stressed the correlation between the growth of language and the maturation of society: communication was the essence of civil society. Men invented terms to express what they distinctly perceived or strongly felt; because a "man of speculation" did not interpret words in the same sense as the vulgar, ambiguity confused issues.[12] Similarly Sir James Stewart insisted that imperfection of language caused disputes and Lord Kames emphasized that the words must fit the meaning.[13] Hume was even more occupied with precision, as evidenced by his dedication to explicit terminology, the right word to convey a particular impression; he knew that artful manipulation could shape opinion and policy. Monboddo wrote six volumes to prove that language had evolved as had man, and Thomas Reid, influenced in part by Monboddo, stressed the relation between communication and the growth of knowledge: language must keep abreast of knowledge.[14] At the same time Reid cautioned that new words aroused prejudice and led to misconstruction. Because men often differed not in judgments but in expression they debated meaning instead of issues; imperfections led to errors and ambiguities.

It was in this environment that Anderson lived and wrote, though there is no evidence that he owed anything to the men

12. *An Essay on the History of Civil Society*, 1767, 5th ed., London, 1782, pp. 23-24. This whole essay is in some degree an explication of words. Similarly between 1771 and 1774, eight brief "Miscellaneous Observations on the English Language" by *Scoto-Britannus* appeared in the *Weekly Magazine or Edinburgh Amusement. Containing the Essence of all the Magazines, Reviews, etc. With a variety of Original Pieces by Men of Literature, both in Prose and Verse. Also Extracts from New Publications of Merit, on whatever Subject of Science, Being an entertaining Record of the Writings and Transactions of the Times* (1768-1784), XIII (1771), pp. 35-36, 68-69, 173-74; XIV (1771), pp. 108-110, 130-32; XV (1772), pp. 131-34; XXI (1773), pp. 357-59; XXIII (1774), pp. 65-69. Anderson sometimes wrote pieces under *Scoto-Britannus* but I am inclined to believe that he did not write these; as will be seen below he did concern himself with such matters. To some extent both Ferguson and *Scoto-Britannus* anticipate Raymond Williams's suggestive *Culture and Society, 1780-1950*, Penguin, 1961, especially the Foreword and Introduction.

13. Sir James Stewart, *Inquiry into the Principles of Political Economy*, 2 vols, 1767, preface; Lord Kames, *Elements of Criticism*, 1762, New York, 1833, pp. 189, 215; *Sketches of the History of Man*, Edinburgh, 1774, *passim*.

14. Lord Monboddo, *Of the Origin and Progress of Language*, 6 vols, Edinburgh, 1774-92; *Antient Metaphysics or, the Science of Universals*, Edinburgh, 1779; *The Works of Thomas Reid*, 2 vols, ed. by Sir William Hamilton, 6th ed. Edinburgh, 1863, I, pp. 70-72, 98-99, 245; II, pp. 515-17, 605-6.

cited.[15] He spoke his own convictions and he often did so in essays unrelated to language *per se*. Alive to dynamic society and knowledge, he would have language reflect, even promote change. Language was discovery, and a revolution in thought meant a revolution in language. The essays he wrote, the periodicals he edited — and largely wrote — attested implicitly and explicitly his belief in communication. What distinguished men from animals was speech, the faculty that supplied the defect of knowledge by reasoning. Having that faculty, men should use it if they wished to learn; they would profit from reducing ideas to words, since until they did so they were not likely to attain the degree of accuracy requisite for utility. The Baconian gospel that writing maketh an exact man permeated Anderson's counsel as did many Baconian injunctions, linguistic and otherwise.

Recognizing his own verbosity, which he attributed in part to faulty education and in part to anxiety to convince others no better educated, he sought, not always successfully to avoid ambiguity and achieve lucidity. The man who knew must educate those who did not, and in terms they could understand; he must inform rather than entertain. It comes as no surprise then that Anderson continually stressed the obligation of the informed to *publish* their knowledge: "one observation, founded on actual experience, is undoubtedly worth five hundred plausible theoretical conjectures," especially when such were shrouded in jargon. Here, then, is his central emphasis, whatever the subject, namely the creative quality of language and its relation to ideas and institutions. Unhappily it did not, he felt, keep pace with the gradual, often imperceptible but nevertheless perpetual evolution of knowledge and progress of society.[16]

In order to appreciate the extent and constancy of Anderson's emphasis we can profitably examine five specific facets, all interrelated, some very closely: words in particular, language in general, grammar, style, and universal character and language. Although, as already suggested, he had much company in the first

15. I have omitted attention to the contemporary Scottish rhetoricians since I am particularly concerned with men whose major interest lay elsewhere.
16. *The Weekly Magazine*, XIII (1771), 1; *Interest of Great Britain with regard to her American Colonies* (1782), *passim*.

four, for the last it is necessary to go back a century to find an English parallel.[17]

Throughout Anderson's literary career of some thirty-five years he was sensitive to the necessity of clothing the thought and the thing in the proper word. Names remained but the things denoted by them were extremely diversified at different periods, with consequent misapprehension in meaning and error in practice. Furthermore, mistakes often arose from annexing modern meanings to words originally of quite different, even contrary, signification; men must guard against being misled by ancient terms, and loose ones too.[18] In this context he urged the need for classification, an emphasis very marked in contemporary medicine; once men knew what was being talked about they could investigate the "real qualities of natural objects."[19] He obviously agreed with Lavoisier's insight, voiced about the same time (1789): "as ideas are preserved and communicated by means of words, it necessarily follows that we cannot improve the language of science without improving the science itself."

Although Anderson never achieved literary distinction himself — as he recognized and his critics noted — he sought it in others, as manifest in brevity, elegance, clarity, and above all precision.[20] Consequently his attack on the "prevailing rage for inventing new names" causes no surprise. When men found it necessary to invent words to express new ideas they should, instead of compounding words, borrow from other languages and so assist the migration of words, a suggestion that at least in part prefaces his later plea for universal grammar. Compounds, he went on, became ill-founded because once the ideas they expressed were superseded they were

17. Particularly to John Wilkins, *Essay towards a Real Character and a Philosophical Language* (1668) and George Dalgarno, *Ars Signorum* (1661).

18. *Recreations in Agriculture, Natural-History, Arts and Miscellaneous Literature*, V (1801), p. 331. Here he anticipated Richard Whately and William Whewell half a century later, men like himself concerned less with grammar *per se* than with logic and meaning. See the present writer's "Cant Language, Common Language and Ambiguity: English Churchman, Linguistics and Social Change," *The Historical Magazine of the Protestant Episcopal Church* 40, 1971, pp. 311-13, 451-54.

19. *Recreations* I (1799), "Natural-History," p. 2, "Miscellaneous Literature," p. 87.

20. *Monthly Review* LVII (1777), p. 317; LVIII (1778), pp. 52-60, 375; LXXV (1786), pp. 131, 466-67; LXXVI (1787), p. 258; LXXVII (1787), p. 103; LXXVIII (1788), pp. 15, 361-70; 2 ser. I (1790), pp. 387-404.

not fitted to a dynamic society.[21] Words formed when ideas were immature lingered on when they were compatible neither with the original ideas nor with existing knowledge. He might have said with Horace:

> The liquors that a new vessel first contains
> Behind them leave a taste that long remains.

The problem was by no means simple. Men needed a proper nomenclature based on philosophical principles, but was a day of rapid change a fitting time to establish one? Who knew what tomorrow would bring?

Not only ideas but their application could be improved by the proper choice of words. In agriculture unless men applied the correct term to different kinds of soil, agriculture as a science stood still. In navigation men continued to use *latitude* and *longitude*, legacies of a day when the earth was presumed flat, with obstructive consequences. In imperial affairs because men differed over the meaning of *colony*, manifest at different periods, they differed over policy, with disastrous consequences. In social structure Anderson would replace *master* with *landlord* as less conducive to subservience. He ridiculed the delicacy that translated breeches into "small clothes" or "inexpressibles" and attested not delicacy but grossness. Finally, although humor was not his long shot, he indulged in linguistic japery in "Thoughts on the great Benefit to be derived from Want of Health": a cabinet minister retires only because of the "precarious state of his health"; a bankrupt nobleman goes abroad "merely for the recovery of his health"; a lady "whose shape has met with an untimely distortion retires to the country . . . for the recovery of her health." These latter items, and others like them, led him to emphasize how word-inventors sought to hide their intellectual poverty behind verbiage that bred ambiguity and confusion.[22]

---

21. *The Bee, or Literary Weekly Intelligencer, consisting of and selections from performances of merit, foreign and domestic, a work calculated to disseminate useful knowledge among all ranks of people at a small expense*, I (1790), pp. 90-95. Perhaps it was this conviction that prompted him to publish in a later number, IX (1792), pp. 173-76, "A Word to the Wise" by A. A. L., which attacked the prevailing spirit of linguistic innovation.

22. *Bee* V (1791), p. 265; *Recreations*, I, "Agriculture," pp. 2-3; *Bee*, I, pp. 90-95;

This same emphasis permeated more general reflections on language as it did his animadversions on grammar, style, and universal language. In an account of Scottish antiquities he contended that to appreciate the historical process the historian must study language as a source: nothing was better calculated for throwing light on the origin of nations. Therefore he strongly regretted that the description of fundamental social change had often fallen to an "inferior class of literary laborers" who neglected this source and at the same time hid the poverty of their thought under elegant phrases.[23] He also complained that although attention to language was the "surest proof of the progress that any state has made in civilization," Britain by that criterion would be among the least civilized. In comparison to other countries Britain had no protection against the caprice of individuals; while men could not create language they could improve it and so promote learning.[24]

The absence of an academy, the inadequacy of lexicography, and, most of all, the deficiencies of grammar inspired Anderson to stop the gap. He fully recognized that English was a baffling language and that of all sciences grammar, especially English grammar, was the most intricate.[25] Although no subject ought to interest English youth more than their own language, nearly all the attention had consisted of learning by rote the parts of speech. Because grammar was a practical and necessary art, instruction by precept and example should begin early; since people learned their common tongue by imitation errors were compounded. To combat that situation required a trained, skillful teacher who always spoke correctly and corrected promptly, and who never wearied his pupils with hard words that they did not understand. To elucidate, not perplex, was his goal. Throughout pupils must distinguish between reading words and reasoning about what they read; once the powers of reflection and judgment were awakened

---

"Thoughts on the American Contest," *Weekly Magazine*, XXXII (1776), pp. 321-25; *Interest of Great Britain with regard to her American Colonies*; *Bee*, III (1791), pp. 158-61, 317-21; *Recreations*, III (1800), pp. 54-66.
    23. *Bee*, VII (1792), p. 132.
    24. *Bee*, VII, pp. 57-65.
    25. *Bee*, VII, pp. 271-82; IX (1792), pp. 146-50; XV (1793), pp. 41-47, 84-95, 162-68, 232-39.

they would see the need for clear ideas. Clear expression meant clear thinking, as good words followed clear ideas. The man who thought would never rest with slovenly phraseology.

In his discussion of grammar Anderson must be accounted an ally of women's lib., for he found female compositions natural. Did the pedantry of male writers follow attempts to fetter the common tongue with the rules of Latin grammar? Women knowing no grammar wrote English more naturally than the "great lords of creation" who would only be content with "props borrowed from Greek or Latin authors." To deck out English grammar in Roman dress was absurd. More puerilities had been "gravely uttered by learned men on this subject than perhaps on any other" that could be named. Because language was the medium of creating as well as communicating ideas grammars should ever be pointed to that end. A good grammarian was a boon to society.

Equally so was a good lexicographer, though the task was too big for one man. Because of that, the English language, in Anderson's opinion, lacked a good dictionary, Johnson's being no exception since it often misled rather than informed readers. Like grammars dictionaries were built upon their predecessors, each one retaining the old defects and adding new ones, which made for obscurity and inelegance. One of the gravest errors was the careless use of synonyms. Although interchange often made no difference, on occasion one word alone was fitting. What a treasure a dictionary that defined a word and indicated its difference from commonly used synonyms would be. To achieve that goal the authors should not only attend to etymology but know the subject signified by the word well enough to supply the precise meaning; they should also include obsolete words. Given these assets the product would at once provide a fund of historical knowledge and guarantee accuracy in communication.

Having on numerous and diverse occasions criticized imprecise usage, inadequate grammatical terminology, the impropriety of the genitive, and related deficiencies, Anderson proposed solutions to these ills in installments of a dictionary and grammatical exercises.[26] He discoursed on the distinctions between *melt*,

26. *Bee*, VIII (1792), pp. 179-84; X (1792), 146-52, 177-82, 239-45, 274-84,

liquefy, and *dissolve*, between *immediately*, *instantly*, and *presently*, and several others. He thought *noun* meaningless, made more so by the absurdities of gender and case, the latter especially since many words had no genitive. He was vastly upset by pronouns where he again found gender a sticky point, most of all the third person plural. He complained about the use of a word in two utterly different senses: "He laid in a bed. Did he?" Where is the egg? He emphasized the limits of translation, though recognizing that knowledge of languages, the tools of learning, prefaced the acquisition of substance. Nevertheless, like Locke he believed that differences in culture could not be bridged in translation which rendered the peculiarities of idioms meaningless; moreover parts of speech essential in one language were suppressed in others.

All these matters convinced Anderson of the need for universal grammar and language, a conviction strengthened by current interest in anthropology and evolutionism and by awareness of non-European languages, particularly the Chinese, which had fascinated English devotees of universal language from Bacon forward. Indeed, some years before he formulated his own project he wrote "Hints respecting the Chinese Language" wherein he pursued several of his favorite themes, most of all that the circumstances affecting the language of a people were worth tracing because the history and character of a language were inseparable from the history of the human mind.[27] Chinese peculiarities of expression, he said, were owing to the mode of writing which in turn influenced thinking. Since the Chinese had no alphabet they denoted words by characters and left much to the imagination. This was the feature that he chiefly invoked in defense of his scheme for a universal language, an ideal that spanned several years ranging from casual reference to a German scheme through insistence on rational grammar to the full-dress project which he first presented to the American Philosophical Society.

It was on 17 July, 1795 that he subjected the members of that society to what may have been the harshest ordeal — not

311-18; XI (1792), 120-30, 193-204, 240-50, 226-74; *Transactions of the Royal Society of Edinburgh* I (1788), 23-24; *Monthly Review*, LXXVIII (1778), p. 493.

27. *Bee*, XI, pp. 48-52.

excepting the recent epidemic of yellow fever — of their lives, a 10,000 word "Heads of a Plan for removing the obstructions that the diversity of languages have hitherto thrown in the way of direct correspondence between the individuals of different nations." How long, one wonders, might the Plan itself have been? Anderson had been elected to the Society fifteen months before, through the good offices of George Washington and Thomas Jefferson — sponsorship that tells something about the man — but he was not present to read his proposal, nor is there any record of its reception.[28] Although the Society did not publish the paper, presumably the reason was not lack of interest. In June and November, 1788, two essays, one in French, were submitted for a prize medal which was awarded to one in December 1793. Both essays were published in the *Transactions*.[29]

In February, 1795 Anderson had sent an abbreviated version of his proposal to the Manchester Literary and Philosophical Society, of which he was a member, which was read on 4 November, 1796 and published in its *Memoirs* in 1798.[30] Four years later he published another version in his own journal *Recreations in Agriculture, Natural-History, Arts, and Miscellaneous Literature,* under the title, "Disquisitions respecting Language, and the qualities and uses of the different modes of writing that

---

28. The Plan was neither his first nor his last contribution to the Society. On 6 December, 1794, he sent "A Disquisition on wool-bearing animals" which was read 3 April, 1795, and published in the *Transactions of the American Philosophical Society, held at Philadelphia for promoting Useful Knowledge,* IV, Philadelphia, 1799, pp. 149-153; later on he sent "Additional Observations" on the same subject, also published, and books and samples of wool and nuts. *Trans.,* IV, pp. 153-54. See also *Early Proceedings of the American Philosophical Society for the Promotion of Useful Knowledge,* Philadelphia, 1884, pp. 220, 232-33.

29. *Early Proceedings,* pp. 161, 165; *Transactions,* III, pp. 262-310; IV, pp. 162-73. The recipient of the gold medal was "Cadmus, or a Treatise on the Elements of Written Language, illustrating, by a Philosophical Division, the Power of each character, thereby mutually fixing the Orthography and Orthoepy. With an Essay on the Mode of Teaching the Surd, or Deaf and consequently Dumb, to Speak" by William Thornton, M.D. The author, a resident of the Virgin Islands, owed a great deal to seventeenth-century English writers for both parts of his essay. For early English interest in teaching the deaf and dumb see the present writer's "An Arte to Make the Dumbe to Speak, the Deafe to Heare: A Seventeenth Century Goal," *Journal of the History of Medicine and Allied Sciences* 26, 1971, pp. 123-49.

30. *Memoirs of the Literary and Philosophical Society of Manchester,* V, part 1, London, 1798, pp. 89-101.

have been hitherto devised."[31] The three versions differ chiefly in the trimmings though the American Philosophical one warrants priority if only for its completeness. None departs in its essentials from the doctrines Anderson had been preaching for a quarter of a century; rather they represent his solution to the ills to which he thought the mind was heir.

He began his Philadelphia and Manchester papers on a personal note, seeking rapport with the audience. He reminded the Manchester society that he had of late employed his time chiefly in facilitating physical communication between places, still in a primitive stage, reminiscent of children beginning to walk, and expensive too. Now he was turning to intellectual communication between minds, for however primitive physical communication, intellectual was much more so. He informed the Philadelphia society that one of the principal amusements of his leisure hours for many years had been to discover how best to remove the barriers that separated nations and prevented general intercourse between individuals, of which one of the greatest was diversity of languages. Every literary person, he said, knew the difficulties implicit in the multiplicity of languages; the hours spent in acquiring them consumed more than half the time set apart for study, so that persons with a taste for learning could never apply their full time to the pursuit of real knowledge, because of the difficulty of discovering what others had said on the subject. Moreover, even if men did spend half their days in acquiring languages they, with few exceptions, could master but three or four. Every other person was stopped in his inquiries the moment he extended them in the smallest degree beyond his native tongue. And what did this "prodigious waste of mental exertion" profit a man? It permitted a rich correspondence between a small number of literary characters who, being unacquainted with the common

---

31. VI, pp. 1-23, 79-101, 310-20. Here he proposed three modes of writing, hieroglyphic, alphabetic, and symbolic, of which he preferred the last, not least because Chinese was symbolic and demonstrated remarkable facility. He suggested a symbolic system that had no connection with the sound of words, one that permitted arranging all words of every language in a few general classes. He incorporated some symbols he had devised for earlier papers, and proposed marks to denote number, gender, verbs, nouns, and other parts of speech with variations for moods, persons, and tenses, and even the age of animals.

business of life, were unable to distinguish how they could apply their knowledge to the benefit of society, while the people occupying the important stations in public affairs were precluded from intercourse with their fellows in other nations. Yet these men, possessed as they were of common sense, the discriminative faculty that tended above all others to promote the general good of mankind, could put that intercourse to best use.

To meet these problems Anderson had a solution "so perfectly simple" that it was inconceivable why it had not been adopted long before. (Simple solutions for complex problems which Lovejoy found characteristic of the Enlightenment). The solution was a new art of writing which by enabling two persons, ignorant of one another's tongue, to communicate with one another, would continually improve the conveyance of ideas to mutual improvement. What could be done for two could be done for five hundred, for it presented no greater difficulty than learning one's own language, a difficulty neither Anderson — nor any teacher since — underestimated. Henceforth it would be possible for every individual who knew his mother tongue to read and understand the books of every other nation and correspond with their nationals.

With uncharacteristic modesty Anderson laid no claim to discovery, even allowing that his "device" might be thought a "gasconade," but emphasized that he was only applying principles long known. Since Arabic numerals were equally intelligible to all Europeans why could not signs be devised to convey ideas. Although spoken language might be unintelligible, written was not; various nationalities used the same characters. Men tended to persevere in the track they were accustomed to and so were loath to consider, let alone to try, something different. They were committed to syllabic writing but when impartially examined that mode was found more difficult than symbolic writing wherein the Chinese demonstrated remarkable facility. Although Europeans dismissed the Chinese mode of writing as "unwieldy chaos" five minutes reflection demonstrated the absurdity of that dismissal. French academicians had found the Chinese written character accurate and precise even when dealing with the most abstruse questions. Far from running up to 100,000 words, that character amounted to 240 radicals, all the rest being modifications.

Although Anderson admitted that "characters" did stand at the center of the communication problem, he also asserted that only so long as he contemplated the problem from the outside did it seem insurmountable; characters seemed so difficult to form and to master. To express the ideas words express, would it not be necessary to devise an impossibly large number of signs, too large for the mind to master, even to invent, too numerous for a printer? On further consideration the difficulties were more apparent than real, especially when one allowed for derivatives and compounds. Once that was recognized and the signs devised usage followed readily. Both the sound and the sight of the characters must be mastered, but to learn them required no more time or difficulty than a strange language. A perfect knowledge of the signs would in no way exceed human capacity since several men had learned ten languages, each with individual words, and the number of signs would not equal one tenth the number of words in one language or one fiftieth of what many literary persons bestow on languages. A child could acquire them as easily as his mother tongue. Five hundred characters would satisfy all demands.

In forming his signs Anderson began with the perpendicular straight line as a base from which he thought it easy to form at least 1000 characters — twice as many as necessary — no two of which could possibly be confounded. Were one to adopt other forms as bases one could readily create 100,000,000 characters, all "perfectly distinct" from one another, but indeed 1000 was more than enough to express all the ideas of the mind and with far greater precision than hitherto attained. The same basic sign could be used to denote contrasts or opposites, cope with words that sounded alike orally, add precision to words that conveyed none, solve the deficiencies of gender — masculine, feminine, neuter, indefinite, castrated, spayed — and give meaning to personal pronouns in case, number, and gender. Writing was intended to communicate ideas by means of certain marks, speech by means of sounds, but it seemed more natural to denote ideas to the eye than to the ear. In whatever way men wrote they sought to excite ideas, but the attempt to do so by articulate sounds was useless unless men knew the language in which the words were couched.

It was obvious, he continued, that every language must be proportioned to the ideas of the people who need it. As ideas were enlarged language became more copious, and as the mode of thinking became more distinct language became more accurate and refined. Allowing for such distinctions, all languages were radically identical. The same ideas were clothed in a variety of dresses called words, so disguised that they were not recognizable among different nations. Were the dresses laid aside the ideas would be universally recognized. What was necessary was a universal written character to denote every distinct idea and place it in a dictionary of easy reference. Then the most sophisticated people would express their ideas by signs appropriate to their discrimination while the less sophisticated would disregard the signs for which they had no use; they too would think more precisely and express new ideas. All would be perfectly accommodated. Because the number of signs could not exceed the number of ideas they could never be more numerous than the words of any language. Since one idea often had ramifications, the same sign might be modified by differential marks to indicate the variations without altering the general idea.

For all his insistence on the practicality of his proposal and the ease with which it could be consummated, Anderson had no confidence that its adoption would come easily. Yet how obvious were the benefits – "free literary intercourse among all nations," ease of teaching children to read and write, diminution of space in writing and printing, permitting economy and increased circulation, rapidity of transcribing academical lectures, legal arguments, public harangues; noting ideas that flash upon us without loss of time, much more accurately and precisely than shorthand with its "half words and mutilated sentences, liable to be mistaken." Admittedly to state these benefits without evidence was "like putting down a parcel of enigmas" but, he bade his readers, think what had been accomplished with ten "trifling" Arabic numerals.

With this situation in mind Anderson avowed his readiness to help anyone who would undertake to complete what he had sketched. In addition he had asked a gentleman more skilled than himself to turn his attention to notation. The gentleman, unnamed, responded with great ardor and, though ignorant of Anderson's particular scheme, devised a mode equally comprehensive and "arranged with the most beautiful simplicity," which so pleased Anderson that he requested the gentleman to proceed. The gentleman as he advanced found that not only did the signs become more simplified but the ideas became more precise. He concurred with Anderson that five hundred characters would suffice and that these could be varied by movable signs denoting general ideas which became particular when connected with individual signs. Although unnamed, this ally was Dr. William Brown of Edinburgh whose "Hints on the Establishment of an Universal Written Character" was read to the Manchester Society on 26 January, 1798, and published in its *Memoirs* the same year.[32] Suffice it to say here that the two projects complemented one another. Brown, however, carried his proposal no further, and Anderson returned to the problem in the last volume of the *Recreations* in 1802.

What was the response to the project? Skeptical or, perhaps better, non-existent. The *Monthly Review* described Anderson's address to the Manchester Society as a "slight sketch" of a design, the difficulty of which did not consist in the general idea, which several ingenious men had already conceived, but in the particulars and, even more, in the execution — a difficulty exceeding not only that of a learned individual but probably of a union of all the learning of an age. Similarly Brown's proposal was conceded to contain many ingenious remarks but on a close view the difficulties rose faster than ingenuity could remove them. Another writer thought Anderson's later "Disquisition" valuable but doubted its adoption and pleaded for more explicitness. Anderson replied characteristically that a symbolic script could easily be devised.[33] And so the matter ended.

In relating Anderson, and some of his fellows, to the proper study of mankind, several items warrant mention. The thirty years spanned in these remarks embraced many interrelated revolutions — in politics, economics, thought. It would have been strange had

32. Pages 275-97.
33. *Monthly Review*, 2 ser. XXVIII (1799), pp. 49-50.

they not been reflected in the rhetorical environment. Hans Aarsleff, *The Study of Language in England, 1780-1860*, has characterized 1786 a crucial year in the history of language, chiefly because of *Diversions of Purley* by John Horne Tooke and "On the Hindus" by Sir William Jones.[34] Although both were important two publications do not make a revolution. When John Logan, an obscure philosopher of history, perceptively anticipating Cassirer, observed in 1781 that the "arrangements and improvements which have taken place in human affairs result not from the efforts of individuals but from the movement of the whole society,"[35] his words apply readily to the study of language, and to Anderson's concern with language as a means to an end. Whatever his emphasis at a given moment — grammar, lexicography, universal language — it reflected the contemporary transformation in knowledge and society. His lust for knowledge, his recognition of the need for clarity and precision in communicating that knowledge, his awareness of social tensions, all drove him to think in terms of *community*, the kingdom of man.

In this respect he was a good Lockean: "men were the masters of their own destiny; their happiness or misery is most part of their own making." He was a good Montaignist too in his recognition of human limits and potentialities: "a man may sit on the throne of God, but he must sit on his own ass." Finally, in this listing, he was a good Lucretian: men should use to the utmost the capacities they had. Among these capacities were getting the facts, getting them straight, and reporting them precisely. Ambiguity seemed so great an ill because in a revolutionary society it would compound confusion; if there was to be communication definition was essential since that was the beginning of knowledge as well as wisdom.[36] He was fully cognizant of the nursery of confusion but

34. Hans Aarsleff, *The Study of Language in England, 1780-1860*, Princeton, 1967, especially the Introduction and Chapter 1. See also James T. Boulton, *The Language of Politics in the Age of Wilkes and Burke*, London, 1963.

35. *Elements of the Philosophy of History*, London, 1781, quoted in J. R. Hale, *The Evolution of British Historiography from Bacon to Namier*, Cleveland, 1964, p. 35.

36. These ideals were registered throughout the pages of *The Bee*. To satisfy their need to read, people could resort to circulating libraries and book societies. The "middling and poorer ranks" could resort to periodicals. Before the advent of printing no individual could witness any remarkable "intellectual melioration in society" but now social man had improved "beyond all the calculations of philosophical historians," which

he worked all his life to make that confusion a school for studying life.

Charles F. Mullett

testified to the "power of aggregate existence." Anderson's mention of book societies recalls an eighteenth-century passion which he sought to nourish. In 1791 he projected a "general assembly of the learned of Europe, to be formed of the representatives, chosen by all the philosophical and literary societies for the time being"; it should circulate its transactions, report on the state of learning, and establish a press. Two years later he hailed the Newcastle Philosophical Society: when men united to disseminate knowledge, promote free discussion, nurse citizenship, and explore every useful art rather than wrangle over religion and politics, only benefit could result.

The Enlightenment & Social Structures

The Enlightenment[1] was very much a product of the urban culture of the late seventeenth and eighteenth centuries. Of course there were from the plantations of Virginia to the estates of Moscovy non-urban *philosophes* but these men usually looked to a city or cities for stimulation, guidance and for the standards to which they conformed or which they might seek to surpass. But, when we think of the enlightened, we think of them in the cities which provided varying social contexts in which the majority of them lived and worked, cities like London and Paris, Bordeaux and Edinburgh, Geneva and Weimar, Leyden and Königsberg, Glasgow and Amsterdam. Such cities were the nurseries of enlightened thought and the places in which the concerns of their surrounding hinterlands were most effectively discussed. Because of this it is worth asking how their size and institutional complexity affected their intellectual milieu, how in fact their enlightenments were limited and skewed by social determinants. That is the principal problem with which this study deals. I shall

---

1. By *Enlightenment* I mean the willingness of Europeans between c. 1660 – c. 1780 to dare to know, and within limits, to act on their rationally grounded knowledge. During this period enlightened Europeans came to assume that human problems of all kinds could be solved and that the answers to them could be unified in a general science of nature which ought to guide all actions which made claims to rationality. To support these views "the origin, extent and certainty of human knowledge," traditionally questions of rational psychology, had to be established. The investigation of these yielded new views of human nature but more importantly a methodological revolution which sanctioned empirical or quasi-empirical procedures. Skeptical doubts and an increased interest in facts and inductions based upon them could be and were brought to bear on an every aspect of thought, action and expression. This was a dynamic and progressive process which knew no end because nothing was held to be beyond doubt or the possibilities of confirmation or disproof. *Enlightenment* denotes a manner of thinking and acting, not a set of specific doctrines. To define *The Enlightenment* as a complex of beliefs is to fail to understand that it possessed an immanent teleology of its own shaped by its mood, methods and its general interest in practical problem solving and improvements. It is obvious that my view is taken from Ernst Cassirer's *The Philosophy of the Enlightenment*, trans. F. C. A. Koelln and J. P. Pettegrove, Princeton, 1951, and from various discussions of the period by Sir Isaiah Berlin.

try to show that real differences existed between metropolitan centers and three kinds of provincial cities. While my examples are British, I believe that the same relationships were to be found on the continent, particularly in France, and even in the American colonies.

The size of a city and the scope and quality of its cultural life are closely related for economic, demographic and political reasons. Only the largest cities provided markets for certain cultural goods. Theatres, opera houses, presses not only existed there but existed competitively. Novelty, variety and tension were elements of the literary scene in any metropolitan center. Paris or London offered artists and professional men of every kind a chance to live by their talents, skills and wit. They attracted the pre-eminent men of every field for such cities provided the greatest remuneration in money and prestige because they were the resorts of the wealthy and usually the seats of government. Economic causes insured that the recruitment of the best available men in every field would be maintained without the creation of institutions to train and induct men into their urban intelligentsia. The same causes guaranteed that the range of intellectual work would be broad both in kind and quality for amongst the competitors would be producers of everything for which there might be a market large or small, good or bad. The economic attractions of the metropolis meant that cities like London would find in their intelligentsias men from the remote and perhaps semi-independant parts of the country such as Ireland, Scotland and the colonies. Connecting their regions to the life of the metropolis, they were likely to bring to the largest cities perspectives not native to them. However much they might share theoretical views, they were not likely to agree on social issues. A great city could sustain diversities of outlook and the feuds which in the eighteenth century resulted from them. The size of a city virtually decided whether a city was to be a leader or an imitator of fashions and standards set by others. Provincial cities in Britain followed London; even the brilliance of Edinburgh was the reflected brilliance of selective adaptation and imitation. What they could do largely depended on the kinds of men they possessed and these were determined by the institutions they contained. Qualitative differences came also from the fact that provincial cities were training grounds for those who would eventually emigrate; their permanent and rooted intellectuals were different men from those who competed in the hurly burly of London or Paris. Those who stayed were not always mediocre but they were men with land, places, and security, men with reasons to conform.

Some peculiarities of metropolitan intellectual life derive from the size of its enlightened intelligentsia. In large cities this inevitably fragmented because of the opportunities for increased specialization and because no one group could embrace and serve the various interests of its members as could the Academy at Bordeaux[2] or a couple of societies with overlapping memberships as in provincial cities like Edinburgh, Aberdeen or Glasgow. A fragmented intelligentsia could not offer one coherent viewpoint but presented several which might be mutually incompatible although equally enlightened.[3] London to a gentleman in Lincolnshire in 1760 could have conveyed no definite ideology even though he might accept his standards of taste and intellectual accomplishment from its artists, critics, academicians and improvers. Edinburgh provided such a coherent viewpoint to the men living in the hinterland it dominated; so did Bordeaux.[4] Coherence in both cities came from an undivided intelligentsia possessed of bodies which could articulate a distinctive regional view. And, in both cities it was the view of men related by blood and family ties who shared a common background, who saw one another almost daily and who were men of property and office, securely rooted in their province. The pressures to conform in such a city where the intellectual élite might include only two or three hundred men were much greater than they could have been in Paris or London. In the metropolis a man could if he wished remain anonymous or

---

2. Cf. *Bordeaux au XVIIIe Siècle*, tome V of *Histoire de Bordeaux*, ed. F. G. Pariset, Bordeaux, 1968; D. Roche, "Milieux académiques provinciaux et société des lumières ..." in *Civilisations et Sociétés: Livre et société dans la France du XVIIIe Siècle*, Paris and La Hague, 1968; P. Barrière, *L'Académie de Bordeaux*, Paris, 1956.

3. Paris in the 1760s offers the example of the *physiocrats* and the *encyclopédistes*. In London one might point to various political thinkers ranging from the commonwealthmen on the left to Burkean conservatives on the right.

4. *Histoire de Bordeaux*, t. V, p. 97; Barrière, *op. cit.*, p. 35.

work in undisturbed isolation. In smaller cities this was less likely and for the same reasons it was likely that provincial intellectuals would write scandalous books like *The Memoirs of A Woman of Pleasure*. The effect which numbers had on the quality of city life was noticed by Dr. Johnson whose comments on Ladyday 1776 Boswell reports as follows:

> I observed that it was strange how well Scotchmen were known to one another in their own country, though born in very distant counties; for we do not find that the gentlemen of neighbouring counties in England are mutually known to each other. Johnson with his usual acuteness, at once saw and explained the reason of this: "Why, Sir, you have Edinburgh, where the gentlemen from all your counties meet, and which is not so large but they are all known. There is no such common place of collection in England, except London, where from its great size and diffusion, many of those who reside in contiguous counties in England, may long remain unknown to each other."[5]

While Johnson's remark is about gentlemen, it applies equally well to that portion of the gentry which composed the enlightened élite of the city. Moreover, it suggests that the enlightenment of some provincial cities may have had a greater impact on their hinterlands than did that of the large centers. The gentlemen collected in Edinburgh managed Scotland just as they sustained its intellectual life. This could not be said of the London intelligentsia or of those in smaller British cities with the possible exception of Dublin. Such a situation was conducive to the study of issues which directly affected the lives of the landed gentry and was congenial to the city's professional men who came mainly from their ranks. Knowledge and the power to act on it was maximized in provincial capitals. The lack of fragmentation in their élites presupposed a lack of political division not to be found in the metropolis but necessary to the preservation of provincial independence. Independence to be kept had to be asserted in socially useful ways. The élite of Edinburgh studied their history, collected

---

5. James Boswell, *The Life of Samuel Johnson*, Oxford, 1924, vol. I, p. 678.

and expounded their laws and promoted trade and industry partly because these were necessary to their survival as Scots. The improvement of agriculture became a national concern in Scotland long before it did in England and this was possible because of the collection of gentlemen in Edinburgh. London had a local influence over the home counties and a sporadic one over the whole of Britain, while Edinburgh's sway was more uniform, albeit, over a smaller hinterland consisting principally of the Lowlands but in some cases ranging as far south as Yorkshire.

Having said all this it is equally important to point out that size alone did not determine whether or not a city would have an enlightenment or precisely what kind of an enlightenment it would be remembered for. Where political or religious opposition to enlightened thought was too strong nothing happened. Where the aristocracy or urban middle classes were unmoved or unsympathetic, little was achieved. Where the hinterlands were small, poor and unable to supply recruits for the cities' intellectual life, it might wither. Where deep cultural divisions existed within a country, as in Ireland, where the religion and language of the peasantry was not that of the literate classes, the enlightenment never rooted. Even in Dublin it never flourished perhaps because the majority of its large population could not be touched by the culture of the élite. In some areas, like Germany, there was not really a metropolitan city to function as London and Paris did. Moreover, German provincial towns were often the seats of minor courts which looked to Paris and imitated what their rulers could afford. Sometimes they had periods of forced and hectic brilliance, as Weimar did, but this was due to the interests of the prince and to their institutional complexity. Some cities like Copenhagen, which was culturally German, lacked the linguistic base requisite to self-expression. Holberg's decision to write in Danish for a small and not particularly cosmopolitan audience was analogous to the opposite choice made by Scots to write in standard English and to be part of a larger world.[6] In Scotland

---

6. In 1727 Holberg wrote, "My name might perhaps have obtained some celebrity in foreign countries, if I had not written in the Danish language, which is confined within such narrow limits, that even in parts of Denmark I am scarcely known; but I am satisfied with having deserved well of my native language, and with having at any rate

high literacy rates, a relatively good school system, considerable social mobility and after c. 1730 a flourishing economy had something to do with the brilliance of this period of Scottish history.[7] So too did the presence of an aristocracy which felt compelled to become as polite as the English and to emulate them in other ways while at the same time maintaining their character as Scotsmen and their paternalistic stance toward the lower orders. All of these factors had some bearing on the fortunes of eighteenth-century cities. They help to explain why Madrid had fewer enlightened men to boast of than did Geneva, why Copenhagen and Stockholm with populations larger than those of Edinburgh and Glasgow could point to no cluster of men of comparable brilliance. Perhaps they make it clearer why Naples and Dublin were less fruitful places than Bordeaux and Birmingham, why Weimar outshone Vienna.

The institutional complexity of a city, like size, set limits on the intellectual activities which could be sustained within it because its institutions determined the kinds of men from which the intelligentsia could be recruited and the number of places in which they could be supported. Eighteenth-century cities can be classed in four groups possessing quite different levels of complexity. To the first class belong the metropolitan cities which were centers of national life and possessed the most diverse array of places. Here we could put St. Petersburg, Stockholm, Copenhagen, Berlin, Munich, Leipzig, Vienna, Paris, London, Madrid, Venice, Turin and Naples. To the second rank belong the capitals of formerly autonomous areas which in the eighteenth century possessed the remnants of independant establishments which were still being assimilated into states which were not yet thoroughly unified nation states. These cities possessed relatively diverse types of men though one type might predominate as did the men of the

---

secured my name from oblivion among my countrymen." A generation later he complained that "most of the prominent people would rather read rubbish in French than the most excellent of compositions in their own tongue, it is little wonder that the best of Danish literature lies unsold." *Ludvig Holberg's Memoirs*, ed. S. E. Fraser, Leiden, 1970, pp. 153, 261.

7. T. C. Smout's *A History of the Scottish People 1560-1830*, London, 1969, pp. 500-14 and D. Daiches's *The Paradox of Scottish Culture*, London, 1964, are the best short discussions of the Scottish Enlightenment.

law in Edinburgh and Bordeaux. To this rank we could assign Königsberg, Dresden, Strasburg, Edinburgh, Dublin, Geneva, Lausanne, the parliamentary cities of France, Milan, Bologna, and Padua. Thirdly, there were towns which had regional importance and some culturally supportive institutions such as church establishments, courts, or universities. Cities like Upsala, Aberdeen, Utrecht, Leyden, Göttingen, Bayeux and Montpellier might be included here. Finally there were cities whose civic and cultural life was more closely connected to commerce and industry and whose enlightenments reflected the importance of these. Glasgow, Birmingham, Manchester belong here as does perhaps a city like Lyons. When cities are grouped in this way it is easy to see that their intelligentsias will be recruited from very different bases and that the scope and quality of their work is likely to differ. Given the kind of city, its enlightenment can to some extent be predicted for the enlightened will concern themselves with topics of professional interest to them and express themselves in forms they are used to handling. Plays are unlikely to be written in cities which lack theatres and legal works will probably not be written in university towns lacking courts and lawyers. Professors will write textbooks but not hack journalism unless the university is in or near a printing center. Works of all kinds are probable in a metropolis, but not in a small city where the only culturally supportive institutions are the churches and university. In Britain, London, Edinburgh, Aberdeen and Glasgow can be used to illustrate the ways in which institutional complexity helped to determine patterns of intellectual activity. Similar examples could I am sure be found in France and elsewhere on the continent.

Eighteenth-century accounts of Britain sometimes included a kind of institutional inventory of its component kingdoms and of their principal cities. Anyone who has looked at such an account, or at a civil list from the period, cannot help but be struck by the degree to which the national cultural life of Britain was centered in London, particularly in the first half of the century. London possessed as any capital would, the court, Parliament, the centers of the civil, ecclesiastical, military and naval administration. This meant that at any given time, a large if not a preponderant portion of "the rich, the well born and the able" people of the country, were there to enrich its life and to benefit from the opportunities the city provided.[8] In addition to the hundreds of government places available there, many others existed to be filled. Charities, schools, hospitals, colleges, municipal and gild organizations as well as professional bodies like the College of Physicians, the Inns of Court or foundations like Sion College, all provided jobs and were sources for the recruitment of the enlightened intelligentsia. Chartered bodies like the Royal Society, or the Society of Arts, clubs like that of the Antiquaries in the 1720s or the Literary Club of Dr. Johnson's old age provided opportunities for the like-minded to discuss their views or even actively to promote them. Patrons throughout the century dispensed their largesse there. Not all were worthy of the support they received, nor were all the worthy supported, but the establishments found room for a surprising number of enlightened men throughout the eighteenth century. In 1715, on the abbreviated civil list printed by Guy Miege in his *Present State of Great Britain*, one easily finds the names of at least twenty distinguished men holding patronage jobs in London. The scientists include Newton, Halley, Cotes, Hans Sloan and among the doctors one notes Arbuthnot and Garth. Sir Christopher Wren, Sir John Vanbrugh, Grinling Gibbons and Sir Godfrey Kneller represent architecture and painting, while Nahum Tate, Sir Richard Steele and Dr. Bentley might be said to uphold the claims of poetry, prose and criticism. Peter LeNeve, Roger Gale and Thomas Maddox, antiquaries and historians found places as did Robert Molesworth, Benjamin Hoadly, William Popple, Jr. and Lord Bolingbroke who, like them, was later to write on politics and public policy. At least fifty others included on the roster of the Royal Society in that year could be added to this list which even then would be incomplete. Later in the century Johnson's Club would display a similar diversity and would include only a few men without some place secured in London.

When one turns to Edinburgh in 1715 one finds none of this

---

8. Dorothy Marshall's *Dr. Johnson's London*, New York, 1968, has a good discussion of the importance of London in eighteenth century British intellectual life. She has noticed that the London intelligentsia was "A world of coteries and groups and individuals" but underplays I think the importance of the institutions from which the intelligentsia was recruited and in which many of its members were supported.

rich variety; only two enlightened men appear on Miege's lists. What is important, however, is not the lack of intellectuals holding office, but the fact that offices of various kinds existed for enlightened men to fill. Even the truncated Scottish establishment preserved in Edinburgh a more diverse mixture of institutions and people than could be seen in any other British city save Dublin. Court offices were reduced to a few sinecures and hereditary positions, but the civil administration was large enough to provide men throughout the century who could realistically consider practical problems of government as well as to provide places for others like Adam Smith who did so. While the city's religious establishment was smaller than the English bench of bishops, the General Assembly of the Church of Scotland and its standing committees met in Edinburgh. The Castle garrison had soldiers some of whom were always included in most of the significant intellectual circles in the city. Only the judiciary and the lawyers were comparable to the establishments in London. There Miege listed over 350 offices connected with the courts of Chancery, Exchequer, King's Bench and Common Pleas and he gave the names of 144 Sergeants and civilians at Doctors Commons. In Edinburgh the judicial functionaries numbered about 110 while the lawyers (advocates and writers) came to 175. The city possessed a few foundations, municipal and guild organizations as well as a College of Physicians and two corporations of lawyers one of which possessed a great library. Edinburgh in 1715 lacked a Royal Society but such a body had been promoted at the end of the seventeenth century and several would flourish in the eighteenth century. Patrons were not numerous but in the university Edinburgh possessed a cultural asset which London lacked. From the perspective of many Scots, then and now, these remnants of an independant past were pitiful, but they were sufficient to insure that the intelligentsia of this city would be diverse in its composition and that it would embody something like a national consciousness.

When we turn to Aberdeen and Glasgow the civil authorities become minor customs and revenue officials and town councillors. The church is represented by a synod whose appellate court is the General Assembly. Military presence is insignificant and the corporations of lawyers and doctors were relatively unimportant. The colleges are the only institutions which are comparable to those in Edinburgh. Nevertheless Aberdeen was of regional importance in ways difficult to define. Isolated from the rest of Scotland, linguistically somewhat different, episcopalian and non-juring to a greater degree than the rest of the kingdom, more than a little Jacobitical and somewhat more Latin in their culture, even different in their eating habits and trading to ports not frequented by Edinburgh or Glasgow merchants, different even in their schooling and philosophy, Aberdonians lived in a distinct region and a city which had almost the status of a minor capital. But, it lacked the institutions through which to articulate its distinctness. Throughout the century its intelligentsia was recruited from the university, the local gentry and the ministers. Glasgow was too close to Edinburgh to be so distinctive. Its major difference when compared to Aberdeen is to be found in its commercial life but this was not without intellectual consequences. Growing from 12,000 to 85,000 people during the eighteenth century, its merchants were men of importance and played a larger role in enlightened circles within the city.

The effects which institutional complexity had upon the recruitment of the intelligentsias of eighteenth-century cities can be seen when we compare clubs in the four British cities during the latter half of the century. The groups I have chosen are Johnson's Literary Club, the Edinburgh Poker Club, the Aberdeen Philosophical Society and Gordon Mill's Farming Club and the Glasgow Hodge-Podge Club and Literary Society. These groups were equally enlightened and typical of other groups in their respective cities.

The Literary Club[9] was a general discussion group in which only one topic was proscribed. To exclude politics was not unreasonable when among the members were to be found opposition Whigs like Burke, Fox, Sheridan and Dunning, near radicals like Sir William Jones, and various men holding important

---

9. I have taken my information about it, including the membership list, from Boswell, *op. cit.*; Sir John Hawkin's *The Life of Samuel Johnson*, New York, 1961; the *DNB*; G. E. Cokayne and V. Gibbs, *The Complete Peerage*, London, 1910-53, and G. E. Cokayne, *The Complete Baronetage* London, 1900-9.

THE ENLIGHTENMENT & SOCIAL STRUCTURES • 109

posts in government. The Club's members were men whose interests in literature and whose accomplishments made it desirable for them to have a place in which to talk about their ideas, their books[10] and the studies which they pursued. It could be a relatively specialized group because others in the city existed to cater to the needs to improve, agitate or to consider the arts, sciences and history. Most members belonged to at least one other such body. This can explain why men were members but it does not explain why they were in the city in the first place. When we try to answer that question we return to the kind of city London was. Twelve of the members were Irishmen, half of whom made a political career in England. Christopher Nugent and Goldsmith were drawn to the city by the opportunities it offered to men of letters and perhaps by the hopes of patronage. Three Irish bishops may be harder to account for but Lord Charlemont and Agmondesham Vesey undoubtedly came for social and political reasons. Edward Malone expected to practise law in London, where instead, he became one of the century's great book collectors. The five Scots in the Club had similar professional motives. Bishop Douglas held lucrative London livings. George Fordyce was a fashionable doctor, while Adam Smith was in London working on and then overseeing the publication of the *Wealth of Nations*. Boswell was Johnson watching, dining at the Inns of Court and seeking opportunities to come to London. Sir William Hamilton's diplomatic career had depended on his residence in London. For the thirty-one Englishmen who belonged only seven were native Londoners. (Banks, Hawkins, Chamier, Coleman, Fox, Hinchcliffe, Shipley.) Dunning, Lord Stowell, Sir Robert Chambers and Sir William Jones had been drawn to London by the courts in which they practised and in which they got jobs. Reynolds, Burney, Johnson, Garrick and Dr. Richard Warren could not have reached the top in any other setting. Ten others in the Club were MP's, two were on the Board of Trade, one was the Receiver General of the Duchy of Cornwall, the Duke

---

10. Several members had notable private libraries including Earl Spencer, Sir Joseph Banks, Topham Beauclerk, Garrick, Malone and Stevens, while Chambers and Jones were collectors of Sanskrit MSS. The Literary Club members jointly probably had more books than the Advocate's Library in Edinburgh.

of Leeds was Chief Justice in Eyre North of the Trent, Richard Burke was for a while Deputy Paymaster, Anthony Chamier became Under Secretary of State and Samuel Dyer had a job in the War Office. Thomas Warton was the Poet Laureate and his brother not only the Headmaster of Winchester but the holder of several church livings as well. Altogether these places meant a subsidy to learning and show the degree to which recruitment of the intelligentsia of a metropolis was affected by size and the institutions available.

In the 1760s and 1770s the Edinburgh Poker Club[11] was the only group in that city comparable to Johnson's Club. It was a general discussion club with an avowedly political aim, the establishment of a Scots militia and the promotion of legislation favorable to Scotland. In 1768 there were seventy-eight members who can be categorized as follows: twenty-four were judges or lawyers, ten were or had been soldiers, five were attached to the civil administration, eight were university professors and an equal number were merchants or bankers, four were clergymen including the Clerk of the General Assembly and three other leaders of the Moderate party. Among the remaining gentlemen were John Hume and his cousin David, Adam Smith and John Adam an Edinburgh architect and government contractor. Collectively these men exercised more power in their city and perhaps in Britain than did the members of the Literary or any other London club. They and they alone led Scottish public opinion, they controlled local politics and formed a sizeable parliamentary interest. The Poker Club failed in its main political objective but during its twenty-two years it admirably served the needs of men who required some institution in which to meet, to discuss and plan the improvement of their city and region. Moreover, like the Edinburgh Philosophical Society or the Academy at Bordeaux, it articulated a provincial

---

11. Information on the Poker Club can be found in Alexander Carlyle, *The Autobiography of Alexander Carlyle*, ed. J. H. Burton, Edinburgh, 1910, pp. 282, 291, 439 *et. seq.*, 466, 482, 483; Harry A. Cockburn "An Account of The Friday Club" in *Book of the Old Edinburgh Club*, vol. III, June, 1911; D. D. McElroy, *Scotland's Age of Improvement*, Pullman, 1969; D. D. McElroy, "Literary Clubs and Societies in the Eighteenth Century," unpublished Ph.D. thesis, University of Edinburgh, 1952. *The Minute Book of the Poker Club* is at the University of Edinburgh Library, MS. Dc. 5. 126.

viewpoint shared by most enlightened Scots. It expressed a kind of civic and national pride which reflected the positions held by its members and it gave them the feeling as one of them said that they were the equals of the "literati of Paris" and were to be counted among "the ablest men in Europe."[12] They could not, however, find among their members any artists, musicians, actors, great aristocrats or holders of high offices, nor had they men of letters who lived by their pens or adventurers drawn to Edinburgh as Burke had been drawn to London.

In Aberdeen and Glasgow the intelligentsias were drawn from much more limited sources. Prior to the founding of the Philosophical Society or Wise Club[13] in 1758, Aberdeen seems to have lacked a significant enlightened group. During its first ten years that club gathered seventeen members only two of whom were not members of one of the two colleges — the minister of Nigg and the tutor to Lord Deskfoord's son. During these years a farming club flourished in the vicinity, eighteen of whose members are known.[14] Five were professors, three were merchants including the town's principal bookseller and printer, two were advocates, one a minister and the remainder gentlemen with estates in the area, including the Rector of King's College. Glasgow was richer in clubs but had none of the importance of those in Edinburgh. The Hodge-Podge Club founded in 1752 began as a serious intellectual venture for the discussion of political and literary questions but within two years it was washed to the whist tables on waves of punch, toddy, porter and brandy.[15] Between 1752 and 1783, it admitted thirty-one members of whom twenty were merchants, four professors, two surgeons and one gentleman of means. The Glasgow Literary Society,[16] a more significant group founded

---

12. Carlyle, *op. cit.*, p. 442. The man he quoted was James Edgar, a Commissioner of Customs who in this way declined an invitation to dine with the Baron Holbach.

13. Information on the Wise Club can be found in McElroy, "Literary Clubs," I, p. 128; the *Minute Book, Rules and Questions* and *Notes of Discourses in the Philosophical Society* (kept by David Skene). These are all in the King's College Library, the University of Aberdeen: MSS 539-1-2-2a; MS 145; MS 540. A list of its paper topics is also contained in James McCosh, *The Scottish Philosophy*, New York, 1875, pp. 467-73.

14. J. H. Smith, *The Gordon Mill's Farming Club 1758-1764*, Edinburgh, 1962.

15. T. F. Donald, *History of the Hodge-Podge Club*, Glasgow, 1900; McElroy, "Literary Clubs" I, p. 550; J. Strang, *Glasgow and Its Clubs*, Glasgow, 1857.

16. *Minutes of the College Literary Society 1790-1799*, Glasgow University

in 1752 or 1753, had initially no members unaffiliated with the university. By 1796 it had admitted one hundred men of whom nine were merchants, twelve ministers, four doctors, five advocates, thirteen gentlemen and peers and fifty-seven professors and officers of the university. In neither Aberdeen nor Glasgow do we find judges, civil administrators, soldiers, or even so many gentlemen. They were lacking because the places for them were not there.

The enlightenments of the four British cities reflect the complexity of their institutional bases. Aberdeen's was a professional enlightenment coming from the classroom and pulpit and the Wise Club sessions. Thomas Blackwell, Marischal College Professor of Greek, converted his expertise into three works on ancient history including one of importance on Homer. George Turnbull, moralist and divine translated a famous text book by Heineccius and wrote on morals, religion and in 1740 produced a *Treatise on Ancient Painting*. Alexander Gerard's essays *On Taste* and *On Genius* were products of the Wise Club and his theological writings owe something to his professorship of divinity. James Beattie's poetry may stand outside this rule but his *Pamphlet on Scotticisms* and the work up of his lectures entitled *Moral Science* were from and for the classroom as well as the general public. The very interesting *Essays on the History of Mankind* by James Dunbar included Wise Club papers and covered topics on which any regent would lecture. The algebra book and the edition of Robert Simson's *Porisms of Papus* with a biography of Simson by William Trail were again what might be expected from a professor of mathematics. Thomas Reid, the greatest of the Aberdonian philosophers, published what were sophisticated versions of his lectures, portions of which were also read to the Wise Club. One looks in vain for significant works on law, medicine, science or even politics for Aberdeen lacked great professors in these fields and had no one else.

At Glasgow the scope of the enlightenment was greater not only because the university was better but because its personnel

---

Library MS gen. 4; *Transcript of Laws and Minutes*, Glasgow University Library, Mu 21-Y.33, MS Murray 305.

was different and responded to the bustle of city life. One reason for that is perhaps the port, another is to be found in the fact that Glasgow was a more fashionable university, famous for its teaching which prior to 1760 Edinburgh could not equal. It had a more pious and less distracting environment which brought to it the sons of the gentry. Fashion to be maintained requires an outer-directedness which was lacking in more remote Aberdeen. In Glasgow it was assured partly by the placing in the university of gentlemen who had been abroad with the sons of noblemen who had influence in the college. The Muirs of Caldwell in two generations placed their tutors there and helped a cousin to a professorship as well. Lord Cathcart secured for his secretary and the tutor of his son the Professorship of Humanity. James Moor, the editor of the Foulis Press classical works, was the tutor of the Earls of Selkirk and Kilmarnock; he got the Greek chair. The Dukes of Hamilton were in part responsible for placing Robert Hamilton in the Chair of Anatomy and for making William Cullen an academic. Had he wanted it they could have found a chair for Dr. John Moore who accompanied the eighth Duke on the Grand Tour. Such appointments meant a professoriate which had seen and done more and was willing to talk about it in lectures which were perhaps more exciting and relevant than those given at Aberdeen. Moor's classics courses concerned themselves with the rise and fall of civilizations and empires, the nature of civic greatness and the genius and national institutions of the Greeks.[17] His colleague in the history chair, William Ruat, gave a course which was a preparation for the Grand Tour and a public political career. He also gave public lectures on the newly discovered art works of Herculaneum. Both men had an eye on Montesquieu as well as on their audience. Smith's change in the logic course to include rhetoric and *belles lettres* was a nod in the same practical direction as were his lectures on police, justice, revenue and arms which formed a part of moral philosophy as he taught it.[18] Finally,

17. Some of Moor's and Ruat's lecture notes are preserved at the National Library of Scotland: Adv MSS 23.6.18; NLS MS 4992.
18. Glasgow men were not wholly innovative in these matters. Charles Mackie's history course at Edinburgh was also given with the grand tour and the study of the civil law in mind. John Stevenson, the Edinburgh logic professor, had turned his course into

although the great works of the Glasgow enlightenment — Hutcheson's philosophy, Simson's mathematics, Smith's Theory of *Moral Sentiments* and John Millar's *The Origin of Ranks* — were all the products of classroom teaching, as they were at Aberdeen, they did not exhaust the enlightened activities of the professoriate.

Glasgow professors were not inward looking but when they looked inward they saw different things from what was visible in Aberdeen. The scientists Black, Cullen, Robison and Hope, all began their academic careers in Glasgow, and all were active men whose professional interests escaped the lecture hall and the laboratory. Black not only practised medicine and taught chemistry, but he was interested in steam engines and in the commercial and technical work of the Foulis brothers whose press like Watt's instrument shop, was within the university precincts. All his life Black was consulted on problems as disparate as the qualities of mineral waters from wells which might be improvable as spas to the testing of ore samples. He analysed the Edinburgh drinking water, new dyes and kelp ash. Cullen had shipped out as a surgeon on a voyage to the West Indies; he had been a magistrate at Hamilton and was interested in salt making and the linen trade. He wrote on bleaching and on agriculture as well as medicine. Robison too went to the West Indies, to Canada where he helped to chart the St. Lawrence in 1759 and after he left Glasgow he spent several years in Russia. He was for a time attached to the Board of Longitude; he was as fascinated with electricity as with the engine of his friend Watt. Later in life he was to encourage the building of lighthouses and to give at Edinburgh a tough science course which would enable his students to apply their scientific knowledge to the solution of industrial and technological problems. A manuscript memoir of him in the Glasgow University Library describes his work in Russia in terms that apply equally well to his career in Scotland:

> [He travelled] to obtain for [Catherine] a more thorough knowledge of the situation, soil & natural productions of

something more than logic chopping. The classicists and others, however, had not yet begun to study Montesquieu or other French writers nor were the moralists teaching economics as had Smith's predecessor at Glasgow.

these immense tracts of widely extended Empire; that from the information so acquired she might be enabled to form & bring forward plans for improving Arts, establishing Manufactures, extending the Commerce & bettering the condition of her Subjects inhabiting those distant regions.[19]

Hope's discovery of strontium in 1791 was but another evidence of academic concern with the problems of mining development. Among others who made academic careers in Glasgow, John Anderson and Alexander Wilson deserve mention. Wilson, a protégé of the Duke of Argyle, was the first Professor of Astronomy and the operator of a type foundry which supplied the Foulis Press. In his son's will £1000 was left to the university for the purchase of optical instruments to advance the study of astronomy, navigation and related fields. John Anderson, the eccentric and short tempered Professor of Natural Philosophy from 1756-1796, left an even larger bequest (£1500) to found the Andersonian Institute (now the University of Strathclyde) which was to cater to the needs of Glasgow craftsmen and the town's industries.[20] Anderson's science was not all theoretical. In 1759 he was the engineer in charge of fortifying Greenock and he continued to be interested in cannon, for in 1791 when in Paris, "He presented to the French people the model of a gun of his own design which was hung up in the hall of the Convention with the inscription 'The gift of Science to Liberty.'" Professor Meikle who tells this story goes on to note that the guns were effective as were balloons invented by him and used by the French to send revolutionary propaganda over enemy lines.[21] Glasgow after all was not far from the Carron Co. Finally it would be wrong not to mention the Foulis brothers' attempt to run a school of design and fine arts in the city. This was meant to promote business as much as it was hoped it would refine taste.[22]

---

19. Glasgow University Library, MS Murray 303. Edinburgh University has various papers relating to Joseph Black, MSS Black 874: I-V.
20. For an account of Anderson's earlier activities in this direction see C. G. Wood's "The Royal College of Science and Technology," pp. 308-9 contained in *The Glasgow Region*, ed. R. Miller and Joy Tivy, Glasgow, 1958.
21. H. W. Meikle, *Scotland and the French Revolution*, Glasgow, 1912, p. 75.
22. This venture was supported by important Glasgow merchants such as John

One would like to think that trade and commerce in Glasgow had a direct reflection in the writings of the city's intellectuals. In two cases it may have for Adam Smith and Sir James Steuart were both members of the Political Economy Club which existed there from c. 1743 to sometime after 1762.[23] Much has been written about Smith's connexion with this club but little seems to be known about it. Steuart left not only a great economic work, largely written during his years of exile, but also a plan for an ever-normal granary to provision the grain-poor west of Scotland.[24] Club discussions may have influenced his work: the leader of the Club Lord Provost Andrew Cochrane seems to have left no published works. Another sign of the city's commercial life, perhaps of the Club's influence, can be discerned in the lectures of William Wight Professor of Ecclesiastical History who was also a member. Annually after 1762 Wight gave a kind of western civilization course in which he spent time on topics such as agriculture, navigation and commerce in the ancient world, the renaissance and the modern period. Lecture 95 has the following outline: "Agriculture and populousness in the different nations of Europe — the state of fisheries in different countries — origins and progress of some of the most remarkable manufactures in Europe — progress and good effect of manufactures in the British dominions."[25] Sir John Dalrymple, another probable member of the Political Economy Club, was interested in chemistry and even wrote on soap boiling. The merchant members however seem to have left no traces of club discussions nor did the Foulis brothers who also belonged to it.[26]

Glasgow University men dominated the intellectual life in their

Glassford, the tobacco king, Archibald Ingram banker and calico printer and John Campbell of Clathic Lord Provost 1784-6. Campbell was a member of the Hodge-Podge while Glassford belonged to the Literary Society.

23. John Rae, *Life of Adam Smith*, London, 1895; New York, 1965, pp. 92-94; S. G. Checkland, "Adam Smith and the Biographer," *Scottish Journal of Political Economy*, 1967, pp. 75-76; W. R. Scott, *Adam Smith as Student and Professor*, New York, 1965, p. 81; S. R. Sen, *The Economics of Sir James Steuart*, London, 1957, p. 12.

24. Sir James Steuart, *The Works*, London, 1805; reprinted New York, 1967, Vol. V, "A Dissertation on the Policy of Grain," pp. 347-77.

25. William Wight, *Heads of a Course of Lectures on the Study of History*, Glasgow, 1767.

26. For a general discussion of the Club see McElroy's thesis cited above.

city but their work owed something to the merchants who shared in it. In the life of enlightened Edinburgh the university men were far less important and really led only in the sciences. This is not to say that the University men behaved differently than their colleagues elsewhere for they did not. The doctors published what they lectured on and what they did for their learned societies. So did the others. John Erskine's *Principles of the Laws of Scotland*, Adam Ferguson's *Essay on Civil Society*, Hugh Blair's *Lectures on Rhetoric*, the *Works* of Dugald Stewart and Tytler's *Elements of History* all testify to the effects of the classroom on the literary scene. In Edinburgh, however, it was a scene not monopolized by the professoriate. Hume's philosophy, while academic in nature, was the work of a man of letters. Lord Kames' works of criticism, philosophy, history and law were the productions of an urbane judge and those of his colleague Lord Hailes the diversions of an antiquary concerned with the national past. Lord Elibank, a retired soldier, wrote on economics and the Reverend Robert Wallace on various risky topics from sex to politcs and religion. Perhaps the best way to show the relative unimportance of the Edinburgh professoriate is to look at the leadership of the culturally innovative institutions within the city: its clubs and corporations which over the course of a century provided a small community with facilities for the pursuit of rational amusements, the furthering of the arts and the general improvement of Scottish society. From 1778 on Edinburgh possessed a musical society[27] which had three functions. It provided a weekly opportunity for amateur musicians to play for their own pleasure; it insured that a professional and competent body of musicians would be present in the city to direct and to perform difficult and elaborate compositions, or to sing works which required special training, and, lastly, it provided teachers of a polite and socially useful accomplishment for the wives and children of the élite. Throughout the century the Musical Society was presided over by lawyers and noblemen. Its deputy-governors were a surgeon, a lawyer, Lord Provost Drummond, the Earl of Kelly and Sir William Forbes

27. W. F. Gray, "The Musical Society of Edinburgh and St. Cecilia's Hall," *Book of the Old Edinburgh Club*, vol. XIX, December 1933; D. F. Harris, *Saint Cecilia's Hall*, Edinburgh, 1899; R. A. Marr, *Music for the People*, Edinburgh, 1889.

the banker. Its Treasurer was always a Writer to the Signet. Among its forty-some Directors during the century only five professors are to be found — most were lawyers or merchants. This was the largest and most comprehensive, and the most expensive of the Edinburgh societies, one which included most of the city's enlightened men. It was not beyond the means of the professors but its minute books make it clear that they had less to do with it than civil functionaries or the soldiers of the garrison.[28] The same thing can be said (with more reason) about the Edinburgh theatre which was supported by men like Kames, Monboddo, writers like James Carmichael and even clergymen such as "Jupiter" Carlyle who opened it to the clergy. The second most comprehensive enlightened groups in the city were the various improvement societies which began with the Honourable the Improvers in the Knowledge of Agriculture (1723-1745). As one might expect the improvers were recruited from the nobility and landed gentry who often appear in the members list of 1743 as advocates, judges, and sometimes as soldiers. The professors were not important in this group as they were in the Gordon Mill's Farming Club at Aberdeen, but even so it is surprising to find only three on the list, half as many as the number of doctors and merchants. When the Secretary came in their *Transactions* to praise individual improvers all were noblemen or advocates, but he did hope that agriculture would be made scientific and taught "in a College-way, as other Sciences are."[29] In the great improvement group of the mid-century, the Select Society and its affiliated societies the Edinburgh Society for the Encouragement of the Arts, Sciences and Manufactures of Scotland and the Society for the Encouragement of the Reading and Speaking of the English language,[30] the case was somewhat different. Among the thirty-two founding members of the Select Society, none had yet become professors though seven were to achieve this distinction. The Reverend

---

28. *The Minute Books of the Edinburgh Musical Society* are in the Edinburgh Central Library.

29. *Select Transactions of the Honourable the Society of Improvers in the Knowledge of Agriculture in Scotland*, Edinburgh, 1743, p. X.

30. See R. L. Emerson, "The Social Composition of Enlightened Scotland: the Select Society of Edinburgh 1754-1764," *Studies on Voltaire and the Eighteenth Century*, vol. cxiv, 1973, pp. 291-329.

Alexander Carlyle, whose name stands tenth on the members' list, thought of Allan Ramsay jr. as the Select's founder and mentioned Dr. Alexander Monro, Sir Alexander Dick, Patrick Murray, an advocate, Lord Monboddo and Lord Elibank as well as William "Potatoe" Wilkie as the man who did much to make it a success. He could have added the names of Lords Hailes and Kames, Alexander Tait a Writer to the Signet and Principal Robertson. Of these only three were university men, five were lawyers and judges, one a retired soldier and the other a former army doctor who had married an heiress.

In 1755 the Edinburgh Society was created at the suggestion of General Oughton of the Castle garrison. This body was run principally by lawyers and two merchants. The Language Society had the sponsorship of the professoriate but was after two years a failure. The Select Society broke up around 1764 with most of its élite going into the Poker Club. Only when one turns to the scientific societies do we find the university men playing a role in intellectual life comparable to that of their Glasgow colleagues. Yet even there they were not the sole leaders. The first scientific society, the Medical Society of 1731 was a project of Professor Alexander Monro and some of the members of the College of Physicians and the Chirurgeons Company. As a club, but not as a medical journal, this group died within two years.[31] In 1737 Monro and Professor Colin Maclaurin founded the Philosophical Society which became in 1783 the Royal Society of Edinburgh. From the beginning this society drew much of its leadership from the gentry and advocates and without their support it would probably have died a casualty of the '45. In 1740 it could count among its members half a dozen noblemen (including the Earl of Morton later President of the Royal Society of London), nine advocates, eleven doctors and three surgeons (i.e. the Medical Faculty plus three others), the Professors of History and Mathematics and a miscellany composed of a priest, minister, instrument maker, mine manager, printer, architect and iron master.[32] In its

---

31. H. D. Erlam, "Alexander Monro, Primus," *University of Edinburgh Journal* 17, 1953-54, pp. 87-88.
32. *Transactions of the Royal Society of Edinburgh* Vol. I, Edinburgh, 1788; *Proposals for the Regulation of a Society for Improving Arts and Sciences and*

early years the work done by its President the Earl of Morton and his protégé James Short was perhaps as significant as that of Maclaurin or its chemist Dr. Plummer. When the Society revived after the '45, it was reorganized with David Hume as one of its secretaries and Lord Kames as its leading man. Throughout the century the professoriate supplied it with papers and analytical skills, and put the resources of the university in which it met at the disposal of the society. Much of its activity, however, was concerned with topics of interest to its amateur members — agriculture, geology and mining, Scottish antiquities, even the Northeast Passage.

There remains one other club in Edinburgh which is of interest after 1775, the Pantheon Society in which artisans, businessmen, and shopkeepers met as they did at the Robin Hood in London to discuss political and literary questions.[33] Its existence is significant because it shows that enlightened ideas had penetrated further down in society here than was usually the case. Scottish education perhaps in this instance balanced the effects of numbers out of which the Robin Hood society could flourish. Finally it is worth noting that student clubs in the three Scottish cities initiated boys into one of the patterns of adult social and intellectual life. This training of the young which associated academic standards and polite societies helped to insure the perpetuation of the clubs as a prop to the provincial enlightenment. Indeed they may have given an academic cast to Scottish thought and have provided the nurseries for Scots' "feelosophy."

The articulation of a Scottish viewpoint and the improvement of Scots' culture was an unstated purpose of most of the eighteenth-century Edinburgh clubs. Even the doctors were seen as upholding the honour of Scotland by outshining Leyden and were thanked for attracting students to the city. When improvements were conceived in these terms even the most professionally oriented clubs served a provincial purpose. But the societies did more than this and were somewhat different from their London counterparts. They related their members to the European world

particularly Natural Knowledge, Edinburgh, n.d. (c. 1740).
33. Cf. McElroy, "Literary Clubs."

of learning and certified them as citizens of the Republic of Letters thus increasing their status, mobility, and perhaps making them more effective at their work. A society like the Edinburgh Philosophical Society, or later the Society of Antiquaries, provided Scots with an opportunity to contribute to European science and letters while retaining a sense of regional consciousness.[34] Astronomical observations made in the north were useful, plants and animals were still to be discovered; Scottish feudalism was as interesting though different from the brand about which Montesquieu wrote. These studies were career furthering for doctors and lawyers and interesting to the amateurs who expected them to yield knowledge in some way useful. The clubs facilitated the communication of foreign ideas and their aristocratic and well-placed members ensured that they would be acceptable and applicable within Scotland. There was probably a more thorough acceptance of the enlightenment in the Scottish cities for this reason than there could have been in a metropolis like London. Clubs and societies were however not the only institutions through which enlightened ideas were transmitted and made effective. The Enlightenment everywhere built on, and extended, old institutions and created new ones. Without these the brilliance of a provincial city like Edinburgh would have been considerably diminished.

Clubs and Societies can show how institutional complexity affected the recruitment and work of city intelligentsias but they do not show the degree to which older corporate bodies affected the enlightenments of these towns. Edinburgh offers a good example of how a handful of far sighted men in the dominant institutions could effect great and important changes. Perhaps one should begin with the Town Council, for its members were willing

34. The Society's "journal," *Essays and Observations, Philosophical and Literary* 2, Edinburgh, 1756, has the following statement of this idea: "One great design of the institution of *this* Society being faithfully to record every remarkable phaenomenon in nature that occurs, it has been thought proper to insert the following accounts of the effects of the late earthquakes, as they have been observed in our district of North Britain; nor do we regrete, that they are not more singular or interesting in their kind. When all the facts and circumstances shall be collected by the united labours of the learned in different places, there is reason to expect, they may furnish materials for a more complete and accurate history, than hath been transmitted of any like event that ever happened in any preceeding age of the world," p. 423.

to approve of most of the changes in the city, to keep politics out of the university to some extent and to take the advice of George Drummond, merchant, placeman and five times Lord Provost, a man to whom Scotland owes a great debt of gratitude. The Town's university was reformed in 1708 under Principal Carstairs and from 1717 on added new chairs in all of its faculties except divinity. The impetus for change came partly from the college itself but the medical chairs were due to the College of Physicians, to the Chirurgeons' Company and to individuals like Dr. John Monro and his descendants. The chair in history had probably been projected by Carstairs (it was filled by his kinsman Charles Mackie) but the real pressure for it came from those who wished Edinburgh to emulate the French, German and Dutch schools in which history, like *belles lettres*, was already being taught. The law chairs were sought by the Faculty of Advocates whose members filled them. One of their number late in the century endowed the chair of agriculture. The advocates and doctors did not stop there in the doing of good works for virtually every civic improvement owed something to them — the Royal Infirmary, the Dispensary, The Botanical Gardens and observatory, the new college buildings, the Exchange, the improvements at Leith harbor and other civic works. With the support of the gentry, the merchants, lawyers, doctors and even the clergy, virtually every aspect of civic life was improved because the corporations were numerous, possessed of talented men and able to effect change in a city which was not so large as to swallow them or so small as to make their existence impossible.[35] By the end of the century growth may have so changed this optimum size that they could no longer function as they had in the second and third quarters of the eighteenth century. In 1793 William Creech set down the changes which thirty years and the expenditure within the city of £3,000,000 had brought. He did so with mixed emotions for while the city boomed it had grown luxurious and progress had

---

35. Aberdeen and Glasgow spent much of the century elaborating their institutional bases. Both improved their colleges, paved streets, built hospitals and theatres, port and harbor facilities, churches and workhouses. Both had by the century's end legal and medical corporations as well as many more places for doctors. It is worth noting that both cities produced more societies and clubs of greater pretensions after 1790 than they had before that date.

destroyed an old way of life. Reading his account one senses that the city had lost its old intimacy, that its cultural élite was in some way or other breaking up and that wealth and class interests were replacing patriotism and civic pride which had played so large a role in the outlook of the enlightened men of Edinburgh. New suburbs, the bridge, mound, Register House, a riding academy, an Assembly Hall, the new college, a water system, the harbour at Leith, a second playhouse added to the one existing in 1763 — the money had bought all these and more. Six newspapers and sixteen printers were working in the city rather than the two and six of thirty years before. Mills, banks, ships, students, goods of all kinds were in greater supply. So too were whores, the poor, criminals and other evidences of moral laxity. The center no longer held; with social complexity and growth had come division, the loss of the pressures to conform and a city which resembled London but which really had less to offer to its citizens.

Edinburgh came to resemble London in the quality of its intellectual life as the conditions in which the provincial enlightenment flourished caused to obtain. Its intelligentsia began to fragment in the 1780s with the founding of the Society of Antiquaries, (1783), over the objections of all the city corporations. The city had now enough men to support two circles. The establishment of the Chamber of Commerce (1784) began to take part of the old improving activities out of the hands of those who had traditionally fostered them. Increases in size meant a loosening of the pressures to conform, while the increasing assimilation of English ways and the encroachments of English governments upon provincial autonomy sapped the civic idealism which had inspired so much enlightened activity. Growing specialization and professionalization in the arts and sciences dissolved the common ground upon which advocates, doctors and gentlemen had met. To some extent all this had occurred earlier in London and had affected its cultural life throughout the century. There life and enlightenment had been different. London could boast of every activity which the Scottish cities showed with the exception of the work of the university men whose classroom experience had forced them to think systematically and had enabled them to publish in fields which were of common concern.

While the Scottish enlightenment tends to be academic that of London suffered from the lack of rigorous and systematic work particularly in philosophy. Market conditions and competition told against the English producers of the very genres in which the Scots excelled.

If I am correct in thinking that we can discriminate four kinds of enlightened cities in the eighteenth century with rather different preoccupations, it makes sense to ask if there was a common European, a cosmopolitan enlightenment. I believe there was and that it is to be found in the questioning, the daring to know and the willingness to act upon rationally grounded knowledge which came to Europeans between c. 1660 and c. 1780. Needless to say the eighteenth century saw a great deal of thinking and action which was unenlightened. Indeed, those who were wholly and consciously committed to enlightenment were few (as Kant noted) and sometimes they experienced a despair to which Hume gave eloquent expression. Many were only partially enlightened and were not always daring in their inquiries. Everywhere the numbers concerned with reason and nature varied, as did the time of their appearance. Nevertheless the enlightenment as a style and fashion of thinking and acting informed the outlook of most of the first rate thinkers and doers who made lasting contributions to European culture during this period. But the cosmopolitan enlightenment did not affect every city at the same time or in the same way. The size and complexity of cities put limits to the problems which occurred to men in different circumstances just as they restricted the actions of the enlightened. To observe those limits is to gain a deeper understanding of what enlightenment meant to men in the eighteenth century.

Roger Emerson

Towards a Definition of the Scottish Enlightenment

The Scottish enlightenment remains one of the most puzzling phenomena of eighteenth-century cultural history. It is true that the last two decades have seen a steady flow of scholarly books and monographs on particular Scottish thinkers and upon some of those particular areas of thought — such as metaphysics, the social sciences, literature and criticism — for which enlightened Scots were so justly celebrated. Yet it is still difficult to see exactly why Scotland should have developed so vigorous a cultural life in the eighteenth century and why it was that by the second half of the century, she should have become one of the major sources of contemporary western culture.[1] As Joseph de Maistre once said of the Port Royal and its intellectuals, "Je vois bien des abeilles mais point de ruche."

In this paper I want to think about the hive rather than the bees and more especially about the development of the relations between Edinburgh's intellectuals and the wider society of which they were part during the eighteenth century. I shall confine my discussion to Edinburgh not simply for reasons of convenience, but because there is an important sense in which the history of the Scottish enlightenment *is* the history of Edinburgh. Throughout the century the cultural life of the city dominated that of Scotland. It attracted intellectually-minded peers and country gentlemen, learned country ministers, professors from Aberdeen

---

1. The literature on the origins of the Scottish enlightenment is modest in proportion and variable in quality. The most generally held view is that summarised by D. Daiches in *The Paradox of Scottish Culture: The Eighteenth Century Experience*, London, 1964. More fruitful are the following: H. R. Trevor-Roper "The Scottish Enlightenment," *Studies on Voltaire and the Eighteenth Century*, LVIII, 1967, pp. 1625-58. J. Clive, "The Social Background of the Scottish Renaissance," in *Scotland in the Age of Improvement*, ed. N. T. Phillipson and R. Mitchison, Edinburgh, 1970, pp. 225-44. Various aspects of the argument presented in this paper are developed at greater length in my essay "Culture and Society in the Eighteenth Century Province: The Case of Scotland and the Scottish Enlightenment" in *The University in Society: Studies in the History of Higher Education*, ed. L. Stone, Princeton, 1973.

and Glasgow and ambitious young men in search of intellectual excitement as well as a career. From the city's clubs, salons, class-rooms and taverns emerged a dominant cultural style built on distinctive ideological and intellectual foundations to which learned Scotsmen might respond or against which they could react. Indeed by the 1750s, such was the vigour, sophistication and reputation of learning in Edinburgh, that some of its citizens, like the dramatist John Home, were beginning to think of the city as a modern Athens in which men sought fame through learning rather than through politics or war.[2] Others like the painter Allan Ramsay thought of it as the Athens of Britain, the source of those polite and useful values necessary to guide the leaders of a progressive society.[3] Soon a romantically minded European public would think of Edinburgh, more ambiguously, as the Athens of the North.

Why did Edinburgh society take intellectuals and their work so seriously in the second half of the century? Did this influence the way in which philosophers and poets thought about the highly technical business of writing philosophy and poetry? Such questions are, in the last resort questions about the function of culture in the elite society of Edinburgh; they require us to consider that society's changing image of itself and its place in the world around it, the particular hopes fears and anxieties this aroused and the part intellectuals played in provoking and allaying them. It is only in this context that the status of intellectuals and the importance of cultural activity to Edinburgh's society becomes comprehensible.

Eighteenth-century Edinburgh, like Dublin, Boston, Naples, Bordeaux or Nancy, was the capital city of a province of a great monarchy. That is to say it was the centre of the legal, administrative and political life of the surrounding province and the focal point of the collective life of a provincial governing elite. Provincial capitals normally possessed some sort of representative assembly, governors' courts, law courts and perhaps a bishop's

2. See the prologue to the Edinburgh production of "Douglas" in *The Works of John Hume Esq.*, Edinburgh, 1822, I, p. 291.
3. A. Ramsay to Sir A. Dick, 31 Jan. 1762. *Curiosities of a Scots Charta*, Chest ed. Hon. Mrs. A. Forbes, Edinburgh 1897, p. 198.

palace and a university and their social life was dominated by those landed and mercantile interests who controlled these institutions and much of the political life of the province. Moreover, the remarkable degree of autonomy most provinces enjoyed by the middle of the century, meant that provincial elites were free to govern their province in their own way with only minimal interference from the metropolitan centre of government. Ideologically this meant that some elites — and notably those in the cities just mentioned — had a strong sense of local pride. They thought of themselves as the legitimate guradians of provincial liberties and as agents of improvement who would modernise their province by means of energetic, intelligent and public-spirited leadership and draw it from a state of rudeness to one of cosmopolitan refinement.*

At the beginning of the eighteenth century, Edinburgh fitted this pattern fairly closely. It was the seat of a provincial assembly (the Scots parliament), a Privy Council, the Court of Session (the supreme Scottish court of law) and the General Assembly of the Scottish church. It possessed a small and impoverished university whose primary function was to prepare boys from humble backgrounds for the ministry. It was the focal point of the collective life of the Scottish governing elites — which may be defined as those landed and mercantile interests which controlled the institutions of local and central government and were represented in the Scots parliament. In the last quarter of the seventeenth century it is clear that this elite had begun to think of Parliament and Privy Council as institutions which could be used to promote the economic improvement of their country. At first their campaign was desultory, spasmodic and of limited practical

---

* My use of the term "ideology" derives from Erik Erikson. An ideology provides members of a group with a sufficiently coherent and convincing pattern of legitimate forms of action to support the individual as well as the collective sense of identity of its members. But the possession of such an ideology necessarily predicates the existence of the institutional forms necessary to provide the group with the means of acting collectively. For in this sense institutions and ideology have complementary functions. An institution without an ideology is a contradiction in terms; an ideology unsupported by an institution is simply the generalised expression of a desire to act on the part of an incohate collection of individuals whose capacity to act collectively can only be realised once the institutional mechanisms which translate hopes into action have been discovered.

consequence. It was intensified at the turn of the century after a decade of economic disaster in the 1690s. Already tenuous trade routes were dislocated by international war; famine in the latter years of the decade resulted in the death of perhaps ten per cent of the population and acute hardship for the rest and the disastrous attempt to found a trading colony on the swamps of the Darien isthmus provoked a sense of acute frustration and failure.

By the early 1700s it was taken for granted that the economy was desperately backward and in need of improvement. It was now assumed, in true Harringtonian fashion, that the possibility of future political and social stability and even of national "independence" depended upon the success of the governing elite in stimulating economic growth. By 1707 it had come to be assumed that the only conditions which would make that growth possible was free trade with England and her colonies. And it was assumed that in the last resort, only the cupidity of the English parliament stood between the Scots and the attainment of that growth upon which their country's future and their own sense of self respect depended. In other words, by 1707 Edinburgh was a provincial capital dominated by an elite which was deeply conscious that it was the source of legitimate government in the province, that it was the proper agent of its improvement and that the only obstacle which stood in the way of improvement was a corrupt, metropolitan, English parliament; ideologically it is a story which bears striking similarities to that between the New England Colonies a generation later. The Scottish story reached its climax between 1703 and 1707 when the Scots deliberately precipitated a crisis in their relations with England which was resolved more or less to their own satisfaction. The Act of Union of 1707 gave them the right to free trade with England and her colonies and ensured that nothing much would be done in the immediate future to undermine the existing political ascendancy of the governing elite. However the price of this settlement was high — many thought exorbitant; it involved the abolition of the Scots parliament and the assimilation of its functions to that of England which would be modestly reinforced by the presence of forty-five Scots M.P.s and sixteen representative Scottish peers.[4]

4. Phillipson, "Culture and Society."

The Union had a decisive though rather unexpected effect on the social life of Edinburgh. The terms of the Act of Union ensured that the city would remain the centre of church government and of the legal system. What was more surprising was that it remained an important political centre. Contemporaries had feared, reasonably enough, that without a parliament and privy council to draw them to Edinburgh the Scottish governing elite — and particularly the nobility — would spend their time in London and leave Edinburgh stripped of its aristocratic society as well as its traditional political function.[5] However although the Union involved the dismantling of the Scots parliament and Privy Council, English ministers soon found it convenient to leave Scottish political and administrative business to a "manager" who had no constitutional existence but who contemporaries looked on as "the uncrowned king of Scotland"; the most notable of these were Archibald, 3rd Duke of Argyll who "reigned" almost continuously from 1725 to 1761 and Henry Dundas who "reigned" from 1784 until 1801.[6]

The reasons for this development are not hard to discover. As far as the English were concerned, Scotalnd was a long way from London (fourteen days expensive travel at a cost of around £12-14 in the early part of the century). And anyway Englishmen knew little about Scotsmen and Scottish affairs and tended to react as John Wilkes reacted to a Scottish election case; "I'll have nothing to do with it! I care not which prevails! It is only *Goth* against *Goth*!"[7] But the main reason was more fundamental than English insularity. Only the richest of Scots could afford to play the expensive game of aristocratic politics in London and given the backward state of the economy that meant that only the greatest nobility could afford to take the high road to London in 1707 and leave their great houses in Edinburgh's Canongate to degenerate into slums. The sixteen representative peers and forty-five M.P.s made their way south more reluctantly, heavily subsidised from secret

---

5. *Ibid.*
6. J. M. Simpson, "Who Steered the Gravy Train?" in *Scotland in the Age of Improvement*, pp. 47-69.
7. J. Boswell, *A Letter to the People of Scotland on the Alarming Attempts to Infringe the Articles of the Union and Introduce a Most Pernicious Innovation by Diminishing the Number of the Lords of Session*, London, 1785, pp. 70-71.

service funds which paid for visits to the metropolis they could ill afford to make. Until the 1750s the minor nobility and more substantial gentry were content to lead Scottish-oriented lives focussed on the familiar, cheerful and economical pleasures of Edinburgh.[8]

From 1707 to the 1780s the entire life of the city was dominated by successive generations of around 400 families of minor nobility and substantial gentry, closely knit by kinship and by marriage. This landed society monopolised the bench of the Court of Session and the Scottish bar (the Faculty of Advocates).[9] After the passing of the Patronage Act of 1712, they could provide ministers with livings and schoolmasters with employment. They could offer doctors lucrative practice and professors prestigious pupils and the prospect of well-paid tutorships which would rescue them from the hurly-burly of university life. It was the fact that Edinburgh remained the focal point of the collective life of much of the Scottish landed class that ensured that Edinburgh would function *de facto* if not *de jure* as a provincial capital. And it is Edinburgh's elite society, its collective needs, its expectations and its cultural life that we need to understand if we are to understand the social foundations of the Scottish enlightenment. I want to discuss Edinburgh's elite society first of all with relation to the period 1720-40 when their poverty confined expectations to Scotland and to Edinburgh. Then, I want to discuss the changes that the prospect of increased landed wealth brought to the following generation which came to dominate the social life of the city in the 1750s, the high period of the Scottish enlightenment.

II

The position of Edinburgh's aristocratic society immediately after the union was certainly perplexing. After all, the men who had been left stranded in Edinburgh formed the rump of a once homogenous and highly motivated governing class, which had been deeply aware of its role as the legitimate guardians of a province

---

8. Phillipson, "Culture and Society."
9. N. T. Phillipson, "The Scottish Whigs and the Reform of the Court of Session," (unpublished *Cambridge University Ph.D.*, 1967) pp. 349-54.

and as the proper agents of its improvement. Their poverty confined their expectations to a life in Scotland; their inherited ideology encouraged them to believe that the Union was a necessary precondition for attaining progress and that their own role in securing that progress was of great importance. But from 1707 until the early 1720s problems of economic readjustment and a lack of any real economic growth coupled with political and ecclesiastical unrest as disturbing as anything they had hitherto experienced, showed them that the Union was not the instant panacea they had hoped it would be. Some voiced their disappointment in Jacobitism, but not all found much to satisfy them in an ideology which was associated with despotism, catholicism and a tribal, highland society which most lowlanders despised. It was not until the worst of these upheavals were over that the minor nobility and substantial gentry found the collective self confidence to assert that they, after all were the legitimate heirs of the old Scottish governing elite. They did this by establishing an institution which not only gave them a formal collective existence but became associated with an ideology which derived from that which had animated the old parliamentary elite in the years immediately before the union. This institution was the Honourable the Society for Improvement in the Knowledge of Agriculture.

The Society was founded in 1723 and lasted until 1745.[10] It was the first of its kind in Britain and the model for those that followed. Its 300 members were drawn almost exclusively from the nobility and more substantial gentry. Its primary function was to provide instruction in scientific agriculture according to the best examples the modern world could provide and, more generally, to encourage the spread of agricultural improvement throughout Scotland. But soon its horizons widened and it began to advocate a more general programme of economic improvement — notably in the fields of linen manufacture and fishing — and, once again, they sought to do this by emulating the best models

---

10. The main source for the history of the Society is the *Select Transactions of the Honourable the Society for Improvement in the Knowledge of Agriculture*, ed. R. Maxwell, Edinburgh, 1743. See also D. D. McElroy *Scotland's Age of Improvement: A Survey of Eighteenth Century history Clubs and Societies*, Washington, 1969, pp. 7-9.

that the modern world could provide. What is interesting about this programme is the way in which the interests of the Society gradually extended from the improvement of agriculture — to advocating a general programme of economic improvement which was the same in substance and ideological form as that which had been persued before the union by the Scots governing elite. In doing this, they were quite aware that they were setting themselves up as a modern-minded, patriotic elite, responsible for their country's fortunes. As their secretary, Robert Maxwell of Arkland, wrote,

> If the Agriculture and Manufactures were improved and carried on to the height they could bear, we might be near as easy and convenient in our circumstances as our sister kingdom of England, seeing neither our soil or climate is unfriendly and since we enjoy the same Priviledges of Trade with them. If we are far behind, we ought to follow the faster.

If the society were to be judged solely by its success in stimulating economic growth, it would be of little interest to the historian. Its importance lies in what it tells us about the image the Scottish governing elite had of itself as the legitimate rulers of a province for whose improvement they felt responsible. It is important to realise that this development was not peculiar to Scotland. Similar societies were appearing at much the same time in the west; those of Dublin and Bordeaux are notable examples. Moreover in considering the cultural life of Edinburgh in this period, we must remember that it, too, was developing in much the same way as that of similar provincial capitals. In other words, to anticipate part of my conclusion, I shall argue that by 1740, Edinburgh's cultural life was exactly what one would expect to find in a western provincial capital possessing a vigorous, self-consciously modern-minded elite.[11] And I shall want to go on to argue that the

---

11. Provincial culture is one of the seriously neglected areas of Enlightenment historiography. But see D. Mornet, *Les Origines Intellectuelles de la Revolution Française*, Paris, 1933, D. Roche, "Milieux academiques provinciaux et société des lumières" and "Encyclopedistes et Academicians; Essai sur la diffusion sociale des lumières" in *Livre et Société dans la France du XVIIIe Siècle*, vols I and II respectively,

extraordinary upsurge of intellectual vitality that took place in the 1750s, which is unique to Edinburgh, was a function of an ideological crisis within the governing class, precipitated by an important change in their expectations of life which was itself the function of rapid economic growth.

The characteristic institutions of Edinburgh's cultural life between the 1720s and 40s were the club and the college. From the 1710s onwards, Edinburgh began to proliferate a myriad of tiny clubs and societies. They were seldom more than ten or twelve strong and seldom survived for more than two or three years. They were highly formal in structure, hedged in with elaborate rules to prescribe the correct manner in which debates should be conducted and essays prepared. Their members came from every section of Edinburgh society. There were gentlemen and artisans, whigs and jacobites, presbyterians and episcopalians, advocates and ministers, professors and doctors. Their only common characteristic was their youth and the fact that they were about to embark on careers which would probably confine them to Scotland. In other words, like the aristocratic improvers, they were men whose expectations of life were firmly confined by the limits of the life of provincial Scotland. The College, for its part, had undergone a root and branch reorganisation. In the 1690s it had been little more than a backwoods presbyterian seminary; by the 1720s a secularised institution, modelled on the university of Leiden, seeking to cater for a clientele of gentlemen. Soon it would emerge as Leiden's successor and would be recognised as one of the most influential centres of higher education in the west.[12]

Through these institutional channels Edinburgh society absorbed all the essential attributes of western polite provincial culture. The *Tatler* and *Spectator* were widely studied, and local imitations, like the *Tatler of the North* by "Donald McStaff" proliferated. So did elegant editions of classical and neo-classical authors, periodicals devoted to the production of polite verse and

Paris, 1965 and 1970. Bordeaux provides a particularly good point of comparison with Edinburgh. See P. Barrière, *L'Academie de Bordeaux: centre de culture internationale du XVIIIe siècle, 1712-1792*, Bordeaux, 1951.

12. The following discussion is based on Phillipson, "Culture and Society."

polite journalism by local authors and authoresses. The philosophy of Locke and Newton, Shaftesbury and Butler, courses in universal history and useful sciences like mathematics and experimental medicine came to be seen as fundamental to the values of a polite society and to a proper education. At the same time, polite Scottish intellectuals developed distinctively Scottish preoccupations. Some looked anxiously backwards to a Scottish past that seemed in danger of becoming forgotten and wrote lengthy treatises to remind themselves of the antiquity of the Scottish nation, of the valour of its soldiers and of the vigour of its learned men. More confident modern-minded patriots like Allan Ramsay were anxious to rediscover the forgotten glories of the Scottish verse of the renaissance and of a vernacular culture that seemed to be in danger of disappearing and to refurbish it according to the correct taste of a polite world. The philosophically and theologically minded, their intellects sharpened by the teaching of Francis Hutcheson at Glasgow, explored the structure and working of the moral sense and, more dangerously, the sceptical marshes of Berkelian metaphysics – an important point to which I shall return later.

Ideologically these clubs were to the intellectuals much as the Honourable the Society for Improvement in the Knowledge of Agriculture was to the aristocrats. In both cases, members saw themselves as members of modern-minded elites, the one civilised by the pursuit of literature, philosophy and science, and the other by the pursuit of agricultural improvement. In both cases it was believed that these pursuits would lead to the improvement of society at large. For intellectuals and aristocrats both believed, in a way that was becoming commonplace in the west that the economic, social and cultural fortunes of society were interconnected and that improvement in one area would accompany and reinforce improvement in others. In this way society would progress as a totality from a state of rudeness to that state of refinement which they believed all modern-minded societies had it in their power to attain.

What social function did such cultural activity serve in a city whose life was dominated by an aristocratic provincial elite? Here I want to make only two very simple and obvious remarks. In the first place, if we are to judge from the behaviour of the most prominent of the early literati such as the poet Allan Ramsay, and the mathematician Colin McLaurin, and, from general contemporary comment, the literati set out to reinforce and encourage the improving zeal of the provincial elite they regarded as the natural leaders of society. University reformers had set out quite deliberately to supply the nobility and gentry with the sort of polite education they had hitherto only been able to obtain in Holland. Again, in 1737, Colin McLaurin went to considerable trouble to encourage his medical colleagues in the University to encourage not only medical research, but research into the sciences in general and even into anitquities, not simply to secure aristocratic patronage, but aristocratic participation in the pursuit of polite knowledge.[13] And Allan Ramsay, who was generally regarded as the poet laureate to polite society, devoted much time to the composition of large quantities of exhortatory verse to encourage improvement of which the following, addressed to the Society for the Improvement in the Knowledge of Agriculture, is a typical example:

> Continou Best of Clubs Long to Improve
> Your native plains and gain your nation's Love
> Rouze every Lazy Laird of each wide field
> That unmanur'd not half their Product yield.[14]

My second point concerns the most obvious ideological attribute of polite culture — the faith that polite society had in the creative value of collective action in stimulating social progress. No-one doubted for a moment that by the selection and emulation of suitably progressive models, and by mutual self-education, the natural leaders of society could turn themselves into a modern-minded elite whose collective efforts could bring about the improvement of society. Such an ideology ultimately rested on a fairly optimistic view of free will. To be sure, polite society knew

    13. D. D. McElroy, *Scotland's Age of Improvement*, pp. 27-30. W. Maitland, *A History of Edinburgh from its foundations to the Present Time*, Edinburgh, 1753, p. 151.
    14. "The Pleasures of Improvements in Agriculture" (c. 1723) in *The Works of Allan Ramsay*, ed. A. M. Kinghorn and A. Law, Scottish Text Society, 1961, III, pp. 171-72.

enough about Locke to realise that the individual depended upon his perceptions of the external world for his knowledge of it, for his values and for his knowledge of the God he worshipped and that he was in some sense a psychologically determined agent. Nevertheless, polite society also assumed, with Shaftesbury and Hutcheson, that in addition to possessing the five traditional senses of sight, touch, hearing, taste and smell, man had a moral sense which allowed him to choose virtue and to eschew vice, to show public spirit or to relapse into selfishness. He thought of the happy man as one who understood the workings of human nature and recognised the limits in which he was free to act. And he took it for granted that such purposive actions would play a decisive part in increasing virtue and personal happiness and the happiness of society at large.

But say you doubted whether the individual himself, was simply a bundle of perceptions, made coherent by a process of association and habit over which his reason and will had little or no control. Did that not threaten the idea of the individual as a free agent or even of the individual as an entity with an objective personal identity? Say you went further and suggested that the structure of society and the course of social progress was determined by mechanisms of which we have little knowledge and over which we have little control? Did such doubt not strike at the ideological heart of polite culture with its optimistic faith in the improveability of man and his environment? In contemporary philosophical terms, these sort of questions were discussed by the followers of Bishop Berkeley (if not always by the Bishop himself). Edinburgh had a circle of Berkeleians who formed the Rankenian Club, a little society which was founded in 1716, flourished until 1746 and survived until 1774.[15] It was an exceptionally vigorous club, by all accounts and was in contact with Berkeley himself, whose doctrines they were said to have pushed "to amazing lengths";[16] and although the young David Hume was not a member, he knew most of its members. As George Davie has observed, it was the Rankenians who brought

15. McElroy, *Scotland's Age of Improvement*, pp. 22-23.
16. *Scots Magazine*, XXXIII, 1771, pp. 340-41.

him into contact with the world of contemporary metaphysics.[17]

Although intellectuals and some ministers and college students found plenty to intrigue them in Berkelian determinism their discussions do not seem to have aroused much interest in wider aristocratic circles. This is not surprising. It is easier and more sensible to ignore uncongenial philosophy or to laugh at what seem to be the self-evident absurdities of philosophers than to attack them. Philosophers are worth attacking only if it is believed that what they write (whether or not it is understood) constitutes a threat to good order and good morals. That situation is only likely to arise when a philosopher and his writing is treated with respect by powerful social interests. In this early period Berkelian determinism can be regarded as a deviation from the accepted ideological norms of polite culture in a city which was a perfectly conventional example of a provincial capital with a lively but fairly conventional cultural life. What is interesting is that determinism suddenly emerged as the ideological norm of polite culture between 1750 and 1780. We must see how this came about and try to discover why it did so.

III

By the 1740s the first important evidence of the economic progress that the Scots had hoped for, would be seen. Not only were there signs of commercial expansion but rent-rolls were beginning to rise significantly. As far as landed society was concerned, it meant that the poverty which had confined their expectations to Scotland and to Edinburgh was now on the wane. Young men, raised in the polite culture of the 1720s – 40s were now feeling the liberating effects of long-promised wealth for the first time. By the 1750s this new generation was becoming prominent in Edinburgh society and to their normal Edinburgh season they began to add the sort of periodic visits to London that James Boswell and his friends loved to make. By the 1770s and 80s street directories make it clear that they and their sons were

---

17. G. E. Davie "Hume and the Origins of the Common Sense School," *Revue Internationale de Philosophie* 6, 1952, pp. 213-21. See also G. E. Davie "Berkeley's Impact on Scottish Philosophers," *Philosophy* 40, 1965, pp. 222-34.

beginning to give up the Edinburgh season altogether, leaving the direction of its social life in the hands of a professional bourgeoisie and petty gentry. As far as the minor nobility and substantial gentry were concerned, by Walter Scott and Francis Jeffrey's day, Edinburgh was what Lady Sinclair of Duntreath called "An inn or a halfway house between London and Highland muirs."[18]

Changing expectations inevitably raised ideological problems. The long campaign to stimulate economic growth seemed at last to be bearing fruit and it was natural that this new generation should want to see themselves as the legitimate heirs of their fathers, the rightful guardians of their country's liberties and agents of its improvement. The difference was that while their fathers had necessarily confined their expectations to life in their impoverished province, they could look forward to a more expansive London-orientated life of the sort that English noblemen and substantial country gentlemen led. In other words they needed an ideological formula which would identify them as a legitimate governing elite but which would not identify their fortunes with their country as closely as that of their fathers. Their fathers had articulated their collective identity in an institution with para-parliamentary characteristics. Their sons however did not revive this institution when it became defunct in 1746 or found an alternative to it; instead they became parasite upon the little club of intellectuals called the Select Society. To put it metaphorically, while the fathers had built an ideological house in the city, the sons merely chose to rent ideological rooms in a house which did not belong to them.

The Select Society began life in May 1754 as a club of fourteen of the younger literati led by David Hume, Adam Smith and the painter Allan Ramsay (the poet's son).[19] Like the younger aristocrats these men had been raised in the polite culture of the 1720s – 40s. They met, so it seems to discuss the sort of sociological and aesthetic problems on which Hume had written and on which the others were soon to publish. In so doing, they believed, in the conventional way, that they would promote their

18. *Cassell's Old and New Edinburgh*, ed. J. Grant, London, 1880-83, III, p. 63.
19. McElroy, *Scotland's Age of Improvement*, pp. 48-67. See also E. C. Mossner, *Life of David Hume*, London, 1954, pp. 272-85.

own improvement and that of their country. In other words, it seems clear that they expected the Select Society to be to them what the Rankenian Club had been to an earlier generation, the institution which gathered together the more deterministically minded men of their generation. However, no sooner had the club come to life than it was bombarded with applications for membership from the young aristocrats of Edinburgh and soon, not without some misgivings on the part of its original members, the society had acquired a highly aristocratic membership of 135 and there could have been many more. As Hume reported to Allan Ramsay, in the spring of 1755,

> It has grown to be a national concern. Young and old, noble and ignoble, witty and dull, laity and clergy, all the world are ambitious of a place among us, and on each occasion we are as much solicited by candidates as if we were to choose a Member of Parliament.[20]

The Society's social structure is fascinating. By the end of 1754, the average age of its members was 32 and well over half were closely connected by ties of kinship and marriage. A majority were heirs soon to come into estates and over three-quarters were men who were well on the road to careers which would take them into significant and active offices in national and local government, in the military, naval and ecclesiastical establishments. As Mr. R. L. Emerson has put it, "Their roles were conditioned by the expectation of inherited titles, places, responsibilities, wealth and power — the very stuff that human confidence is made of."[21] At first, under the aegis of the literati, they discussed the type of institutions, economy manners and culture proper to a progressive society, the relations between different stages of society and the mechanisms which caused them to progress from one stage to another. More particularly, they discussed local problems relating to economic improvement legal and political reform. Soon their activities became more practical and they resolved to sponsor a

---

20. D. Hume to A. Ramsay, April—May 1755, *Letters of David Hume*, ed. J. Y. T. Grieg, Oxford, 1932, I, pp. 219-21.
21. R. L. Emerson, "The Social Composition of Enlightened Scotland: The Select Society of Edinburgh 1754-64," (unpublished paper).

programme of economic and social improvement which closely resembled that which their fathers had undertaken a generation before which was itself derived from the programme of the governing elite before the union. As their prospectus observed:

> To encourage genius, to reward industry to cultivate the arts of peace are objects deserving the attention of public-spirited persons.[22]

The situation which had developed was paradoxical and significant. While Edinburgh was an aristocratic city, the focal point of its social life was a society run by the literati. Between the 1720s and 1740s the function of the literati had been to encourage the improving energies of the natural leaders of society. By the mid-1750s the literati were providing them with the institutional means of articulating their identity as a governing elite; they had become the guardians of the *virtù* of an aristocratic society. Naturally this gave the literati remarkably high status. The novelist Henry Mackenzie later recalled that "men of fashion were proud of their connection and acquaintance with men of letters."[23] The banker Sir William Forbes observed that "The circle of society in which (David Hume) moved in Edinburgh was not only extensive but the most distinguished for rank and fashion and literary merit of which Scotland could boast."[24] And Hume, along with Lord Kames and Lord Elibank, found themselves exercising what contemporaries saw as a complete dictatorship over the literary life of the city.

Ideologically the situation which had arisen was very curious. The high social status of Hume and his friends necessarily meant that their writing acquired a social significance it would have otherwise never enjoyed. The godly thought that this involved legitimising religious scepticism and in many respects they were right. However a much more important consequence was the legitimisation of a highly determinist view of man and society.

---

22. *Scots Magazine*, XVII, 1755, pp. 127-29.
23. H. Mackenzie "Account of the Life of Mr. John Home," in *The Works of John Home*, I, p. 28.
24. Sir W. Forbes, *An Account of the Life and Writings of James Beattie, LL.D.*, 2nd. ed., Edinburgh, 1807, I, pp. 209-10.

This is not the place to discuss the well-known psychological and sociological determinism of Hume and Adam Smith, or the less well-known but equally significant determinism of the neo-classical dramatist John Home or the sentimental novelist Henry Mackenzie — arguably the four most conspicuous and influential members of Edinburgh's polite society between 1750 and 1780. Let me simply stress the emphasis Hume and Smith gave to man as an agent who is, psychologically and sociologically deeply determined, whose purposive actions have little creative value in a world which functions according to mechanisms which he has little capacity to control. The determinism of John Home and Mackenzie derived from classical tragedy as much as from contemporary psychology and sociology. Each had a Sophoclean realisation that self-knowledge can only lead us to see that the world in which we act is one which we may understand, but in which we can never be free. The trouble was that such a view of human action necessarily posited that improvement does not and cannot result from the sort of organized pursuit of progress that aristocratic society had undertaken in the 1720 — 40s or that which their successors wanted the deterministically orientated leaders of the Select Society to patronise. In other words the aristocratic members of the Select Society seemed to want simultaneously to identify themselves with the ideology of their fathers and to adopt one which would undermine it.

Given the first signs of real economic growth in the 1750s and the ideological importance the Scottish landed classes had for so long attached to the attainment of such a goal, it was scarcely surprising that young aristocrats should have wanted to identify themselves as the traditional ideology of the Scottish governing elite. But the prospect of wealth also promised to open up the expensive high road to England to members of their class for the first time and threatened to arouse a guilty sense that they were betraying the patriotism and virtue which had inspired their ancestors to pursue the course of improvement. Thus it was not surprising that the Select Society frequently debated such subjects as this: "whether a nation may subsist without public spirit"; "whether commercial and military spirit can subsist in the same nation"; "can a body politic be virtuous" etc. What was reassuring about the determinism of the literati was that it reassured them that the liberties and future welfare of their country lay not in their care but in that of the Invisible Hand.

It is axiomatic that attacks on free will and thus on personal identity are capable of arousing deep anxiety and if one can understand why aristocrats patronised a determinist brand of polite culture and in so doing, gave it and its practitioners considerable social importance, we must remember that not every Edinburgh citizen was an aristocrat with swelling rent-rolls. The gradual alienation of landed society from the city exposed the fact that there were many lawyers, doctors, ministers, professors, bankers, merchants and petty gentry whose lives and expectations had always been as firmly rooted in the city as those of the aristocrats of an earlier generation. Moreover, as I have indicated, these largely bourgeois interests would soon dominate the social life of the city. An emerging social elite of this sort could hardly be expected to look with favour on an ideology which denied them any real creative role in governing and improving their country. However, as civilized and intelligent men, anxious to seek legitimisation as the heirs to a successful aristocratic elite, they could scarcely derive much ideological comfort from the vulgar clerical bigotry that tried to defeat polite determinism by sheer abuse, by calling Hume and his friends "the imps of hell" and the aristocrats "the idle loose, useless catives, falsely called nobility and gentry, and especially those called judges and lawyers."[25] What this rising bourgeois oligarchy needed was an ideology of their own, a new variant of the polite culture of 1720 — 40 which Hume nd his friends had undermined, which would affirm, once again, the creative value of the collective leadership of a governing elite. The course that much of Scottish culture took in the second half of the eighteenth century was determined by the anxiety which many intellectuals and members of this newly-emerging elite felt with a culture, associated with Hume and his circle,

---

25. *The Players Scourge: or a Detection of the Ranting prophanity and frequent impiety of stage plays, and their wicked encouragers and frequenters; and especially against the nine prophane Pagan Priests, falsely called ministers of the gospel, who counternamed the thrice cursed tragedy called Douglas*, Edinburgh, 1758. (National Library of Scotland H. 1. a. 15).

which, through force of historical circumstance had acquired a social and ideological importance of disturbing proportions. It was their need to allay these anxieties by discovering satisfying ways of coping with polite determinism which provided intellectually-minded Scots with a powerful impetus to creative thinking.

In time I hope I shall be able to trace the ways in which this crisis worked itself out in the fields of metaphysics, sociology, history, literature and even physiology. I hope that I shall be able to show that the ideological common denominator to the reaction to polite determination in each of these fields was a defensive concern on the part of philosophers, scientists and men of letters with the problem of showing that man was a free agent and a creative being, capable of shaping his own environment according to his needs, in spite of the powerful determinist forces which threatened to overwhelm him. Here I would simply like to indicate, very briefly, how I think that this reaction affected two important areas of learning, the social sciences and metaphysics.

Adam Ferguson was deeply disturbed by Smithian determinism. Were all men's actions really directed towards assimilating himself passively to the dominant value system of those around him as Smith had so brilliantly argued in the *Theory of Moral Sentiments*? Had man no active principle to prevent him from becoming thus enslaved? Ferguson thought that he had. Man acquired his liveliness and humanity from a restless pursuit of a perfection he could never define. It was a pursuit which involved him in competition with nature, with his fellow men and with himself, which, once relaxed, would leave him prisoner of the passive, comfortable, prudential values he most feared. No doubt, said Ferguson in one of his most interesting moments, Hume and Smith were right to think political activity seldom achieved anything you could define in utilitarian terms. But all societies and tribes love politics and do so because its quarrels and its struggles help them to preserve that tribal sense of identity which is daily threatened by the division of labour and the progress of luxury.[26] For John Millar, Smith's most accomplished pupil, the problem

---

26. There is a particularly valuable discussion of Ferguson's moral philosophy in Duncan Forbes' introduction to his edition of Ferguson's *History of Civil Society*, Edinburgh, 1966.

was rather different. Millar understood Smith's sociology as well as anyone and he understood how small a part chance, foresight and the activities of great men played in determining the course of social progress. But he was a political animal and a Foxite whig at that. As such, it was difficult for him to find comfort in a sociology that denied creative power to the reforming politician. As one of his pupils, Francis Jeffrey noticed, Millar was ultimately unable to reconcile the demands of sociology and politics. His justly celebrated attempt to treat the history of England sociologically, the *Historical View of the English Government* is brokenbacked; its early chapters are more a study of feudal society in general than that of England and its later chapters are brilliant political pamphlets.[27] But the work as a whole is an extraordinary fitting monument to the ideological tensions built into the culture of the Scottish enlightenment.

The second and historically most important reaction to polite determinism came from the Common Sense philosophers, Thomas Reid, James Beattie and Dugald Stewart. The Common Sense reaction to determinist polite culture came from Aberdeen University and the Aberdeen Philosophical Society which was founded in 1758. This, in itself, is significant as Aberdeen was the centre of the "non-conformist" north-east. It was a city strongly associated with episcopalianism and jacobitism rather than the presbyterianism and whiggery of Edinburgh and lowland Scotland. Traditionally difficult to govern, with a distinctive cultural tradition, the Common Sense reaction to the polite determinism of Edinburgh can be seen as the reaction of the province to the capital. Philosophically this reaction took the form of a deliberate, conscious attempt to combat Hume's determinism and, by extension to question the value of the sort of anthropological and historical evidence upon which his theory of human nature ultimately rested. Resting upon the proposition that those truths which our common sense makes known to us are necessarily true, Reid could bypass Hume and Smith's devastating critique of free will by asserting that if we know our will to be free and if this belief is shared equally by every living person then it is so and all

27. *The Edinburgh Review* 3, 1803-4, pp. 154-81, esp. pp. 162, 176.

reductionist attempts to explain it away are perversions of science. In the same way the objective existence of the external world, the necessary existence of God, the existence of personal identity could all be postulated as axiomatic.[28]

This critique, coupled with a sophisticated, even penetrating, examination of the mechanics of perception and association and a deep respect for the creative possibilities of science properly conducted, provided the intellectual foundations for a new variant of polite provincial culture which quickly took root in Scotland. By the 1780s Common Sense philosophy had taken over the philosophy schools in Edinburgh and all the other Scottish universities. In 1764 Reid moved the chair of moral philosophy at Glasgow in succession to Adam Smith (to Smith's evident annoyance) and while Beattie refused the moral philosophy chair at Edinburgh in 1773, Reid's best pupil, Dugald Stewart was to occupy it in 1785. Soon it was to underpin the critical style of that most influential of all nineteenth century journals, the *Edinburgh Review*.[29] It was the cultural triumph of provincial Aberdeen over metropolitan Edinburgh. Outside Scotland, Common Sense philosophy spread to restoration France[30] and, most strikingly to revolutionary and post-revolutionary America where it was the philosophy of Common Sense and not the determinist polite culture of Hume and his circle that was to work its way into the college curricula and into the cultural life of New England elites immediately before the Revolution and for nearly a century after it.[31] Perhaps common sense philosophy attracted Americans

---

28. G. E. Davie, "The Scotch Metaphysics," (unpublished D. Litt., Edinburgh, 1954) is essential reading. See also, J. McCosh, *The Scottish Philosophy Biographical Expository, Critical, from Hutcheson to Hamilton*, London 1875: S. A. Grave, *The Scottish Philosophy of Common Sense*, Oxford, 1960.

19. This point was first noticed by Philarete Chasles in *Revue Contemporaine*, 1853, p. 87.

30. The leading French exponents of common sense Philosophy were Victor Cousin, P. P. Roger Collard, T. Jouffrey, M. F. P. G. Maine de Biran and C. de Remusat. The attraction of "la philosophie ecossaise" for such philosophers and teachers is best approached via C. de Remusat's "L'Ecosse depuis la fin du XVIIe siecle et la philosophie de Hamilton" in *Revues des Deux Mondes*, April 1856, pp. 465-507. See also V. Cousin, *Cours de l'Histoire de la Philosophie Moderne*, 1st series, IV, Paris, 1846, esp. pp. 4-30.

31. On which see L. A. Cremin, *American Education: The Conolial Experience 1607-1783*, New York, 1970; D. Sloane, *The Scottish Enlightenment and the American College Ideal*, New York, 1971, esp. ch. iv, vii. D. W. Howe, *The Unitarian Conscience: Harvard Moral Philosophy 1805-61*, Cambridge, Mass., esp. ch. 2.

for the same reason that it attracted the newly emerging bourgeois and petty-gentry elite of Edinburgh in the second half of the eighteenth century. Perhaps they, too, could find in it a means of legitimising their role as members of an elite composed of sensible, modern-minded, Godfearing men of affairs, who dealt in the realities of ordinary life and in the day to day business of running the society of which they were the natural and legitimate leaders. Scottish common sense philosophy traded in such needs just as much as the provincial culture of the early eighteenth century had done and offered an extraordinarily durable variant of polite culture which was ideologically able to withstand a psychological determinism which was, as James Beattie put it,

> The bane of true learning, true taste and true sense; [It is] to it we owe all this modern scepticism and atheism; [it] has a bad effect upon the human faculties and tends not a little to sour the temper, to subvert good principles, and to disqualify men for the business of life.[32]

IV

In this paper I have tried to explain why Edinburgh, of all the various centres of western provincial culture, should have developed a cultural life of such richness in the eighteenth century and why it should have been at its richest between the 1750s and 80s. My explanation has placed great weight on the social effects of the Anglo-Scottish union on one particular section of the Scottish landed class and upon those ideological needs it called upon a literati to satisfy. And I have suggested that the ideological purchase which some purely intellectual problems received in the process gave those problems a capactiy to arouse anxiety and stimulated men to seek to ally it in particular ways. This, I have suggested, is the hall-mark of the Scottish enlightenment and it is the function of a historical situation that was peculiar to eighteenth-century Edinburgh.

But the interest of explanatory models lies as much in what they do not explain as in what they do. And while I think I can

---

32. Forbes, *Life of Beattie*, I, p. 171.

explain a preoccupation with determinism in the 1750s, I cannot explain the precise form of the cultural debate which took place in Edinburgh. No doubt the infertile condition of Scottish presbyterianism ruled out the possibility that the debate would be cast in theological form and that a Scottish Jonathan Edwards would emerge to dominate the country's ideological and cultural life. No doubt the state of professional philosophy and literature dictated that intellectual parameters of the debate would be fixed by Berkelian metaphysics, moral sense philosophy, the thought of Montesquieu, and by the conventions of classical tragedy. But the most striking characteristic of Edinburgh's cultural life in the 1750s is its sense of urgency and the sense that intellectual inquiry was socially vitally important. That was due, quite simply to the genius of Adam Smith and above all, David Hume. Their analytical brilliance, their rhetorical force and clarity, their ruthless intellectual honesty, made it exceptionally difficult for intellectuals, working in a civilised environment, to produce satisfying means of allaying the anxieties which a deterministic ideology aroused. Given the social importance of polite determinism this was a situation designed to call forth powerful reserves of ambitious, creative energy. The intellectual power of Scotland's determinists set in a distinctive and complex social environment was the trigger which detonated those social and cultural forces which turned Edinburgh into the Athens of Britain.

Nicholas Phillipson

Music & the Court in the 18th Century

Music, because of its particular sensuous effect and great capacity for symbolic representation, became Europe's special and characteristic art. Only Western music developed harmony and counterpoint, all the ancient high civilizations of the Near and Far East remained monophonic in their music. Being least susceptible to naturalism, music is able to express the abstract, for which reason it became known as the handmaid of religion, *ancilla theologiae*, not only as an aid or ornament like the visual arts, but as an integral part of the liturgy itself. Since the Catholic Church, and after the Reformation the Anglican and the Lutheran were state religions, the courts always kept elaborate musical establishments, the so-called chapels, for the display of royal example in devotion. But since music is also a prime source for entertainment, the courts, royal, aristocratic, and ecclesiastic, maintained considerable forces of musicians as well as opera houses for that purpose. In none of the other arts was the influence of the ruling class so pervasive as in music, and it remained so until the end of the 18th century. The commissioning caste of society, its internal organization, and what we today call life style, determined the nature of the composition to such a degree that we could almost construct a theory of socio-cultural aesthetics. The compositions, their thematic material, their shape, had to be scaled to the etiquette of royal gatherings. Here let me underline an important fact: the European courts, especially those in Central Europe, were highly sophisticated in musical matters; as we shall see, emperors, electors, princes of the Holy Roman Empire, as well as cardinals and archbishops were excellent and well-trained musicians who were amateurs only because they did not have to make a living by music. When the King of Prussia, who was a good cellist, ordered a set of string quartets, the composer knew that he must write an elaborate cello part, without, however, upsetting the delicate equilibrium of the genre. The emperor in Vienna would call in his court composer and, score in hand, would discuss with him details of the opera to be performed. Similarly, the Archbishop of Salzburg would lay down the law about the Masses and vespers to be composed for his court. It was these courts that made possible the great development and expansion of all genres of music, because the rulers' understanding and appreciation of the emerging large symphonic forms encouraged the composers to expand their offerings.

With the advent of sociological studies many socio-cultural theories concerning music have been advanced. The range is wide, extending from hermeneutics borrowed from theological exegesis, to Marxism with its contorted deductions. Many of the social facts that influenced musical style are obvious and easily explained, but while such correspondences and analogies can be found at every turn, we must be careful and recall what Corot said to someone who advanced some fancy theories about painting: "Non, Monsieur, la peinture est plus bête que cela." To cite an example of the fallacy of these far-fetched social interpretations, it was seriously suggested that Bach's monothematic fugues reflect the absolutism of Frederick the Great! The East German Marxists managed to discover in Handel's oratorios a protest of the people against the institution of the monarchy, which is rather amusing considering Handel's staunch support of the House of Hanover and his devotion to the capitalist system. He was more successful in the stock market than most professional brokers.

The basic nature of social life in the times we are concerned with made the professional musician, usually of lower middle class origin, almost entirely dependent on the ruling class and understood only by them. Unfortunately, this high society appears as a double-edged weapon in musical history, for while through its wealth and power it promoted music, at the same time by its very possession of power it limited its dissemination. Furthermore, court music was somewhat circumscribed, bound to the needs and customs of the institution, and its composers worked under certain restrictions. On the other hand, the techniques and formal aspects of court music were far more highly developed and polished than those of a more popular music would be, and since court art does not depend on the fluctuations in public taste it develops in an isolation that enables it to create compositional principles of universal validity. It is axiomatic that in the eighteenth century (as before) the leading art of the age was the art of the leading class which as long as the ideal of culture is a living force within represents the whole of society. Nevertheless, the boundaries within which music represents the true spirit of "high" Western culture, and beyond which begins the domain of so called popular music, are difficult to draw because the two often overlap. It is true, however, that the higher the cultural and ethical force behind a given musical composition, the more complicated its structure, and it will be properly understood only by persons with the requisite intellectual capacity, education, and musical experience. The public for serious music is a small minority, that of light music the vast majority, and the life of serious music is long, while that of light music very brief. (This last remark does not of course refer to genuine folk art, which is a category by itself.)

The artist's profession is urban and middle class. He has always been looked upon as a bourgeois and until the eighteenth century the official distinction between artisan and artist was mostly nonexistent. The artistic leadership emanated from the court until the bourgeoisie was able to assert itself politically and economically. Indeed, court composers were often classed among the servants; no program note or popular book on music fails to mention the livery Haydn had to wear when performing at the Esterházy court. But those court-appointed composers had financial and social security that enabled them to devote themselves to their art, whereas our free and independent artists cannot make a living as composers. Practically all of them are either teaching, or performing, or even doing menial jobs such as copying music in order to be able to compose in their spare time. Even the relatively emancipated citizens of northern Protestant cities, the quasi-republics of the Hanseatic League, or the municipal and consistorial appointees, like Cantor Bach, could not make a living as creative artists; they were choirmasters, organists, and teachers. Bach was even obliged to teach Latin to the pupils in the Leipzig Thomasschule. As to the liveries, do not today's emancipated artists wear a compulsory uniform when performing in public?

Since the court composer raised the lustre of his patron's house, he was well treated, well paid, and at times befriended. Corelli had a luxurious private apartment in Cardinal Ottoboni's palace, Haydn a house, a servant, a bird dog, and hunting privileges at Eszterháza. The question is, then, how did the musician, member of the bourgeoisie, fit into this world of the court?

As I have remarked before, the artist can work for the culture of the upper strata of society until the culture of his own class becomes conscious and demanding. Still, he cannot deny his middle class origins and, though possessing an incomparable technical mastery of the métier, he seldom misses an opportunity to absorb popular materials into his aristocratic compositions. By the middle of the eighteenth century the courts, formerly leaders in advancing music, gradually become conservative, something unknown heretofore. This aristocratic conservatism was really a form of defense against the rising power of the middle classes. In Italy the earthy and popular opera buffa began its conquest of the musical world, first demoting, then virtually destroying the opera seria, traditionally one of the chief forms of royal entertainment. But in the courts the stylized and stilted seria was maintained. As late as 1791, Mozart's last opera, *La clemenza di Tito*, commissioned for the coronation in Prague, was an old-fashioned Baroque opera seria, complete with a castrato role. By that time the seria was so far out of fashion that even Mozart's genius and his immense theatrical savoir faire could not overcome its inhibitions. When the buffa reached Paris, the home of the highly formal and courtly *tragédie lyrique*, the result was the celebrated "War of the buffoons," and it was no accident that it was the author of the *Contrat Social* who composed the first popular, anti-opera musical play, *Le devin du village*. A similar trend is noticeable in dance music. While in the splendid dance suites of the seventeenth and early eighteenth centuries the harmonic-contrapuntal setting and the original flavor of the dances was in fine equilibrium, in the second half of the century the learned counterpoint faded, the dances became homophonic and more and more popular in tone.

This absorption of the popular elements keeps pace with the advancement of human rights. The new stylistic phases are created when factors coming from a lower social stratum, previously ignored or considered of secondary importance, become of primary significance. One of the socio-aesthetic laws that may be defined is that while the techniques and means of the reigning musical style follow the tastes of the courts, the *materials* come from the lower strata. This "law" is valid all along the social line: the aristocracy takes its new materials from the middle class, the latter from the people below it.

Now we witness an interesting development. While the techniques of musical composition, disseminated by the mutual relationships of the courts, become more and more international, the national traits associated with the middle classes assert themselves more sharply. But since even the autonomous development of music is affected by social factors, the elements moving from lower to higher strata of society never appear in their original shape, they always become reconciled to the techniques currently in use. And since the technique of the craft of composition is governed by the taste of the ruling class these new material are polished, stylized, and refined. Mozart's *Marriage of Figaro*, the peak of the rambunctious opera buffa made fit for royal ears, is full of delectable tunes of a decidedly popular turn, yet the work also represents the acme of aristocratic finesse, elegance, and the ultimate in invention, dramatic insight, and compositional virtuosity.

When we speak of courts in the seventeenth to eighteenth centuries, Versailles naturally comes to mind: its palace, its gardens, its ceremonies, and its manners. Every princeling tried to imitate it and many of its features became standard fixtures in royal households all over Europe. But if we look at the musical aspects of court life, Versailles pales in comparison to the Habsburg court and the palaces of the polyglot Austrian nobility. Their role in the history of music is unparalleled, deeply influencing the very style of music for generations. Until the mid-nineteenth century practically all its emperors were not only fond of music but several were talented and knowledgable musicians. They often married Italian princesses, liked to visit their Italian domains, and Italian music and musicians soon invaded the musical establishments at the courts. Vienna was for a long time known as the city of music, and at times has been the unquestioned capital, harboring some of the greatest composers the world has ever known. The reasons for this eminence are geographic, ethnographic, and politico-cultural, but the Habsburgs themselves deserve the lion's share of credit. We shall skip the rich musical history of the House of Habsburg from the Middle Ages onward until we pick up the thread in the seventeenth century. The Habsburgs celebrated every name and birthday, every patron saint's day as well as marriages and baptisms with original works commissioned for the occasion. There were hundreds of these, among them many masterpieces, performed at the Burg in Vienna, the Hradschin in Prague, or the summer palaces in Schönbrunn and Luxenburg. With the Habsburgs it was a matter of predilection, but also an artistic and political article of faith to support music in church and theater; the population loved the lavish services and performances, but was also kept politically quiet and docile to an absolutism that provided it with such feasts for eye and ear. To give an idea of the extent of the imperial court's musical activities I might cite that during Leopold I's long reign (1658-1705) four hundred new operas and oratorios were performed in Vienna.

At this point I must make a little digression, for if the central position of opera is not sufficiently understood the course of musical history can not be properly appreciated. We see the great literature of sonatas, quartets, and symphonies, and they are glorious, but in the seventeenth and eighteenth centuries the nerve center of music, from which emanated most stylistic ingredients, was opera. And, most interestingly, the chief influence on the formation of the so-called classic style, the music of Haydn, Mozart, and Beethoven, came from the musical idiom of the Italian opera buffa. This is not the place to engage in a lengthy explanation of this complicated stylistic and technical metamorphosis, nor of the musical marriage of church and theater, which is indeed so complicated that no comprehensive monograph exists as yet on the subject; suffice it to say, that whether symphony or sonata or Mass, the operatic influence was pervasive. The Protestant north looked upon all this with contempt — "licentious, trivial, and frivolous" it called the style — but in the end it too succumbed. (As late as *Die Meistersinger*, Wagner has Hans

Sachs exhort *unsere deutschen Meister* to beware of "Latin tinsel.") This influence was so overwhelming that those nations that refused to go along with the new dramatic music streaming out of Italy, like England or the Netherlands, fell by the wayside, though previously they had been in the front rank among musical nations. England did not recover until the late nineteenth century. Curiously enough, while in Italy opera became gradually democratized, even small towns supporting opera theaters, beyond the Alps it remained the chief form of courtly representation among all the arts.

Most of the great Italian composers of the seventeenth century, Monteverdi, Cavalli, Cesti, and others, worked for Vienna and some resided there in the employ of the court. Nicolo Minato (d. 1698) of Bergamo, a distinguished Italian man of letters, was engaged as imperial court poet with the sole duty to supply librettos for the composers. Ludovico Burnacini, a Mantuan architect and scenic designer, was in the service of the court for half a century and became famous all over Europe. When Marcantonio Cesti's *Il pomo d'oro* was performed in 1668 on the occasion of the marriage of Leopold I to the Infanta Margaret, Burnacini built a sumptuous new opera house for the event. These magnificent buildings, decorations, and costumes were altogether in the service of a dynastic ideal expressed more directly in the so called *licenza*. This homage to the ruler, usually a mythological scene transparently referring to the head of the house, might be either an integral part of the opera or a newly composed epilogue. I might add that Handel extended the licenza to comprise an entire large work. The king who rules his realm with wisdom in the oratorio *Solomon* is patently George II; this does not prevent the work from being a masterpiece.

Burnacini died in 1707 and his successor, Galli Bibiena and the latter's son Giuseppe, who came from a long line of theater architects and decorators, raised Burnacini's splendor to unparalleled heights. He was the inventor of the *scena per angolo*, the perspective scene design, which revolutionized the stage. For the coronation in Prague in 1723 he built an amphitheater for six thousand spectators, and designed the decorations for Johann Joseph Fux's opera *Costanza e fortezza*. When the court moved, the elaborate sets were transported by specially constructed barges on the Danube. The Bibiena family ruled the European opera stage for a hundred years.

Joseph I who succeeded Leopold I, was a good musician; some of his church music composition were still heard in Viennese churches in the nineteenth century. Though he reigned only for six years, he managed to raise the personnel of the court chapel to over a hundred, and rebuilt the opera house. Every year twelve to fourteen new operas were mounted. Then Charles VI (reigned 1711-1740), a first-class musical emperor, took charge. He was an excellent violinist and harpsichordist, studied composition with Fux, and was an experienced and knowledgable conductor in the opera house. He assembled a plethora of distinguished musicians, enlarged the Hofkapelle to 140, and engaged the pride of Italy, Metastasio, as court poet — that is, librettist. Every composer was eager to set his librettos, and half a century of operatic history could be called the Metastasian era. Charles commissioned operas, and then in a sort of *jus primae noctis*, conducted the dress rehearsal, though for the court only. On one of these occasions old Fux sat behind the emperor and admiringly told him "it is a shame that your Majesty did not become a professional musician "whereupon the emperor answered "yes, I know, but I made out all right." The musical fame of the House of Habsburg was so great that when Fux was queried for a biographical sketch by Mattheson, the leading German chronicler of music, he answered proudly that it is sufficient to know that he was found worthy to be Charles VI's first court conductor.

Since the male line of the Habsburgs expired with Charles, his eldest daughter, Maria Theresa (reigned 1740-1780) succeeded him. This strong-willed and able woman was a trained singer particularly interested in the theater. She reorganized the court music establishment and attracted many outstanding musicians to the court, among them Gluck. Unfortunately, during her reign, the empress was in the center of wars and power politics which did not leave her much time for artistic pursuits.

Under Joseph II the Viennese school reached its zenith with Mozart and Haydn. Joseph, like his predecessors, was a thoroughly trained musician, a good bass singer, played the cello and the violin, and was much admired for his skill as an accompanist. (Maria Theresa wanted all her children to be what in those days was known as *Kenner und Liebhaber*, that is, amateurs but with a near-professional equipment.) After dinner there was always an hour of music in the emperor's chambers, and three times a week regular concerts by the best artists but without a public. Joseph, the political reformer, carried his activity into music. In his own words, he wanted to "raise the theater to an important means for the education of my people." Though an absolutist to the core, he wanted to broaden the enjoyment of the musical theater so he founded the national *Singspiel* theater where operas in a lighter vein were performed in the vernacular instead of in Italian. One of the first commissions, *The Abduction from the Seraglio*, went to Mozart. Such harem pieces were as popular then as our westerns are today to us. Regrettably, Joseph's ruthless ecclesiastic decrees dealt a serious blow to the great traditions of Viennese church music — he even abolished church choirs.

As we turn to the north and examine the Prussian court, the scene shows much less consistency. The first Prussian king, Frederick I, who started his reign in 1701, was a good flute player and also sang. During his reign the court orchestra became modernized and, with an eye on the future, the king engaged a number of distinguished artists. His wife, Sophie Charlotte, being a daughter of the music-loving Elector of Hanover, Ernest Augustus, was even better qualified, and lost no time in making a home at the court for her father's adored Italians. She also built an exceptionally fine music library (now in the Staatsbibliothek). But Frederick William I, the soldier king, ended all this; within half a year after his assumption of power both opera and the Hofkapelle were dissolved, only military music remaining. His children, under the guidance of their mother, were another matter. All three of his daughters were fine musicians, notably Anna Amalia, who was universally praised by all professional musicians who came in contact with her. All three were outshone, however, by their brother.

Frederick the Great started early with his music, as did all the royal children. Frederick William did not mind what the girls did in their spare time, but he was incensed by the crown prince's absorbing interest in music and literature, and banished him to the fortress of Küstrin, where he isolated him from music. But with the start of his reign in 1740 everything changed, and a totally new spirit invaded the Hohenzollern court. The building of an opera house was immediately begun, and Carl Heinrich Graun, one of the leading German musicians of the time, was dispatched to Italy to recruit a troupe. Carl Philip Emanuel Bach and Joachim Quantz were engaged for the court at high salaries, and there were daily musicals, the king playing the flute for hours on end. The king's involvement in music is the more remarkable because he kept it up during his campaigns, taking his flute and travelling harpsichord with him into the field. His extremely conservative tastes, however, to some extent hobbled his musicians, and, being a Deist, he did little for church music. Frederick's collected compositions, concertos and sonatas, have been published in three volumes in a modern edition. His correspondence, especially with his sisters, shows that he followed musical events all over Europe. At one of the usual chamber music seances at Sans Souci the playing was interrupted when the police minister came with the list of arrivals in Berlin, which the monarch always persued. Suddenly he excitedly said to his musicians: *Meine Herren, der alte Bach ist hier* (Gentlemen, old Bach is here), and Johann Sebastian was hailed to the palace, still in his travelling clothes, where he played for hours for the awed king. Sadly, in his old age, more and more involved in wars and crises, the king gradually abandoned music, turned into a real Hohenzollern, and his top musicians deserted him one by one.

Frederick William II (reigned until 1797) closes the Prussian court music for our purposes. He too was very much interested in music but unlike his great predecessor, he was a patron of German art. "German music should be practised by German musicians, not by Frenchmen and Italians" was his motto. He was a good quartet player, maintained a fine orchestra, and ordered the first performance of *Messiah* in Germany in 1786. All the great composers of the age dedicated works to him.

Before we leave the German orbit, we must single out two from the many excellent court establishments: Mannheim and Eszterháza. Carl Theodore, the Elector Palatine, spent half his fortune on music. His opera house was a showcase where every new opera from Venice, Naples, or Paris was performed within the year, but his pride was the Mannheim orchestra, the most modern and significant in Europe. It was one of the chief factors in the rise of the symphonic style. The Esterházy Princes, premier peers of the Holy Roman Empire, maintained a little Versailles of their own; they are irrevocably immortalized by their employment of and devotion to Haydn. The quartets and symphonies streaming out of their provincial west Hungarian town decided the course of musical history for generations. Though the Esterházys were immensely rich, they followed the custom of the lesser aristocrats in the manner in which they maintained their court music. The servants were engaged with an eye to their musical abilities. Gardeners and foresters would play the violin or the French horn, while chambermaids sang soprano and alto; usually only the first deskmen and the two conductors were professionals. But Haydn's scores show that he drilled his sandlot crew to respectable professional level.

Now to the other great musical nation, France. After king and court definitely settled in Versailles in 1680, the musical establishment, long operating informally, was firmly organized in four branches: the court chapel, the Academy of Music and the Dance (i.e. the opera), chamber music, and military music, called "musique de la Grand Ecurie." Leadership of each of these divisions, acquired through competition, was much sought for because the emoluments were attractive and the positions carried considerable prestige. Under Louis XIV, who not only had a taste for music but had rather stubborn ideas about it, church music assumed a truly royal cast. The great figure who dominated all music in seventeenth-century France, Jean Baptiste Lully, the king's favorite, composed this new kind of church music exactly to the king's specifications. Called *motets á grand choeur*, these were psalm settings for double choir accompanied by the entire opera orchestra, trumpets blaring and drums rolling. The king attended Mass every day and upon his order these magnificent but thoroughly secular pieces were substituted for the old liturgic music. This dynastic ceremonial music had weighty consequences, notably in England. The future Charles II observed it first hand while living in Paris and, dissatisfied after his accession with the staid music in the English Church, sent the most promising members of the Chapel Royal to imbibe the new style at its source. Upon their return these musicians transmitted the style to John Blow (1649-1708) and Henry Purcell (1659-1695), the Orpheus Britannicus. It did not take long for Handel to grasp the meaning of this thoroughly Anglicized ceremonial style and he raised it to superlative heights with his Chandos and Coronation Anthems as well as in his anthem oratorios like *Israel in Egypt*. Actually, even the famous Hallelujah Chorus in *Messiah* is a coronation anthem pure and simple. Upon hearing these anthems every English breast swells, not with religious fervor, because in these grand works there is no more Christian quality than in Lully's Te Deums, but because when they hear the psalm "The King shall rejoice" they recognize that it is less the King of Kings whom Handel commemorates, than their own king. The instrumental music of Louis's band, *les vingt-quatre violons du roi*, laid the foundations for the orchestra as we know it; Charles obviously copied it with his "four and twenty fiddles." The list of the musicians at the French court is an illustrious one, but after Louis XIV the monarchs took little direct interest in their music, though the establishment was maintained. Since the palace at Versailles did not have an opera theater, the Académie used a very expensive movable stage set up in the Trianon palace. It was not until 1770 that an opera theater was built by the architect Gabriel. Here again France set an example, if not of music at least of social customs. The great receptions and balls held in the new theater were copied everywhere in Europe. To this day, even in the republics, visiting heads of state and other notables are usually taken to the royal box and treated to a gala performance, even the communist states retaining the custom as well as the royal box, replacing only the crown with the hammer and sicle.

After the middle of the century the *philosophes*, with their insatiable interest in everything problematical, took over the intellectual direction of music in France. The ensuing debates, the scores of pamphlets and open letters are well known; never was an entire nation involved to such an extent in an arduous altercation about music as in the so-called "Querelle des bouffons." Unfortunately, as Rameau contemptuously remarked, the *philosophes* and other men of letters "have perhaps never listened to anything but ditties," and indeed, French music, bereft of professional leadership (the octogenarian Rameau was an embittered old man) and proper patronage from the court, rapidly declined, and, as in England, languished for almost a hundred years. The brief glory toward the end of the century was the work of a foreigner, Gluck.

Little can be said about the music in the English court. After the great Tudor era, when the sovereigns were connoisseurs of music, a gradual decline sets in because the Reformation eradicated many of the centuries-old traditions of English music. It is unnecessary to recount the ravages caused by the Commonwealth, though its hostility to music was less broad than is usually represented; Cromwell himself liked music — in the home, but not in church. However, since their antipathy closed the theaters just when the new Italian dramatic style was changing the face of the musical globe, a hiatus was created that could not be filled for centuries. The Hanoverians brought from Germany their love for music, but they did not care for the local scene, while their subjects did not care for the foreign dynasty and its foibles. Anyway, with Handel's towering presence, little else mattered. The Chapel Royal was maintained because the king was the head of the Church, but both the first Georges preferred the theater, whether opera, or after 1740, oratorio. There was no real court composer in London; the title of Master of the King's musick, formerly an important post, was indiscriminately awarded to musicians good or bad. Some acted more like caretakers of instruments and copyists than composers, others, lacking any creative ability, employed deputies to compose the welcome and birthday odes. Whenever there was a particularly solemn occasion, the death of Queen Caroline, the commemoration of Dettingen or Utrecht, Mr. Handel was bidden to compose an ode or a Te Deum, and he invariably acquitted himself in the grand manner. He was also the author of the coronation anthems which ever since are heard when a British monarch is crowned. All this was dynastic ceremonial music, superbly euphonious, gloriously effective, and English to the core, even though composed by a naturalized German. Whenever there was a service of this sort in St. Paul's, every shade of Englishman, even the non-conformists, flocked to the cathedral, because it was king and country that were being celebrated. George III came to the throne when the decline of music in England had become quite severe. That closes the story of court music in England, for all succeeding sovereigns lacked both taste and understanding for music.

In Spain, the semi-demented and insomniac Ferdinand VI employed the great castrato Farinelly for the sole purpose of lulling him to sleep every night for years on end by singing the same arias by Hasse. But the Queen, Maria Barbara, who played the harpsichord and loved music, supported Domenico Scarlatti, who spent his mature years at the Spanish court dedicating to her hundreds of his sonatas.

Finally, let us take a look at the least developed of courts, the Russian, which offers a marked contrast to the foregoing but complements the narrative by demonstrating what happened in the absence of a well-appointed and well-led court music establishment. The clergy, supported by the czars, frowned upon any music outside the church, and inside it tolerated only monophonic song, the ancient Byzantine-Slavonic chant. What was missing in Russia was the mainstay of a musical culture: the social class that would support it. The first stirrings of art music took place as recently as the end of the seventeenth century. It was Peter the Great (reigned 1689-1725) who deliberately sought to modernize Russia and its culture. Even though the first musical organizations at the imperial and ducal courts were simple imitations of Western models and all the personnel was imported, a profound change took place as the Russians recognized that music was an essential part of civilized court life. Here we have an example not only of the power of an institution, the court, but what it can achieve when an overwhelming personality is at its head. Peter accomplished in a few years what a whole century before him had been powerless to do. The czarinas who followed him continued Peter's example; there was however a price to be paid for this: the enforced westernization, restricted to the court, the aristocracy, and the higher reaches of the bureaucracy, only increased the vast gulf between the ruling powers and the people.

In closing I might say that the eighteenth century ended with the unquestioned supremacy of the Habsburgs' Vienna. Perhaps it was the absence of a splendid and knowledgeable court in middle and north Germany that prevented the continuation of Bach's great art — his own sons opted for the new style of the south — and undoubtedly Pietism's indifference to the arts hindered the development of music in the Protestant north until the romantic era. However, no matter how we contemplate these historical events, the supremacy of the Austrian imperial city remains an indubitable fact: Haydn, Mozart, and Beethoven testify to that.

Paul Henry Lang

Tobias Mayer (1723-1762): A Case Study in the Interaction between Cartography, Astronomy, & Navigation During the 18th Century

Tobias Mayer is an example of someone who was held in the highest esteem by his contemporaries yet barely remembered by posterity. The eminent Swiss mathematician Leonhard Euler classes him in 1760 as "undoubtedly the greatest astronomer in Europe,"[1] while the critical French historian of astronomy Jean Delambre goes even further and asserts that Mayer was "universally considered as one of the greatest astronomers not only of the eighteenth century, but of all times and all countries."[2] High praise indeed! And praise which is all the more significant on account of the fact that Delambre had previously made an exhaustive study of the entire history of his subject, and published three volumes on ancient and mediaeval astronomy. Twenty-five years later, Delambre's assessment is echoed by Robert Grant in the words:

> Mayer possesses claims to be ranked with the greatest astronomers of ancient or modern times; but, as in the case of either of his illustrious contemporaries, Bradley or Lacaille, his labours are not of a nature to be generally appreciated, and therefore his reputation is less widely diffused than that of many an individual whose contributions to science, though more showy, are infinitely less substantial.[3]

---

1. L. Euler to G. F. Müller; Berlin, 15 July, 1760. This letter is published in *Die Berliner und die Petersburger Akademie der Wissenschaften im Briefwechsel Leonhard Eulers. Teil I*, Berlin, 1959. See p. 153.
2. J. Delambre, *Histoire de l'astronomie au dix-huitième siècle*, Paris, 1827, p. 429.
3. R. Grant, *History of Physical Astronomy*, London, 1852, p. 488.

These laudatory references to Mayer's ability as an astronomer actually represent a small sample of those contained in the astronomical literature of the eighteenth and nineteenth centuries; but they suffice to show that one should not dub Mayer as a "secondary" figure in the history of astronomy on account of the comparative obscurity which now surrounds his name. This obscurity reflects our own lack of appreciation of the nature and scope of Mayer's achievements: it does not necessarily imply that the latter were of little intrinsic value or scientific importance. Grant cites the complexity of Mayer's researches as a reason for the subsequent lack of diffusion of their results, and this is certainly very true. Equally significant, however, was the fact that Mayer lived at a time of rapid growth in the physical sciences; thus his pioneering efforts to improve the precision of astronomical and navigational instruments, the determination of terrestrial and celestial longitudes and latitudes, the lunar theory, etc. were all quickly superseded by the contributions of others who had better means at their disposal.

A further factor is that a large proportion of what he wrote and taught has remained almost totally unknown despite the personal interest shown by George III in his manuscripts. George's desire that all of these should be edited and published was only partially implemented by Georg Christoph Lichtenberg in the years 1773-1775 following a decade of indecision on the part of the Hanoverian authorities who purchased them from Mayer's widow shortly after his death. It has taken me five years to complete this task, and the main fruits of my labors to date are contained in five volumes: *The Euler-Mayer Correspondence* and *Tobias Mayer's Opera Inedita*, both published by Macmillan in December 1971; and *The Unpublished Writings of Tobias Mayer* (3 volumes), published by Vandenhoeck and Ruprecht, in December 1972.

In order to acquire a proper appreciation of the nature of Mayer's researches, it is necessary to examine these in a chronological sequence and not, as his biographer Sigmund Günther has suggested, by drawing a distinction between his purely mathematical works, his physical treatises, and his epoch-making astronomical treatises.[4] To label Mayer as a "mathematician, physicist, and

---

4. *Allgemeine deutsche Biographie*, XXI, 1885, pp. 109-116.

astronomer"[5] may be a convenient means of defining the general area of his interests, but it tends to suggest some kind of methodological split in the character of his individual researches which simply does not exist, and at the same time obscures the true pattern of his intellectual development. A more meaningful introduction to Mayer is to trace the course of his life and work through its four phases: the youthful period in Esslingen, up to 1744; the formative years as a copper engraver and map-maker in Augsburg, 1744-1746; the period 1746-1751 as an employee of the Homann Cartographic Bureau in Nuremberg, where he established a reputation both as a geographer and as an astronomer; and the period 1751-1762 as a professor at the Georg-August Academy in Göttingen.

The earliest piece of documentary evidence to have a bearing upon Mayer's scientific career is an autobiographical account of his early childhood, covering the eight-year period from his birth in the small town of Marbach-am-Neckar on 17 February 1723 until shortly before his father's death in Esslingen on 12 August 1731.[6] In this fascinating document, composed sometime during the last three years of his life, Mayer recalls how his antipathy towards irrelevant or useless knowledge, natural artistic talent, and fascination for military affairs, had all been in evidence even in those tender years.

The first of these three factors originated from the vast but useless amount of memorization that he was obliged to do during his early and unhappy school-days, and is a theme which is found in several of his writings. Lichtenberg recognises this trait, and indicates that it was by no means a sentiment which was peculiar to Mayer himself, when he remarks:

> Someone once said about Tobias Mayer: he himself had not known that he knew so much — and therein lies something [which is] certainly very true. This is the real way to progress in the world. The ordinary scholars approach science teleolo-

---

5. This was the title of a biographical article by Victor Kommerell in the *Schwäbische Lebensbilder*, II, 1941, pp. 351-66.

6. "Bruchstück zu Tobias Mayers Leben...." in Franz Xavier von Zach, ed., *Monatliche Correspondenz zur Beförderung der Erd- und Himmels-Kunde*, IX, 1804, pp. 415-32; reprinted in Johann Friedrich Benzenberg, *Erstlinge von Tobias Mayer*, Düsseldorf, 1812, pp. xxxv-li.

gically, and even already in the title are anticipating something that they still do not know. That is depressing. Mayer himself was always seeking, and everything which he learned was to him a need: thus he could develop his science further. Nowadays one learns just the opposite, and offers syntheses which one will never need, along with a lot of useless things, although they are nevertheless very ingenious. . . . The scholar could be someone who has stored a large amount of knowledge in his head, which may be of no further use to him except that he is able to communicate it again. If, however, someone becomes a specialist in a single subject, and all mankind agrees with him — and [if] he is a man only inasmuch as he is this, then he is no scholar.[7]

This interesting passage may be construed as an attack upon the scholastic mode of thought still prevalent in Germany during the latter half of the eighteenth century, which had been sustained by the philosophical writings of Gottfried Wilhelm Leibniz and Christian von Wolff. Lichtenberg's allusion to Mayer's empirical approach to science is of particular significance since it was derived from his close acquaintance with the latter's unpublished writings.

A significant link between Mayer's artistic ability and his interest in military matters arose from his contact with an elderly non-commissioned officer of the Swabian district artillery by the name of Geiger, whose admiration for a set of architectural drawings of the local hospital which Tobias had made when barely fourteen years of age, caused him to take a fatherly interest in the boy's future. It is certainly more than a mere co-incidence that before the end of the year 1738 Tobias, who was now an orphan, was requesting the town-council to recommend him to the same troop and in the same capacity as Geiger himself. The result, however, was not what he anticipated; for it was decided that he should be sent to the high-school in Esslingen in order to increase his knowledge and develop his talents further. The school curriculum included religious instruction, Greek, Latin, logic,

---

7. *Georg Christoph Lichtenbergs Vermischte Schriften. Neue vermehrte, von dessen Söhnen veranstaltete Original-Ausgabe. Erster Band*, Göttingen, 1844, p. 290.

rhetoric, and some geography and history. Mathematics, however, was *not* taught there.⁸

This deficiency in his formal education was partially compensated by the intensive instruction in geometry and artillery (including fortification) which Mayer received from Geiger during his first three months at the high-school, and he subsequently found an outlet for his talents by giving private tuition in such subjects to the sons of a number of local citizens who were destined for a military career. His youthful enthusiasm for mathematics was encouraged by his headmaster, who gave him access to his own library. He would seem to have been attracted to that subject mainly on account of its aesthetic appeal; for in the opening sentence of the preface to his first printed work, written on his eighteenth birthday, he remarks:

> Since from among all the sciences none gives me more pleasure than mathematics, not only on account of its precision and clarity, but also on account of its charm and delightful versatility; I shall consider myself to be particularly fortunate if I should be given the opportunity of practising it still more.⁹

Significantly, this book (whose theme may be summarised briefly as the application of analytic methods to the solution of common geometrical problems) culminates with the solution of a problem of practical importance in the design of military fortifications: viz. how to inscribe an irregularly-shaped polygon inside a circle.

The next three years saw little change in Mayer's position, or little prospect for the development of his talents. Thus it is not surprising that when he came of age in 1744, he left Esslingen and took up employment in the copper-engraving and map-making firm of Johann Andreas Pfeffel in Augsburg. His elder step-brother Georg Wilhelm was then working in that town as a coppersmith; and a map of Esslingen which he had drawn in 1739 had also been

---

8. The information contained in this paragraph was obtained from Paul Eberhardt, "Urkundliche Beiträge zu der Jugendgeschichte des Astronomen Johann Tobias Mayer," *Literarische Beiträge des Staatsanzeigers*, Nr. 12 and 13, 1908, pp. 177-87, reprinted in *Aus Alt-Esslingen*, Esslingen, 1924, pp. 207-24.

9. T. Mayer, *Neue und allgemeine Art, alle Aufgaben aus der Geometrie vermittelst der geometrischen Linien leicht aufzulösen*, Esslingen, 1741.

engraved there.[10] The story goes that "after many adventures which arose mainly from his inexperience and poverty,"[11] he received a friendly welcome in the home of a printer called Silbereisen where he soon came to be regarded as a member of his host's family. He is said to have learnt a great deal during the course of the next two years from his association with artists and scholars — improving his Latin still further, while acquiring fluency in his writing of French and a reading knowledge of English and Italian. His scientific knowledge was broadened through his acquaintance with the optician and mechanic Georg Brander, with whom he collaborated on the construction of a glass micrometer.[12] A thorough search of the Augsburg archives has failed to throw any further light on Mayer's activities during this formative period in his life, and it now seems unlikely that primary source-materials will be found to substantiate the scanty biographical information which is summarised above.

However, a splendid index of the extent to which Mayer had by now developed both his natural artistic talent and his scientific knowledge is provided by his impressive *Mathematischer Atlas* (Augsburg, 1745) in whose sixty plates he presents the whole range of elementary mathematics with (in turn) astronomical, geographical, military, architectural, and mechanical applications. In the preface to a second edition containing eight supplementary tables concerned with the principles of the differential and integral calculus, he defines his intention as being to place a concise, simple, and clear presentation of the most essential and useful aspects of pure and applied mathematics in the hands of all lovers of these "splendid sciences."[13] Among other things, Mayer illustrates the use of projective methods in representing lunar and solar eclipses, and occultations of planets and stars by the moon. Methodologically, his remarkable skill in projective geometry constitutes the most important link with his earlier researches; but the major significance of this atlas is that it represents the

---

10. This is now the oldest map of Esslingen and its surroundings still extant. It is catalogued by Max Schefold, *Alte Ansichten aus Württemberg*, Nr. 1479, p. 121 of the 2nd volume of *Esslinger Studien*, 1957.
11. D. Hausleutner, *Schwäbisches Archiv*, 1793, p. 390.
12. Kommerell, *op. cit.*, p. 5.
13. This preface is dated 18 January 1745.

culmination of a program of self-tuition begun in Esslingen several years previously, based upon Christian von Wolff's *Anfangs-Gründe aller mathematischer Wissenschaften*.[14] Mayer's presentation was much more likely to appeal to a beginner than the axiomatic arrangement favored by Wolff.

The contents of Mayer's atlas leave no doubt about his full awareness that there was an intimate connection between astronomy and geography, and yet a dearth of reliable values for the latitudes and longitudes of most of the major towns and cities of the world. However, his only *explicit* reference to the contemporary state of cartography occurs in the opening paragraph of a manuscript composed about two years later, shortly after he took up a new appointment in the Homann Cartographic Bureau in Nuremberg, where he says:

> It is only too well known in geography that very many, indeed most, of the numerous known and noteworthy places need to have their latitude and longitude more accurately determined. *To achieve this is one of the most important objects of astronomy*, and those who are occupied with this science have continually made great efforts to obtain the kind of observations from which the geographical position ... can be derived. Few, however, have extended their labors to the problem of how their own observations might properly be applied to this goal.[15]

Thus astronomy was, for Mayer, the hand-maiden of geography; and his initial attraction to astronomy stemmed from his appreciation of its usefulness in providing a more reliable knowledge of the locations of places on the earth's surface.

The urgent need to place German cartography upon a new and more systematic footing was strongly felt by Mayer's employer

---

14. Mayer apparently had access to one of the early German editions of the original Latin work *Elementa matheseos universae*, 2 vols., Halle, 1715-1717, popularly known as the Wolffian Compendium.

15. The title of this manuscript is *Collectanea geographica et mathematica 1747*. The quotation is a translation of Mayer's opening remarks in the section headed "Untersuchungen über die geographische Länge und Breite der Stadt Nürnberg" recently printed in Vol. 1 of Eric G. Forbes, *The Unpublished Writings of Tobias Mayer*, Göttingen, 1972, cf. p. 33.

Johann Michael Franz, who founded at about this same time (1747) a Cosmographical Society consisting of three distinct classes of membership: mathematical, literary-cum-historical, and corresponding, the last being for interested laymen only. Mayer and his colleague Georg Moritz Lowitz, Professor of Physics at the Melanchthon College in Nuremberg, were the founder members of the mathematical class; and as such, they committed themselves to the following tasks announced by Franz in the preface to the *Homannische-Haseschen Gesellschafts Atlas* (Nürnberg, 1747):

1. The search for new and more general principles in geodetic measurement and methods of projection.
2. The demonstration of how these projective methods might usefully be applied to celestial phenomena such as eclipses and occultations.
3. The pursuit of practical astronomical science, both in collating old and new observations by others and in making one's own accurate observations, with a view to preparing a reliable list of geographical co-ordinates.
4. The invention, design, construction, and description of celestial atlases and globes, orreries, and other scientific instruments.
5. The making and collation of accurate measurements of the variation and dip of the magnetic needle for as many places as possible, with a view to discovering laws governing these phenomena and how to apply them in cosmography.

This statement of intent subsumes the whole range of Mayer's scientific activities from this time onwards, and provides the key to our understanding of the character and motivation of his researches.

In accordance with the second of these aims, Mayer made an orthographic projection of the lunar surface as a preliminary to a graphical construction of a partial lunar eclipse due to occur on the night of 8/9 August 1747, which was to serve as a basis for the determination of terrestrial longitude differences.[16] He soon

---

16. This projection was published as Tab. XXI of Johann Gabriel Doppelmaier, *Atlas Coelestis*, Nuremberg, 1752.

realised, however, that the best of the existing lunar maps — those of Johann Hevelius and Giovanni Riccioli — were not reliable enough for this purpose, and so decided to prepare a new map himself. With this end in view, he began to make a series of observations with the aid of his glass micrometer and a nine-foot focal length telescope purchased for the Homann firm by Franz of a considerable number of large and small features on the moon's disc. In preparing his map, he was confronted with the problem of making a quantitative allowance for the moon's libratory motion, and developed an analysis in which he distinguishes the contributions of the irregularity of the moon's orbital motion, the variation of its angular diameter, and the effects of parallax, precession, and nutation.[17] A remarkable feature of his solution to this complex problem was that (due to a lucky inspiration) he correctly formed three normal equations from a system of 27 conditional equations — a procedure which had at that time never been attempted, for which no theory had been developed.[18] The same treatise on the lunar libration is historically important for another reason also: it was the first to contain determinations of the selenographic co-ordinates of features on the moon's surface. Mayer's values of these co-ordinates for 89 prominent lunar markings are listed by Lichtenberg in the appendix to his *Opera inedita Tobiae Mayeri I* (Göttingen, 1775). A photolithographic reproduction of Mayer's 40 cm. diameter lunar map was made by W. Hollmann of Dresden over a century later.[19]

The scholarly reputation which Mayer won for himself both through the publication of his original astronomical researches[20]

---

17. T. Mayer, "Abhandlung über die Umwälzung des Monds um seine Axe und die scheinbare Bewegung der Mondsflecken. Worinnen der Grund einer verbesserten Mondsbeschreibung aus neuen Beobachtungen geleget wird," *Kosmographische Nachrichten und Sammlungen auf d. J. 1748*, Nürnberg, 1750, pp. 52-183.

18. Delambre, *op. cit.* 2, pp. 429-449. Delambre's discussion is the basis of the biographical article on Mayer by James Browne in the 7th edition of the *Encyclopaedia Britannica*, Edinburgh, 1842.

19. This was done at the instigation of the Director of the Göttingen Observatory Wilhelm Klinkerfues, and published in 1881.

20. Five treatises by Mayer, comprising a description of his glass micrometer, his observations of a solar eclipse and lunar occultations, his analysis of the moon's libration, and a speculative essay arguing for the non-existence of a lunar atmosphere, all appeared in *op. cit.*

and also through his skill and industry as a cartographer,[21] was largely responsible for his being called, in November 1750, to a professorship at the Georg-August Academy in Göttingen, a post which he duly took up at Easter of the following year. There was, however, another factor involved; namely, the decision of the Hanoverian Government, whose Prime Minister Gerlach Adolph von Münchhausen had been responsible for this appointment, to establish a formal link with the Homann cartographic bureau, with the ultimate intention of effecting a transfer of that entire firm from Nuremberg to Göttingen. This ambition was partially realised in 1755 when Franz and Lowitz also became professors at the Georg-August Academy, bringing some of their equipment but only a few of their staff with them. By this time, an observatory had been built and equipped, and Mayer had become its first director,[22] thereby establishing the desired union between the sciences of astronomy and cartography. In practice, the fortunes of the cartographic bureau were soon to decline owing mainly to the lack of skilled personnel and Lowitz's inability to complete work upon pairs of celestial and terrestrial globes; for it thereby became impossible for that gentleman to repay a substantial loan from the Hanoverian government and money to a number of rich and influential subscribers to his globes.[23] The ambitious program envisaged by Franz suffered a further setback after the French occupation of Göttingen during the Seven Years' War (from July 1757) which effectively put paid to Mayer's astronomical observations. Nevertheless, to compensate for this, the latter developed during the last four years of his life a mathematical theory of mixing colour-pigments, designed to ensure that the colouring of maps and heraldic devices could be consistently reproduced even

---

21. Articles containing information on this aspect of Mayer's scientific activity are: Sophus Ruge, "Aus der Sturm- und Drang-Periode der Geographie," *Zeitschrift für Wissenschaftliche Geographie*, V, 1885, pp. 249-60; and Christian Sandler, "Die Homännischen Erben," *ibid.*, VII, 1890, pp. 333-55 and 418-48.

22. The circumstances of Mayer's appointment to this post are described in Eric G. Forbes, "The Foundation of the First Göttingen Observatory: a Study in Politics and Personalities," *Journal for the History of Astronomy* (to be published shortly).

23. Details of these troubles can be found in Franz and Lowitz's Personalakte (Ph 1/18 4Vb, Nr. 23, 27) in the Dekanat und Universitäts-Archiv, Göttingen; also in *op. cit.* p. 21.

by apprentices with no natural artistic skill;[24] and (in accordance with the last of the above-mentioned aims of the Cosmographical Society), a theory of magnetism applied to the determination of terrestrial longitudes and latitudes from measurements of the variation and dip of the magnetic needle.[25]

Meanwhile — this time by accident rather than by design — a connection had been established between Mayer's researches on the theory of the moon's motion and the improvement of the so-called lunar distances method of finding longitude at sea. The basic principle underlying this method was that of comparing the local time at sea with the standard time on the meridian of an observatory, such as that at Greenwich. The function of the land-based observer had to be provided by lunar tables calculated prior to the sea voyage from a reliable lunar theory, which would enable the mariner to interpolate the moon's distance from a bright zodiacal star corresponding to that which he observed at sea; the instrument now used for this purpose being a reflecting octant of the type invented by John Hadley in 1731. The difference between the local time and that calculated time was then directly convertible into angular measure by means of the identity 24 hours = 360°. In practice, this comparison was complicated by instrumental errors and by the fact that the observed positions of both the moon and the star are affected by astronomical refraction and parallax. The lunar distances had to be "cleared" of these physical effects, and an accurate estimate had to be made of the value of the moon's angular radius (or semidiameter) if the observation were made on the limb of its disc. This whole procedure would, however, be of no practical value unless the lunar theory itself were capable of predicting the moon's celestial position to an accuracy of within one minute of arc — an accuracy at least five times as high as that which the new analytic theories of Alexis Clairaut (1752) and Leonhard Euler (1755) appeared to be capable of yielding.[26]

24. Eric G. Forbes, "Tobias Mayer's Theory of Colour-Mixing and its application to Artistic Reproductions," *Annals of Science*, XXVI, 1970, pp. 95-114.
25. Vol. 3 of *The Unpublished Writings of Tobias Mayer*, (cf. note 15) is entirely devoted to this theme, about which little has hitherto been known.
26. Details concerning these matters may be obtained from Eric G. Forbes,

This was the state of affairs when Mayer published the results of his independent researches on the theory of the moon's motion in the second volume of the transactions of the Göttingen Scientific Society.[27] Unfortunately, he gave no indication in this article of how he had arrived at his formulae — one is required to read his correspondence with Euler[28] to find this out, yet he was claiming for them an accuracy of within two minutes of arc. As a result of further improvements made during the year 1753, Mayer was able to double this degree of precision, and in the next volume of the Göttingen transactions he explained how his improved tables could be used as a basis for the lunar distances method of longitude determination at sea.[29] He recognised that other known astronomical methods involving the observation of occultations of stars by the moon, or lunar and solar eclipses, were too infrequent; moreover, these were suitable only for establishing a *fixed* longitude difference between two landbased observers on widely separated meridians rather than for providing a general means of finding the *variable* longitude of a moving ship. Mayer had never been to sea, nor indeed had he ever *seen* the sea, yet he was well able to imagine that the errors liable to be incurred if a reflecting octant or similar instrument were to be used on board a ship pitching and tossing on the high seas would be very much greater than those found in terrestrial measurements. For this reason, he remained sceptical of the accuracy which might actually be attainable in practice.

It was only after being continually encouraged by his friends and colleagues in Göttingen and, more significantly, by Euler himself,[30] that he decided to submit a copy of his improved lunar tables and papers relating to the lunar distances method to the Admiralty in London, in the hope of qualifying for one of the three major awards of between £10,000 and £20,000 offered by

"Tobias Mayer's Contributions to the Development of Lunar Theory," *Journal for the History of Astronomy*, I, 1970, pp. 144-54.

27. T. Mayer, "Novae tabulae motuum solis et lunae," *Commentarii Societatis Regiae Scientiarum Gottingensis*, II, 1753, pp. 383-430.

28. Eric G. Forbes, *The Euler-Mayer Correspondence (1751-1755)*, London, 1971.

29. T. Mayer, "Tabularium Lunarium in commentt. S. R. Tom II Contentarum usus in investiganda longitudine maris," *loc. cit.* 27, pp. 375-96.

30. Euler to Mayer; Berlin, 11 June 1754. Cf. *op. cit.* 28, p. 86.

the British government under the terms of the Act 12 Queen Anne (1714) to anyone who could provide a useful and practicable method for finding longitude at sea.[31] Batches of more than fifty letters in the Hanover State archives[32] and thirty-five more in the university library of Göttingen,[33] each pertaining to the period 1754 to 1765, enable one to reconstruct the manner in which Mayer's claim was diplomatically handled by Johann David Michaelis, Secretary for Hanoverian affairs in Göttingen, von Munchhausen and his colleagues in Hanover, and William Philip Best, the Hanoverian government's representative in London. It is clear from Best's reports,[34] and from the praise given to the tables in the *Gentlemen's Magazine* for August and September 1754, that informed opinion in England was at this time strongly in Mayer's favour. His Memorial and the accompanying documents were duly delivered by Best to Lord Anson, the First Lord of the Admiralty and chairman of the Board of Longitude — the body of commissioners authorized to adjudicate such claims — on 20 January 1755, after which they were referred officially to the Astronomer Royal James Bradley for comment. Bradley reported enthusiastically to the Admiralty Secretary on the accuracy of Mayer's lunar tables on two occasions (in 1756 and 1760), strongly recommending them as suitable for the purpose for which they were intended.[35]

No decision was taken on the question of a parliamentary award to Mayer before his untimely death from sepsis at 39 years of age, on 20 February 1762. Shortly before he died, however, he received lunar distances observations made at sea with the aid of a Hadley octant by a former student Carsten Niebuhr whom he had trained specially for this task. These pleased him so much that he

---

31. On this subject see, for example, *op. cit.* 28 or Eric G. Forbes, "Tobias Mayer's Lunar Tables," *Annals of Science*, XXII, 1966, pp. 105-16.

32. "Betr. der von Seiten des Prof. Tobias Mayer in Göttingen gelöste englische Preisfrage über die Bestimmung der Longitudo maris, 1754-1765," *Hannover Des.* 92 XXXIV No. II, 4, a¹.

33. *Cod. Ms Michaelis* 320, pp. 535-671.

34. Four encouraging letters were sent from Best to Michaelis on 13 September, 8 October, 5 and 19 November 1754, and are preserved in *ibid.*, pp. 555-69.

35. Bradley to Cleveland, 10 February 1756 and 14 April 1760, were originally published in *op. cit.* 37, pp. cix-cxv, and reprinted in S. P. Rigaud, *Miscellaneous Works and Correspondence of the Rev. James Bradley, D. D., F.R.S.*, Oxford, 1832, pp. 84-89.

asked his wife to send them after his death to England, along with a copy of lunar and solar tables containing the numerous minor improvements that he had been making since 1755.[36] These "new improved lunar tables" were duly transmitted to London in the summer of 1763 via the customary diplomatic channels, and were thoroughly edited by the Astronomer Royal (now Nevil Maskelyne) before being published in both Latin and English seven years later.[37] Maskelyne was a firm adherent to the method of lunars, since he had employed it successfully with the aid of Mayer's earlier (1755) tables during his voyage to St. Helena in 1761 in connection with the transit of Venus, and had published his results together with instructions for the use of the method in *The British Mariner Guide* (London, 1763). These showed that the method was generally useful and capable of yielding longitudes at sea to within 1° or 60 nautical miles, for which the appropriate parliamentary reward to Mayer ought to have been £10,000. Thus the government's decision in 1765 (Act 5 George III, cap. XX) to grant Mayer's heirs only £3,000 was regarded by contemporary scientists as being most ungenerous. One factor which may have influenced this decision was that Mayer himself had not supplied the appropriate auxiliary tables, instructions, worked examples, etc. These deficiencies were rectified by Maskelyne himself through the introduction of the *Nautical Almanac for 1767* (London, 1766) and subsequent years, and his "Requisite Tables."[38] No new principle was involved in these labours, however, thus the question of Maskelyne's own entitlement to a prize never arose.

By providing, through the medium of the *Nautical Almanac*, the first reliable basis for finding longitude at sea, Mayer's tables played a vital and fundamental role in oceanic navigation for several decades before the rival chronometer method, which John

---

36. C. Niebuhr, "Uber Längen-Beobachtungen im Orient..." in von Zach, *op. cit.* 6, IV, 1804, p. 247.

37. Nevil Maskelyne, ed., *Tabulae motuum solis et lunae novae et correctae; auctore Tobias Mayer: quibus accedit methodus longitudinum promota, eodem auctore. etc.*, London, 1770.

38. Nevil Maskelyne, *Tables requisite to be used with the Nautical Ephemeris for finding the Latitude and Longitude at Sea*, London, 1767.

Harrison had been pioneering, came into widespread use.[39] This is what Robert Grant was implying when he remarked that few other astronomers "have been privileged to contribute so directly to the well-being of their fellow-men."[40]

Eric Forbes

---

39. The relative merits of Harrison's and Mayer's claims for a longitude prize have been briefly discussed in *Sky & Telescope*, XLI, 1971, pp. 3-6. Copies of my more detailed monograph on eighteenth-century developments in longitude determination, *The Birth of Scientific Navigation*, London, 1973, may be obtained on application to the Director of the National Maritime Museum, London, England.

40. Grant, *op. cit.* 3, p. 208.

Newton's Principia as Whig Propaganda

The overall thesis under which this paper is written, maintains that scientific revolutions — whether they be Newton's, or Copernicus's or Darwin's, or Einstein's — are socially generated by a transformation in the intellectual sub-structure of the collective mind. This transformation of the collective unconscious provides the young scientist with a new frame of reference with which to examine nature. Because he is looking with a new perspective, he sees new things, and if he describes the new things he sees, then there is no reason to call his scientific treatise "propaganda," but if he makes some alterations in the descriptions of what he sees, or if he adds some terms which are not really necessary, except in that they propagate a particular faith, such as whiggism, or Protestantism, then the treatise takes on a propagandistic aspect. It is not my intention to assert here that Newton's *Principia* is wholly propaganda. I see, for instance, little that is propagandistic about Book I, but the Definitions, Axioms and Laws of Motion, and the manner of presenting the "System of the World,"[1] are definitely engineered to promote a cause external to the needs of science, and are therefore "propagandistic" in their intent.[2]

As for the term "whig," that is more difficult to define but in as much as Newton sat as a whig in the Convention Parliament, it is fair enough to use the term.[3] Still, it would be misleading to assert that Newton's primary interest in life was politics. Nothing could be further from the truth. His first interest was religion, being consumed by a passionate and, at times, almost irrational

---

1. For the history of Newton's "System of the World" see I. Bernard Cohen's introduction to *A Treatise of the System of the World*, by Isaac Newton, London, 1969.
2. For a bibliography of works on Newton see: I. Bernard Cohen, *An Introduction to Newton's Principia*, Cambridge, 1971, pp. 355-68.
3. I. Newton to Covel, 21 February, 1688/9 in *The Correspondence of Isaac Newton*, III, edited by H. W. Turnbull, Cambridge, 1761, p. 12.

hatred of the Roman Catholic Church.[4] Through most of his early life, his attacks on the Catholics, in general, and on the Jesuits, in particular, were directed on a theoretical plane, but when James II became King, and Newton was forced thereby to take political action, he quickly allied himself with the "whig" cause.[5] It was during this period that the *Principia* was thrown together, and thus, although the *Principia* has its foundations deep in Newton's Protestant theology, his immediate motive for turning the *Principia* into an instrument of propaganda was political.

If we go back to Newton's early manuscripts, we find four pillars on which his universal law of gravity was founded.[6] The first was Galileo's observation of a terrestrial gravitational constant,[7] the second was Kepler's observation of a celestial constant governing the motion of planets.[8] The third was Descartes's law of inertia, and the fourth was Newton's Protestant conviction that God had not given two sets of laws, the one for the heavens, the other for the Earth, but one set of laws.[9]

All these factors were essential to the development of Newton's Law of universal gravitation, but the fourth, the theological one, was the *sine qua non*.

The significance of the Catholic stress on the duality between the laws of the heavens and those of the earth can not be emphasized too strongly. Catholic theology was founded on this duality from the time of Saint Augustine, in the 5th century. When Rome fell to the barbarians, Saint Augustine had abandoned the idea of salvation in this earthly kingdom and held up instead the City of God in heaven.[10] At the time of Saint Augustine, the

---

4. See Frank E. Manuel, *A Portrait of Isaac Newton*, Cambridge, 1968.

5. See, for instance, David Brewster, *Memoirs of the Life, Writings, and Discoveries of Sir Isaac Newton*, 2 vols., Edinburgh, 1855, photo reprint, 1965, Vol. II, ch. XVI, pp. 84-122.

6. For an alternative view to that presented here see: John Herivel, *The Background to Newton's Principia*, Oxford, 1965.

7. U.L.C. Add 3958 fo. 45, published in *Correspondence*, III, p. 46.

8. MS. Add 3996, in Herivel, *op. cit.*, p. 121.

9. Alexander Koyre, *Newtonian Studies*, Cambridge, 1965, pp. 65-79.

10. For Saint Augustine, the concept of heaven is ambiguous: "I extend my finger and, whether it points to some constellation or some star, or to the sun or moon, I say to you: 'Behold the God whom I worship.' He is not merely in the place to which my finger is pointed, but he is wherever my mind is directed." Sermon 261 for the Feast of the Ascension, in *The Fathers of the Church* 38, New York, 1959, p. 382.

power of the papacy over secular rulers was established by default. Rome fell to the barbarians and the Pope was left to rule. Papal authority was reaffirmed by Thomas Aquinas in the 13th Century,[11] by the Council of Trent shortly after the publication of the Copernican Treatise,[12] and again by Cardinal Bellarmine in his work of 1610, entitled *On the Supreme Power of the Pope in Temporal Affaires*.[13]

Although the initial power of the Papacy in the West came by default when the Roman Emperor could no longer hold off the barbarian invaders, the continuance of Papal authority depended on the theological supposition that this world is corrupt and that the heavens are perfect. When Adam sinned, not only he, but the entire earthly paradise fell with him.[14] The heavens, however, remained perfect and God sent his son down to this corrupt earth to redeem man and give the true law. The word of God was then passed down from generation to generation by means of the Apostolic succession to each Pope, who in turn passed the word down to his flock.[15] Because of the corruption of this world, the layman could not find the laws of God by himself by going out into Nature, he could only find them through the Church. It was this assertion that so enraged Protestants in general and Newton in particular. Newton harked back to the Old Testament Prophets who spoke directly to God.[16] Protestants like Newton argued that

---

11. Although Aquinas is not directly concerned with the authority of the Pope, the major theme of the *Summa Theologica* is the establishment of the theological foundations of hierarchy. See for instance 12 Part, Q. 103, Act 3, "Whether the world is governed by one?"

12. *Canons and Decrees of the Council of Trent*, by H. J. Schroeder, London, 1941, Twenty-fifth session, "Decree concerning reform," ch. II, "also that they promise and profess true obedience to the supreme Roman Pontiff."

13. Bellarmine's argument depends on Aristotle's and Saint Thomas's defence of hierarchy over democracy in temporal and spiritual affairs, and on the superiority of the spirit over the body and of the laws of heaven over those of earth, Roberti Cardinalis Bellarmine, *Opera Omnia*, I, 1872, *De Summo Pontefice*, pp. 301-575 and IV, second part, *De Poteste Pape in Rebus Temporalibus*, pp. 251-344.

14. *Commons and Decrees of the Council of Trent, op. cit.* Fifth Session, "Decree concerning original sin," pp. 21-23. While it is clear in this decree that Adam's sin is passed down to all men, it is not clear that it was passed on to the earth as well, yet the acceptance of the Thomistic hierarchy, whereby animals are beneath men, and plants and fossils beneath animals etc., implies that the entire earthly paradise fell with Adam.

15. *Ibid.*, 23rd Session, ch. IV, "The Ecclesiastical Hierachy and Ordination," pp. 161-63.

16. F. Manuel, *op. cit.*, p. 117.

when Adam fell, mankind fell with him, but not the entire earth, and that God could be found in it as much as he could be found in heaven. One did not need to go through the intermediate of the Roman Catholic Church to find God.

The greatest threat to the power of the Papacy since the founding of the Church came not from Luther, who insisted on reading the Bible through his own eyes rather than through those of the Church's, but from Newton, who by demonstrating the truth of the Copernican hypothesis that the earth was flying around in the heavens, destroyed the heavenly earthly dichotomy and with it, the theological foundations of Papal supremacy.

In the short run, Copernicus, whom Newton was to vindicate in his *Principia*, had been easier to deal with than Luther. It had been a simple matter of putting *De Revolutionibus* on the Index and of asserting — with good evidence — that the Copernican hypothesis was mathematically viable, but physically untrue. In this they had the sanction of Saint Thomas Aquinas, who, in his *Commentaries on Aristotle's Physics*, had devoted a chapter to the differences between mathematical truth and physical reality.[17]

In spite of *De Revolutionibus* being on the Index, or perhaps because of it, enemies of Papal authority of the 17th Century such as Galileo, Kepler, Gilbert and Von Guericke, spent an extraordinary amount of time attempting to demonstrate the physical reality of the Copernican supposition, and when we examine the manuscripts of the young Newton, we find him already as a Cambridge undergraduate, working hard to do the same thing.[18]

The physical problems of the Copernican theory involved explaining what held bodies on the earth as it flew around in the heavens, and indeed, what held the earth in the grip of the sun. Von Guericke had experimented with the possibility of electrical forces,[19] Gilbert of magnetic forces, Kepler had suggested the Holy

---

17. St. Thomas Aquinas, *Commentary on Aristotle's Physics*, tr. by R. J. Blackwell, R. J. Spath and W. E. Thirlkel, New Haven, 1963, Book II, lecture III, "How physics and mathematics differ in their consideration of the same thing," p. 77.

18. Letters to Pietv-Desmaizeaux in 1718, Newton writes: "in the two plague years of 1665 and 1666 . . . I began to think of gravity extending to ye orb of the Moon . . . ," and his early manuscripts confirm this.

19. Alfons Kauffeldt discusses the theological significance of Von Guericke's work in: *Otto von Guericke Philosophisches über den leeren Raum*, Berlin, 1968, pp. 71-102.

Ghost,[20] Descartes had put forth the notion of vortices; Galileo had simply suggested that it was natural for bodies to fly around in circles.[21] They all had tried; they all had contributed something, but ultimately they all had failed to destroy the natural foundations of the Catholic universe. In Newton's youth, the foundations of Catholicism were as strong as ever and the Church itself was growing more powerful daily. With the restoration of Charles II to the throne of England as Newton went up to Cambridge, with James II, an avowed Catholic, due to inherit the throne, with Louis XIV on the French throne and ready to revoke the Edict of Nantes, with the Habsburgs growing stronger in Germany as they repulsed the Turkish invasion and held up Catholicism as the defender of Christian Europe, and with the spread of Catholicism to Asia and to the New World, the Roman Church had never been so powerful, but if we probe into Newton's early manuscripts, we see the beginnings of the destruction of Catholic theology and with it the effective destruction of the Catholic Church as Newton makes his first attempts to extend gravity to the moon. Under Thomistic theology, gravity was a quality possessed by bodies belonging to the earth, not to the heavens. Newton's attempt to extend gravity to the moon was not only rank heresy in Catholic eyes, but a termite which would bring the Catholic edifice down.

Newton's first attempts, like those of the other Copernicans, were a failure. In his zeal, he proved not too little, but too much. He proved that the earth's force of gravity was so powerful that it not only had 159.5 times the power to hold trees and rocks onto the earth even at the equator, but 4000 times enough power to hold the moon in orbit as well.[22] The only problem was that if the force of gravity was 4000 times more than was necessary, what was preventing the moon from falling in towards the Earth. Newton attempted to wrest victory from defeat in his 1669 manuscript by pointing out that the earth's hold on the moon was

20. Johannes Kepler, *Gesammelte Werke*, ed. W. V. Dyck and Max Caspar, 1938-1958, 19.2.1599, vol. XIII, p. 286 f., cited in A. Koestler, *The Watershed*, New York, 1960, p. 60.
21. For a more comprehensive treatment of this subject see, "The Case Against Circular Inertia," by Stillman Drake in *Galileo Studies*, Ann Arbor, 1970, pp. 257-78.
22. U.L.C. add. 3958.5 fo. 87, pub. in *Correspondence*, I, p. 297 ff.

much stronger than the sun's hold on it — a hollow victory, unfortunately, as it was based on calculations refuting his own fundamental tenet.

Newton's initial failure in his attempt to extend gravity up to the moon is not, however, the significant thing, for he eventually will succeed in that endeavour. What is significant is that it took him twelve years to succeed. No one is sure exactly how long he was working on the problem because of Newton's priority dispute with Robert Hooke,[23] but the existing manuscripts reveal that he worked on the problem for at least twelve years before solving it. That is a long time to persist in a problem, — unless, and this is the crucial point — he had a prior faith, stemming from his Protestant theology, that he had to be correct, despite the recalcitrant empirical results indicating the contrary.

In 1679, the Catholic menace in England became more acute when the Jesuit confessor to the future Queen was caught out in some "treasonness" correspondence and executed, with a number of Catholic Lords following him to the Tower. The more enterprising Protestants of the Royal Society, among them Christopher Wren, the architect, Robert Hooke, and Edmund Halley renewed their efforts to solve the Copernican problem. They had been inspired by the successes of Borelli over the satellites of Jupiter, and attempted to apply the inverse square law to Kepler's ellipses, but lacked the mathematical expertise.[24] As a result, Hooke wrote off to Newton for help, and Newton, it seems, had already solved the problem of the ellipse or suddenly saw the light and solved it now, but what is more important, he realized the source of his error over his early attempts to extend gravity up to the moon. He had failed, as he put it, to bring Kepler's inverse square law down to earth. This he now proceeded to do, and the problem was solved. It was a great triumph, but Newton was not quite content. He had not worked on the problem for twelve years

---

23. For an interesting discussion of this problem see: D. T. Whiteside, "Before the *Principia*: The Maturing of Newton's Thoughts on Dynamical Astronomy 1665-1684," *Journal for the History of Astronomy*, 1, Part 1, 1970, pp. 5-19.

24. Hooke to Newton, 24 November, 1679, published in *Correspondence*, II, pp. 297 ff., the key thought here is the hypothetical question of what would happen to a stone falling through the earth. It caused Newton to think of a varying force of gravity rather than a constant force as at the surface of the earth. See Whiteside, cited above.

to have the Jesuits snatch the victory from his hands. Once again, he had not proved too little. He had proved too much.

In extending gravity up to the moon, it makes a difference which velocity of the moon one choses. The moon has not one velocity but three empirically observable velocities depending on which background frame of reference one choses to measure the velocity against. If one is a Catholic and holds the earth to be at rest, then one can observe the moon to return over-head every twenty-three hours and fifty minutes, which gives it an extremely fast velocity, far too fast to hold it in orbit if gravity is the force governing it, and therefore Newton rejected this frame of reference.

If one is a Copernican, one can measure the moon's velocity relative to the sun. Again failure. The moon is now moving too slowly. Newton rejected this frame of reference also.[25]

If one is a Stoic and believes that there is an interrelationship between the moon and the fixed stars, then numerical calculations will work out correctly. Had Newton not had any prior theological leanings, he would, no doubt, have chosen the fixed stars as his frame of reference of the moon's velocity. This is what Ernst Mach did in the nineteenth century in paving the way for relativity theory,[26] but Newton's Protestant biases come to the fore once again, and he adopted the theological frame of reference of absolute space, one he had already played around with in 1672 after his initial attempts at extending gravity up to the heavens had failed.[27]

The significance of absolute, universal and uniform space for the Protestants can be understood best if one first studies Thomistic theology which is based on the concept of "Place" rather than of "Space."[28] In Thomistic theology, everything in the universe has its place and its motion depends on its relative

25. U.L.C. Add. 3958.5 fo. 87.
26. Ernst Mach, *History and Root of the Principle of the Conservation of Energy*. Ar. P. E. B. Jourdain, Chicago, 1911, p. 80, note 2.
27. E. A. Burtt, *The Metaphysical Foundations of Modern Science*, makes the connection of Newton's concept of space with the philosophy of the Cambridge platonist H. More, as does M. Fiers in his "Uber Den Ursprung und Bedeutung der lehre Isaac Newtons Von Absoluten Raum," *Gesnerus*, 11, 1954, pp. 62-120.
28. See for instance the great emphasis Aquinas places on "place" in his *Commentaries on the Physics of Aristotle*.

position to that place. For the Thomists the universe is not uniform, but qualitatively different as one goes up from the material earth where motion is governed by gravity in straight lines to the increasingly ethereal heavens, the realm of God where motion is of a different nature, being in perfect and unending circles. For the Thomists, God is not equally everywhere. In his treatise on the "Governance of Things" in the *Summa Theologica*, Saint Thomas Aquinas explains how God works through intermediaries: Archangels and Angels transmit his will throughout the universe without Him working directly.[29] The Protestant notion of absolute space, uniformly the sensorium of God throughout, eliminated all the intervening hierarchy of angels and with it the need for the Church hierarchy as well. It was a concept too precious to Newton's heart to forebear. Already in 1672, he had been attempting to work it into his physics, and once he solved the moon problem, the temptation to pass up the fixed stars as his frame of reference and substitute instead absolute space, was too great to resist, and hence the first error crept into the *Principia*.[30]

Although Newton, by extending gravity up to the moon, had won a battle against his Catholic adversaries, he had not yet won a complete victory. According to Thomistic theology, the lunar sphere was the border between the heavenly and the earthly realms. To prove that gravity extended to the moon, was only to reach the doors of heaven with a terrestial law, it was not yet to enter, and Newton was not so naive as to suppose that he could get away with demonstrating the existence of absolute space on such flimsy grounds: indeed, Bishop Berkeley was to catch him up on this question of absolute space after the publication of the *Principia*. The key now was to bring Kepler's harmonic law into agreement with Galileo's modified gravitational law, and this was no mean task. In fact it could not be done without introducing a new factor, gravitational mass.

When Newton had brought Kepler's inverse square law down to earth, he had produced a new gravitational constant that differed slightly from Galileo's in that it was ameliorated by the

---

29. Thomas Aquinas, "On the Governance of Things" in *Summa Theologica*.
30. Scholium following Def. VIII.

distance of a body from the center of the earth. The new equation looked something like this:[31] $g/r^2 = a$, where "g" is the new gravitational constant, "r" is the radius from the centre of the earth and "a" is the acceleration of the body as it falls towards the centre of the earth, from a distance "r." The problem came when Newton attempted to make Kepler's constant agree with this new gravitational constant. If gravity extended to the planets, then presumably the gravitational constants should be equal, but they were not. Kepler's harmonic law can be written as $K/r^2 = a$, which is the same form as Newton's gravitational law, only the "K" does not equal the "g" and hence whatever it is that makes for gravitational attraction, it is not the same when one passes from the lunar sphere up to the heavens. Once again, Newton and the Copernican cause were in trouble. Once again Newton did a mathematical slight of hand, and proved thereby what he had wanted to prove from the beginning. He introduced a new variable such that $K = GM$ and $g = GM$ where "G" was the new universal gravitational constant and "M" was the new fudge factor to make Kepler's harmonic law and Newton's gravitational law agree. He at last had his law of gravity extended up to the planets. Without further ado, he simply decreed it to extend to the fixed stars by what he called, the principle of "Induction."[32]

There were still some problems. What he had done was some brilliant mathematical manipulations. Bishop Berkeley was later to say "mathematical sophistry," and be not far from the truth.[33] The problem which remained, ironically, was the same problem that had been plaguing the Copernicans all along. It was a mathematically viable representation of phenomena, but was it

---

31. For a discussion of the relationship of Newton's notation to modern notation see: C. Truedell, "A Program Towards Rediscovering the Rational Mechanics of the Age of Reason," *Archive for History of Exact Science*, 1960, Vol. 1, pp. 3-36.

32. "Lastly, if it universally appears, by experiments and astronomical observations that all bodies about the earth gravitate towards the earth, and that in proportion to the quantity of matter which they severally contain; that the moon likewise, according to the quantity of matter, gravitates towards the earth; that, on the other hand, our sea gravitates towards the moon; and all the planets one towards another; and the comets in like manner towards the sun; we must in consequence of this rule, universally allow that all bodies whatsoever are endowed with a principle of mutual gravitation," in *Principia*, Book III, tr. by F. Cajori, Berkeley, 1966, p. 399.

33. See John W. Davis, "Berkeley, Newton and Space," in *The Methodological Heritage of Newton*, ed. by R. E. Butts and John W. Davis, Toronto, 1970, pp. 57-73.

physically real? If it was physically true, what then exactly was the physical object which the new variable "M" represents?[34]

In 1684, Charles II died, the Catholic James II came to the throne and began his attempt to turn Oxford and Cambridge into Catholic seminaries. The pressure was now on. Newton, falling back on his earlier work on Descartes, attempted without success to use the Cartesian vortices to give his mathematics physical reality, but the vortices could not be made to comply with his mathematics. Earlier, in his first treatises on light, he had attempted to associate this mysterious force with a "spirit" or with a mysterious "virtue," emanating from bodies,[35] but this just played into the hands of the Jesuits, for it was manifestly evident that the efficacy of the Holy Ghost emanating from the sun in the heavens was far more powerful than the virtue emanating from the earth.

According to Thomistic theology, motion was the realization of form in matter.[36]

For Newton to associate his fudge factor with pure form, like that of a spirit, was self-defeating. Shortly before throwing the *Principia* together, he decided to equate his fudge factor with matter rather than with form, and to call it "mass," the quantity of matter.

Ernst Mach was later to point out that where Newton had defined "mass" as the quantity of "matter," he had not defined "matter."[37] Newton did not have to. Thomistic theologians knew perfectly well what he was getting at. The spiritual world, with its substantial forms, occult qualities and virtues, had just been brought into the Protestant corpuscular world of Robert Boyle.[38] To be sure, there was still the problem of defining just exactly what matter was, and the major endeavour of science from that

---

34. See Leon Rosenfeld, "Newton and the Law of Gravitation," *Archive for History of Exact Sciences*, 1965, vol. 2, pp. 365-86.

35. Newton discusses this in a letter to Halley 20 June, 1686, *Correspondence*, II, p. 439.

36. Vernon J. Bourke, "Introduction" to *Commentary on Aristotle's Physics*, New Haven, 1963, p. xxviii, a bibliography on Aquinas is appended to this Introduction.

37. E. Mach, *The Science of Mechanics*, tr. T. J. McCormack, Chicago, 1902, p. 241.

38. Marie Boas, "The Establishment of the Mechanical Philosophy," *Osiris* 1952, vol. 10, pp. 412-541.

day to this — whether in chemistry, electricity, optics or biology has been to answer this question. For the time being, however, Newton had provided a viable alternative to Thomistic theology. The only problem left, however, was to disguise his tracks. As things stood, it was so blatantly Protestant propaganda, that it would not have fooled any theologian, least of all a Jesuit. As the stranglehold of James II's reign grew tighter, Newton under pressure from Halley and members of the Royal Society threw the *Principia* together for publication. Instead of beginning at the beginning with his attempt to extend gravity up to the moon, he began by attempting to define "mass."[39] Next he proceeded to attempt to define "force."[40] He distinguished between Galileo's force of gravity at the surface of the earth and his force of gravity ameliorated by the inverse square law. Next he attempted to define absolute space. This makes it appear — indeed, he infers as much — that he began with the concept of mass and force and space and derived his system of the world from them, instead of doing just the opposite — starting from his Protestant theology and plugging in the fudge factors to his equations where necessary, to make it appear viable, but this real stroke of genius came when he broke up his equation of the universal gravitation constant ($GM/r^2 = a$) into two equations by throwing in inertial "mass" on both sides and letting each side be equal to "Force."[41] Half the equation he then introduced in the beginning of the *Principia* as the law of "motion," another dig at the Thomists. The other half he spliced in as Proposition VI — VIII at the very end of the *Principia*. It was a masterpiece of disguise. Little wonder that a Cambridge undergraduate whispered to his friend as Newton passed: "There goes the man that writ a book that neither he nor anybody else understand."[42] Indeed, the book is not altogether understandable unless, of course, one starts with a hatred of

39. Isaac Newton, *The Mathematical Principle of Natural Philosophy*, tr. by Andrew Motte, 1729, definition I, p. 1.
40. *Ibid.*, Def. V, VI, VII, VIII, pp. 4-8.
41. In most standard interpretations of the origin of Newton's system of the World "force is seen as the key concept." See, for instance, Herivel, *op. cit.* and R. S. Westfall, *Force in Newton's Physics*, London, 1971.
42. From D. T. Whiteside, "The Mathematical Principle Underlying Newton's *Principia Mathematica*," *Journal for the History of Astronomy* 1, Part 2, No. 2, Aug. 1970, p. 116 and note 3.

Thomistic theology and the Jesuits, as Voltaire most certainly did, and then the book ceases to be as Bishop Berkeley put it, "mathematical sophistry," and becomes the epitome of reasonableness itself.[43]

My thesis in this paper is that science, theology and social thought are inseparable. Newton made no distinction between his exegesis of the book of Daniel and the *Principia*, why should we? His motive was one, to point out the errors of that "whore of Babylon," as he put it.[44]

In my eyes, this is not an insult to Newton but a compliment. Newton was no man in a white coat manipulating trivia in a laboratory. He was in the social scene and theological scene as deeply as the scientific one. His *Principia* represents not only a synthesis of Kepler's law of the heavens and Galileo's law of the earth, but a synthesis of Protestant theology as well. In appreciation of which Newton was elected to represent Cambridge University in the convention Parliament on January 17, 1689, Cambridge University "giving and granting in this extraordinary juncture to the aforesaid Representative full and sufficient power . . . to do and consent to those things, which then and there shall be determined, by the Lords Spirituall and Temporall and the Commons assembled, for the preservation of the Protestant Religion . . .[45] As if he had already not done enough.

George Grinnell

---

43. Voltaire, *The Elements of Sir Isaac Newton's Philosophy*, tr. John Hanna, London, 1738, reprint 1967.
44. Keynes M.S. 130.5.
45. "Certificate of Election," *Correspondence*, III, p. 8.

The Encapsulated Landscape: An Aspect of Gilpin's Picturesque

It is indeed questionable if the Reverend William Gilpin, M.A., Prebendary of Salisbury, Vicar of Boldre in New Forest near Lymington, connoisseur and amateur artist can lay claim to greatness. Yet few would deny him a modest niche in history. It was he who formulated the concept of the picturesque, a "taste without tears" philosophy which developed into a cult during the late eighteenth and early nineteenth centuries. The concept was really a habit of mind, a mode of vision which deeply influenced the Englishman's aesthetic attitude to nature. It was a theory evolved through a systematic study of both nature and art, reflecting Gilpin's desire to bolster and to expand existing aesthetic categories just as Burke had attempted to do before him in his *Enquiry into the Sublime and the Beautiful*.

Gilpin believed that the picturesque could be defined simply as that kind of beauty in nature which is "capable of being *illustrated in painting*."[2] But this definition is misleading. Gilpin's idea of the picturesque is much more exclusive, and he laid down both explicitly and by inference, qualities which he believed the picturesque should possess. Nature in Gilpin's terms should be perceived mainly in a non-specific or as perfect a way as possible. To perceive in this remarkable way, a person had to be educated in picturesque rules, in order to mentally modify the scene before him. Nature, according to Gilpin, is normally imperfect as a whole but she does possess perfect parts. The educated eye can spot these parts and they are stored in the mind until recalled to assist in locating and correcting scenes subsequently encountered. Essentially, what Gilpin suggests is a kind of "gestalt" of the perfect landscape which the viewer could employ to guide him

---

1. Edmund Burke, *A Philosophical Enquiry into the Origin of our Ideas of the Sublime and Beautiful*, London, 1757.
2. William Gilpin, *Three Essays; On Picturesque Beauty; On Picturesque Travel; and on Sketching Landscape...*, London, 1792, p. 3.

both in the selection and the correction of these views. If the viewer was fortunate enough to possess artistic talents then this "correction" could be pictorially recorded.

For Gilpin, then, scenery viewed aesthetically should normally not be considered in its particularity and imperfection. Deficiencies such as these would be obscured or eliminated in the eyes of the educated viewer by the superimposition of experiences of perfect landscape parts transforming the particular view into one more generalized and one whose appearance approached perfection.

Another essential quality of Gilpin's picturesque was roughness or irregularity of form. This quality, Gilpin believed, distinguished picturesque beauty from other varieties of beauty and could identify an object as being potentially suitable for representation in painting. For this reason roughness or irregularity of form was important as a vehicle for additional qualities, namely, formal variety and light and shade. Indeed so fundamental was roughness, that Gilpin was prepared to suggest the employment of a hammer on objects, in order to assist them in realizing appropriately picturesque states.[3]

Roughness or irregularity usually determined whether or not a subject was potentially picturesque, although as Gilpin explained this quality by itself was no guarantee of picturesqueness. A suitably picturesque view would be embellished by subjects with irregular shapes, such as large rocks, mountains, castle ruins or even cottages, and further could be enhanced by the addition of trees, shrubbery or ivy.

Yet the theory of the picturesque as conceived by Gilpin is neither particularly original nor especially profound. It is not particularly original because it depended heavily on theoretical and practical ideas from the Renaissance and Baroque periods, and in this respect represents the continuation of a tradition rather than the development of a new one. The underlying concept of the picturesque is not especially profound since it lacks consistency and clarity and is often starved of the necessary intellectual elaboration and implication.

---

3. *Ibid.*, p. 7.

It may have been due to the relatively superficial and therefore easily digested character of the picturesque that it gained such widespread attention during the late eighteenth and early nineteenth centuries. Ironically, it was likely for the same reasons that it attracted such vociferous criticisms.

Of the published attacks, one of the most amusing is the poem written by William Combe, entitled *The Tour of Dr. Syntax in Search of the Picturesque,* the first part of which appeared in 1812. Whilst this satirical poem is without real intrinsic distinction it does have historical value. If the poem makes good fun of the picturesque craze, it provides also background information and useful insights into contemporary views concerning the application of picturesque principles.

When in the rollicking verse, Dr. Syntax (who is meant to represent Gilpin) sings forth: "I'll *prose* it here, I'll *verse* it there/ And picturesque it ev'ry where,"[4] Combe is alluding to the many works by Gilpin, both prose (mainly tour guides) and poetry (theoretical disquisitions), which were published between 1782 and 1809. It was these writings embellished by attractive aquatint engraved views which initiated public enthusiasm for the picturesque.

Because of the historical significance of Combe's poem, I have selected a short excerpt which tells us something about contemporary views of picturesque "methodology." The particular episode I have chosen concerns the good Dr. Syntax's journey to York. On the way he stops at an inn and hears from the innkeeper about a ruined castle in the neighbourhood. The Doctor is determined to locate and to examine the remains for their potential picturesqueness. He sets out to find the structure and predictably he does:

> Upon a rock the castle stood
> Three sides environ'd by a flood,
> Where confluent streams uniting lave,
> The craggy rift with foaming wave.
> Around the moss-clad walls he walk'd

---

4. William Combe, *The Tour of Doctor Syntax in Search of the Picturesque*, 3rd ed., London, 1813, p. 5.

> Then thro the inner chamber stalk'd.[5]

After thoroughly examining the ruin, Syntax concludes that the chapel is small because the former occupants spent much of their time gorging in the "festive hall." The Barons, he noted:

> To pray'r preferr'd a sumptuous treat,
> Nor went to pray when they could eat.[6]

Only after reflections of this sort does Syntax get down to the specific purpose of his journey, especially since

> no more remains
> Than will reward the painter's pains:
> The palace of the feudal victor
> Now serves for nought but for a picture.
> Plenty of water here I see,
> But what's a view without a tree?
> There's something grand in yonder tow'r,
> But not a shrub to make a bow'r,
> Howe'er, I'll try to take the view,
> As well as my best art can do.
> An heap of stones the Doctor found,
> Which loosely lay upon the ground,
> To form a seat, where he might trace
> The antique beauty of the place:
> But, while his eye observ'd the line
> That was to limit the design,
> The stones gave way, and sad to tell,
> Down from the bank he headlong fell.[7]

The fall resulted in a thorough soaking and "overwhelm'd with mud, and stink and grief" he returned to the inn without having taken his picturesque view. Despite the ultimate failure of Syntax's mission we can derive useful insights from the episode. We can gather that one of the objections to the picturesque was its specifically conceptual character. For example, poet Combe has Syntax exclaim:

5. *Ibid.*, p. 70.
6. *Ibid*, p. 71.
7. *Ibid.*

> Plenty of water here I see,
> But what's a view without a tree?
> There's something grand in yonder tow'r,
> But not a shrub to make a bow'r.

Here Combe takes issue with the picturesque because it demands that nature be adjusted to suit the ideal form that the viewer has in mind. Syntax had noted the lack of a tree, and the fact that the tower was not suitably framed by shrubbery. But Syntax saw no real difficulty, since tutored in the laws of the picturesque he could eliminate these deficiencies in the sketch he was proposing to take.

The artificiality of the system is remarked on elsewhere. After having completed his scrutiny of the view, Syntax perceptually isolated the part of the landscape with picturesque potential and which he was proposing to sketch. Combe noted that Syntax's eye "observ'd the line/ That was to limit the design." Such perceptual isolation of landscape is one of the fundamental steps in the aesthetic procedure of Gilpin's picturesque, as it assisted in the determination of the view's self-sufficient and contained quality. Indeed, it is the contained quality of the picturesque view which has led me to title this paper, "The Encapsulated Landscape." But in order to understand the full significance of landscape encapsulation, the picturesque must be examined historically.

To find the seeds of the movement one must look to the beginning of the eighteenth century. It was at that time that the Englishman began to examine seriously the aesthetic potential of nature. And it is clear that an appreciation of scenery was predicated on a knowledge of art theory and art but particularly landscape painting. The favoured paintings were of the seventeenth-century classical school, and by Nicolas Poussin, Claude Lorrain, Gaspard Dughet and Salvator Rosa. The classic landscape seems to have provided Englishmen with adequate aesthetic machinery by which to appreciate nature. Jonathan Richardson, painter and theorist, observed that the man of taste with intimate knowledge of painting will gain not only greater insight into art but will learn to see in nature

> the exquisite forms, and colours, the fine effects of lights,

shadows, and reflections, which in her are always to be found and from whence he has a pleasure, which otherwise he could never have had and which none with untaught eyes can possibly discern.[8]

Horace Walpole looked at nature with such eyes when he clambered over the Alps in 1739. A letter written by him to a friend contains a description of this trip in which the topography of the Alps seems to suggest the tempestuous landscapes of either Gaspard or Rosa. He described

> the road. . . . winding round a prodigious mountain and surrounded with others all shagged with hanging wood, obscured with pines or lost in clouds! Below; a torrent breaking through cliffs and tumbling through fragments of rocks! Sheets of cascades forcing their silver speed down channelled precipices and hasting into the roughened river bottom. . . .[9]

Walpole decidedly savours this visual experience which he seems to have conceived as being essentially artful. Indeed on this same journey he made a direct reference to classic landscape painting when he wrote that a view of the Grand Chartreuse reminded him of the landscapes of Salvator Rosa.[10]

Rules derived from painting which directed the traveller or even the artist in the appreciation of nature in Europe, guided him also in his tastes at home. They assisted him in the formulation of a system in the art of gardening where, as Pevsner has observed, the traveller began to "convert his grounds into a sequence of Rosa and Lorrain landscapes."[11] The artist also was affected by classic landscape painting. For example Richard Wilson's views of Italy are palpably influenced by Claude and Gaspard and so are his landscapes of British subjects. Whilst Gilpin stated that nature

---

8. Jonathan Richardson, *The Works of Jonathan Richardson*, London, 1792, "The Science of a Connoisseur," p. 247.

9. Letter to B. West, Sept.-Oct., 1739, as quoted in Robert Wyndham Ketton-Cremer, *Horace Walpole, A Biography*, London, 1946, p. 54.

10. *Ibid.*, p. 53.

11. Nikolaus Pevsner, "Genesis of the Picturesque," *Architectural Review* 95, 1944, p. 146.

Plate 1. *Windermere*, aquatint after a drawing by William Gilpin. Opposite p. 135 in Gilpin's *Observations, relative chiefly to Picturesque Beauty, made in the Year 1772, on several Parts of England; particularly the Mountains and Lakes of Cumberland and Westmoreland*, (London, 1786), I.

should determine her own design, there is no doubt that his vision of nature was conditioned by classical art theory and by the ideal quality of classic landscape. Indeed classic landscape supplied the underlying principles of Gilpin's theory of the picturesque.

The great extent to which Gilpin's picturesque participated in the classic mode of landscape painting, and the success of its participation can be measured by comparing an aquatint landscape[12] (Plate 1) in one of Gilpin's guides with a landscape painting by Claude, *Hagar and the Angel*[13] (Plate 2). Gilpin employs similar balancing coulisses of trees, the various grounds (foreground, middle- and background), the back lighting and the central pool of light, all characteristic of Claude's brand of classicism. Although the limitations of the aquatint medium do

---

12. "Windermere," opp. p. 135 in William Gilpin, *Observations, relative chiefly to Picturesque Beauty, made in the Year 1772, on several Parts of England; particularly the Mountains and Lakes of Cumberland and Westmoreland*, London, 1786, I.

13. It must be admitted that of the painters of classic landscape, Claude was not Gilpin's favourite.

not give us much insight into the actual painting style which Gilpin employs, I can assure you that in his paintings, landscape ingredients are handled with less skill and certainly with less subtlety and sensitivity.

To approach Gilpin more positively, one might say that his landscape is more schematic than Claude's. The degree of

Plate 2. Claude Lorrain, *Hagar and the Angel*. Oil on canvas mounted on wood, 20 3/4 x 17 1/4 in. National Gallery, London.

Plate 3. Richard Wilson, *Snowdon*, c. 1766. Oil on canvas, 39 1/2 x 49 in. Walker Art Gallery, Liverpool.

simplification or abstraction, the hardness of form, seem in certain ways nearer to the landscapes of other painters of classic landscape such as Nicholas Poussin or Gaspard Dughet, or even closer to the classicism of Richard Wilson. Indeed it seems likely that it is Wilson's British form of classic landscape (Plate 3) which influenced Gilpin most profoundly. One quality of the classic landscape which Gilpin's schematisation brings into sharp relief (and especially in the aquatint) is the *isolation* of landscape which, I have suggested, is the basic ingredient of picturesque landscape encapsulation. However encapsulation requires an isolation of a particular kind. It is not simply as Syntax saw it, "the line/ That was to limit the design." Landscape encapsulation implies much more. It demands a reorganization of ingredients, a simplification, an order, a synthesis which invest the separated portion of nature with a tangible *completeness* and *self-sufficiency*, a quality which according to Gilpin is seldom if ever encountered in nature. The traveller who wishes to seek out picturesqueness in nature, therefore must have in the back of his mind the pictorial idea of completeness and perfection to guide him in the selection and subsequent perceptual and artistic adaptation of landscape views.

The processes involved are outlined by Gilpin and are similar to those which Syntax followed when examining his ruined castle. Gilpin makes it abundantly clear that it is from these processes that the aesthetic pleasure of the picturesque derives:

> We examine what would amend the composition; how little is wanting to reduce it to the rules of our art; what a trifling circumstance sometimes forms the limit between beauty, and deformity. Or we compare the objects before us with other objects of the same kind: or perhaps we compare them with the imitations of art. From all these operations of the mind results great amusement.[14]

The aesthetic pleasure of the picturesque is therefore the result of the attempt to fit the scene before the viewer into a pictorial schema (the encapsulated landscape) which is in the viewer's mind.

Up to now "encapsulation" has been discussed strictly in formal terms. Yet the idea embraces simultaneously the concept of time or motion. Although in his tour guides, Gilpin's references to motion are confined mainly to art, they are not entirely, and it is evident that Gilpin implicitly believes that identical criteria operate for both nature and art.

Motion in art has always been a perplexing problem for the artist but especially for the painter. In England one of the first to discuss movement in relation to painting was the Earl of Shaftesbury who, in the early eighteenth century observed that in a history painting what must be represented is the moment which is the most revealing of the episode selected for representation. Shaftesbury states:

> 'Tis evident, that every Master in Painting, when he has made choice of the determinate Date or Point of Time, according to which he wou'd represent his History, is afterwards

---

14. William Gilpin, *Three Essays*, p. 49.

Plate 4. Salvator Rosa, *The Finding of Moses*. Oil on canvas, 48 1/2 x 79 3/4 in. Detroit Institute of Arts. (Gift of Mr. and Mrs. Edgar B. Whitcomb.)

debar'd the taking advantage from any other Action than what is immediately present, and belonging to that single Instant he describes.[15]

Essentially Shaftesbury is saying that the action must be suspended, and isolated from temporal continuity. Now this condition is as applicable to landscape as it is to history, and indeed operates in classic landscape painting. Classic landscape painting normally combines history and landscape and not unexpectedly these exist as mutually reinforcing elements. The sustained moment of history is augmented by a particular and suspended condition of landscape. This landscape "mode" is provided mainly by temporal states; by weather conditions or particular times of day or seasons, appropriate to the action. For example, in the classic landscape *The Finding of Moses* by Salvator Rosa (Plate 4), and I should mention that Gilpin admired Rosa, the relationship between both history and landscape painting can be explicitly illustrated.

---

15. Anthony, Earl of Shaftesbury, *Characteristicks of Men, Manners, Opinions, Times*, 3 vols, London, 1714, III, p. 353.

In this painting the moment selected and sustained is the one in the story in which Pharoah's daughter and her handmaidens discover the infant Moses. It is this moment which simultaneously is the most revealing of the episode and the one which provides the most dramatic impact. And the landscape fully participates in the drama of the event. Wrapped in a turbulent but suspended instant of storm, the landscape is invested with a particular complexion or attitude entirely in harmony with the moment which the story portrays. The instant of storm generates not only the appropriate lighting to dramatize the discovery of the infant Moses, but it also determines the particular wind-blown character of the trees, a character which deliberately echoes the frantic but frozen gesticulations of the women.

Here figures and landscape are interlocked in a close and necessary temporal relationship. One can hardly imagine the shifting or changing of a single object, figure or gesture without undermining the compositional and emotional integrity of the painting. If one speaks of landscape encapsulation, as I have done, then it must be understood to embrace temporal as well as formal elements; time and landscape are isolated from their respective continuities but are inextricably linked together; for it is only through the forms of landscape that the suspended moment of time can be firmly and fundamentally expressed.

Gilpin, whose theory of the picturesque is based on the same principles as those controlling the classic landscape, not surprisingly concurs with this idea of the sustained moment and of temporal and spatial interaction. And although his landscape views are normally bereft of histories (since he found them distracting), he believed that as in the classic landscape, the picturesque view should support defined categories of temporal effect. He observes:

> Scarce any landscape will stand the test of *different lights*. Some searching ray, as the sun veers round, will expose its defects. And hence it is, that almost *every* landscape is seen best under some *particular* illumination — either of an evening, or of a morning sun; or, it may be, of noon-day.[16]

16. William Gilpin, *Observations on the River Wye . . . made in the Summer of the Year 1770*, London, 1782, p. 45.

Therefore particular times of day but also conditions of weather appropriate to and harmonious with the attitude of landscape, are desirable according to Gilpin. For only the sustained moment or condition can be truly picturesque in art. Elsewhere he notes:

> ...in painting I know not, that I should represent any kind of motion in a tree, except that of a violent storm. When the blast continues for some time; when the black heavens are in unison with it, ... an oak straining in the wind, is an object of picturesque beauty....[17]

For Gilpin then, the picturesque is conditional not only on formal containment but on temporal isolation as well. And these elements in a drawing or painting must interact in an intimate and harmonious way.

As I have suggested, the theory of the picturesque and what I have called the "encapsulated" landscape were formulated from ideas and principles derived basically from established classical theory and in particular from the example of the classic landscape. The principles embodied in the concept of the picturesque therefore present a rational and abstracted approach to nature, which identifies Gilpin as being fundamentally an Augustan at heart.

The considerable influence of Gilpin's picturesque is undeniable, yet the extent to which actual theory influenced landscape painting was probably minimal. This of course is not to deny the presence of the picturesque in landscape painting; it definitely exists. But Gilpin's influence in the shaping of the pictorial "gestalt" seems to have been achieved mainly through the aquatint landscapes which abundantly illustrate his travel guides. These plates are illustrations of picturesque theory and since the artist, be he amateur or professional, was more likely to have been attracted to the plates than to theory, it is not unreasonable to suggest their probable importance. One of the most cogent reasons for considering the aquatints important in the dissemination of the pictorial idea of the picturesque is the apparent relationship between the "style" of the aquatint and the style of many picturesque landscapes of the late eighteenth and early nineteenth centuries. The landscapes of the aquatints are simplified and

---

17. William Gilpin, *Remarks in Forest Scenery...*, 2 vols, London, 1791, I, p. 54.

abstract, indeed their forms are almost silhouettes. Such qualities one can often find in landscape drawings and paintings of the period to which often one finds the term "picturesque" applied.[18] For example, compare the aquatint view from one of Gilpin's guides (Plate 1) with a watercolour sketch by George Heriot, amateur landscapist and Postmaster General of British North America (Plate 5). One is immediately struck by the similarities in the tonal stratifications of foreground, middleground and background and the forms in silhouette.

Criticisms of the picturesque, such as Combe's *Tour of Doctor Syntax* were directed as much against the artificiality of the artistic expression as the superficiality of the theory itself. And this criticism was largely due to a change in popular attitudes concerning nature. The conceptual view which the picturesque expressed was giving way to a view of a nature freed from the control of man. Nature gradually released from intellectual bondage assumed a personality of its own. The reaction against conceptuality was expressed widely. Take for example the following excerpt from a guide book written in 1800:

> The old mode of composing pictures by certain formulae, like apothecaries' prescriptions, or receipts in cookery, seems (at least in landscape) to have given way to the study of nature..[19]

No wonder that in 1802 Constable could assert "there is room enough for a natural painter."[20]

I have been concerned to explain the nature of the picturesque and especially that aspect to which I have referred as the "encapsulated landscape." By comparing Gilpin's landscape aquatint (Plate 1) with Constable's *Haywain* of 1821 (Plate 6) a much fuller understanding of encapsulation can be gained.

---

18. Generally, I believe the importance of engraving in shaping British artistic vision during the late eighteenth and early nineteenth centuries has not been sufficiently appreciated. Whilst one would hesitate to attribute the increasingly abstract quality of drawing of this period *solely* to the influence of engraving, yet its impact must have been considerable.

19. J. Stoddart, *Remarks on Local Scenery and Manners in Scotland during the years 1799 and 1800*, 2 vols., London, 1801, I, p. 5.

20. C. R. Leslie, *Memoirs of the Life of John Constable.....* ed. Jonathan Mayne, London, 1951, p. 15.

THE ENCAPSULATED LANDSCAPE • 207

Plate 5. George Heriot, *Lake George*, 1815. Watercolour, 4 x 8 in. New York Historical Society, New York.

Plate 6. John Constable, *The Haywain*, s.&d. 1821. Oil on canvas, 51 1/4 x 73. National Gallery, London.

I have spoken already of the qualities of Gilpin's picturesque; his view of nature was a general, non-specific one; it was a nature simplified, homogeneous, ordered and complete. Constable's *Haywain* possesses quite different characteristics. This painter's nature is specific; he represents a particular location in all its complexity and diversity. It is an ordered nature like Gilpin's but it is an order which nature herself seems to impose. However Constable's landscape, unlike that of Gilpin's, is incomplete. It is incomplete in the sense that what is represented is but a portion of the vast incomprehensible whole of nature, but at the same time a part which nurtures and protects its fundamental spirit. Constable's landscape is a consequence not formally contained, not encapsulated. The landscape seems to extend beyond the format; trees are severed and clouds churn off the canvas unimpeded by the frame in order to imply continuity.

The temporal element in Gilpin's theory, it will be remembered, is suspended and contained; it is interlocked with landscape forms to produce the particular mode or attitude of landscape characteristic of the picturesque. Not so in Constable's landscape. Here, time is continuous and independent. That is to say the painter conceives of nature as being in a constant state of becoming: the immediate past, the present and the impending future, all seem to coalesce in his painting. The water of the stream appears to be moving, its surface disturbed by constant assaults from the breeze. The leaves of the trees are often slightly blurred against the sky, suggesting their agitation by the wind. For Constable, nature has no containment, no frozen attitude; the character of the landscape is complex and changing and can only be savoured through time.

To arrive at Constable's art is to realize how far we have travelled from Gilpin's picturesque. And whilst this comparison may in many respects exaggerate the degree of change in habits of vision which occurred during the late eighteenth and early nineteenth centuries, still it identifies the basic classicism of Gilpin's viewpoint and the fundamental romanticism of Constable's. The old intimate relationship between form and content of the picturesque seems infinitely less important to Constable's art where such distinctions were increasingly being smudged. Natural effect challenged rule and eventually triumphed.

Yet despite the dramatic shifts in the vision of nature which this comparison has illustrated, the picturesque point of view did persist, although in an increasingly modified form.

Even the most illustrious of nineteenth-century British landscape painters like Constable and Turner did not entirely escape the influence of the picturesque. In the early works of both artists, some picturesque ingredients can be identified. At the age of twenty-five Constable's interest in natural effect was developing, as one can see in his early watercolour *Edensor* of 1801.[21] However, in spite of this the work does display the balanced composition, the abstract and also the formal irregularity characteristic of the picturesque landscape. Regarding the latter, notice the appearance of the foliage of the tree on the left, the broken strokes on the roadway and the unevenness of lines of the cottages to the right. There is in the organization of this composition some suggestion of the encapsulated landscape, yet ingredients are not as carefully ordered or as contained as Gilpin would have prescribed. On the other hand, the work of the youthful Turner indicates how deeply he was influenced by the movement. Trained as a topographical draughtsman and illustrator, Turner's early watercolours such as the view of *Captain Fowler's Seat* (1791)[22] and the *View on the Avon* (1791),[23] executed at the age of sixteen!, are clearly vehicles of a picturesque viewpoint. The foreground in each of these landscapes effectively seems to encapsulate the view in a decorative and abstract way. Indeed, although the foreground may contain the view, it does so superficially; for the landscape of the middle and backgrounds appears to extend in continuity from right to left *behind* the foreground coulisses. This configuration also exists in the *View of Salisbury Cathedral* executed two years later,[24] and

21. *Edensor, Derbyshire*, dated 1801. India ink and wash 6 7/8 x 10 3/8 in. Victoria and Albert Museum (247C - 1888).

22. *Captain Fowler's Seat, Durdham Downs*, 1791. Watercolour and ink, 7 3/8 x 10 7/16 in. British Museum, T. B. VI, 17a.

23. *View on the Avon*, 1791. Watercolour and ink, 7 3/8 x 10 7/16 in., British Museum T.B.. VI, 24.

24. *Salisbury Cathedral from the Cloister*, signed; [1793]. Watercolour, 26 3/4 in. x 19 1/2 in., Victoria and Albert Museum (502-1883).

210 • FINLEY

Plate 7. John Constable, *Salisbury from the Bishop's Grounds*, c. 1823. Oil on canvas, 29 3/4 x 37 1/8 in. Presented in 1944 by Mr. Charles F. Martin — The Montreal Museum of Fine Arts. This is one of the versions of the painting in the Victoria and Albert Museum, London.

the only difference is that the framing device is now architectural rather than organic. The superficiality of the framing element in Turner's landscapes becomes much more conspicuous when one compares them with *Windermere* (Plate 1). In Gilpin's view there is a much more effective integration of all grounds guaranteeing an encapsulation both more convincing and complete.

Surprisingly, picturesque elements which one can isolate in the early works of Constable and Turner survive in modified form in the paintings of their maturity. Constable, despite his rejection of picturesque rhetoric, could make use of it. When called on to paint a *View of Salisbury Cathedral*[25] (Plate 7) for its elderly Bishop, the artist apparently accommodated his patron's taste by adopting a

25. *Salisbury from the Bishop's Grounds*, signed and dated 1823. Oil on canvas, 34 x 43 1/2 in., Victoria and Albert Museum (Sheepshanks Gift: No. F.A. 33).

picturesque viewpoint. The attractive bower of elms provides the requisite leafy framework for the lofty Cathedral tower, an effect of which Gilpin would undoubtedly have approved.[26] However here, as in Turner's view of the same subject, the landscape is not really contained by the foreground framing device: it extends once more unimpeded, behind the framing coulisse of trees.

I have mentioned that in the paintings of Turner's maturity, the encapsulation of the picturesque persists also, but it is much metamorphosed. Instead of his landscapes being encapsulated or enclosed by foreground elements, as for example in *Captain Fowler's Seat*, in the 1830s and 40s, they are increasingly contained or spatially insulated by light, as in the *Norham Castle* of 1840-45 (Plate 9) or are imprisoned in a vortex of elemental fury as in *Steamer in a Snowstorm* of 1842 (Plate 8) and *Light and Colour* of 1843.[27]

It must be admitted that to illustrate the persistence and transformation of encapsulated landscape in the paintings of two of the most eminent of British landscape painters is to somewhat distort the general picture of picturesque influence. Less innovative contemporaries embraced the pictorial schema with much more fervour and with greater consistency. Yet even their encapsulated views were metamorphosed, not only by a rising tide of naturalism but by the overwhelming ingredient of Victorian sentiment which often smothered that delicate spirit of landscape which the best of the Romantics, like Constable and Turner, had managed to isolate and intensify.

And now to sum up. I have suggested that at the centre of Gilpin's theory, and underlying his views of landscape, was a particular pictorial configuration which I have referred to as the encapsulated landscape. The character of this configuration,

---

26. In 1823 Constable wrote his friend Fisher about the remarks which Fuseli made about Constable when the latter's *Salisbury* was hanging at the Academy: "I like the Landscapes of Constable; he is always picturesque, of a fine colour, and the lights always in the right places; but he makes me call for my greatcoat and umbrella." (C. R. Leslie, *Memoirs of the Life of John Constable*..., London, 1951, p. 101.) Constable himself saw "picturesqueness" in the paintings he executed although certainly did not understand the term precisely as did Gilpin. In 1824 he wrote about his "Lock": "it is a good subject. and an admirable instance of the picturesque," *ibid.*, p. 120.

27. *Light and Colour (Goethe's Theory) – The Morning after the Deluge*..., Exh. 1843. Oil on canvas, 30 1/2 x 30 1/2 in. Tate Gallery (532).

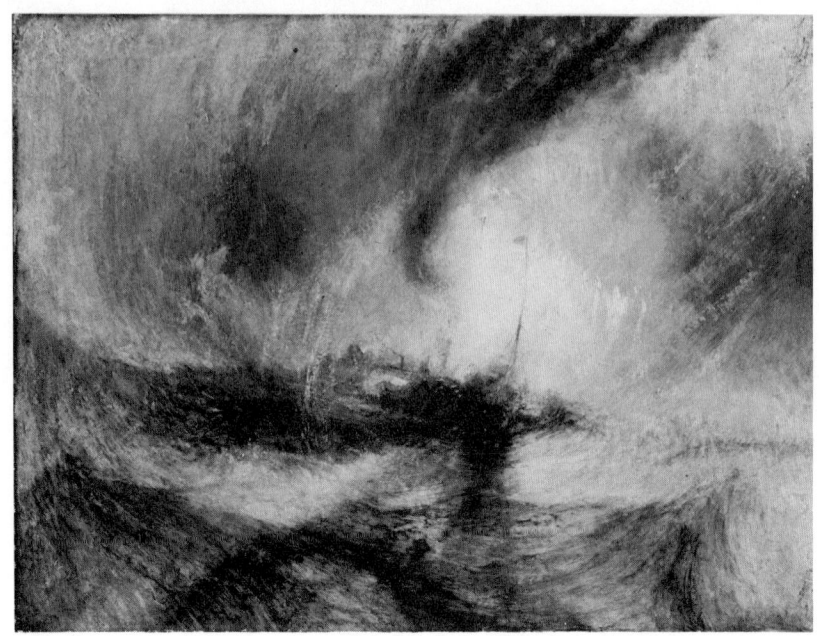

Plate 8. J. M. W. Turner, *Steamer in a Snowstorm*, 1842. Oil on canvas, 36 x 48 in. Tate Gallery, London.

Plate 9. J. M. W. Turner, *Norham Castle, Sunrise*, 1840-45. Oil on canvas, 36 x 48 in. Tate Gallery, London.

shaped mainly by principles derived from classic landscape painting, provided nature with a sense of unity and completeness. This "gestalt" impressed on the minds of eager hordes of amateurs and professionals, armed with pencils and watercolour boxes, served in art to determine the kind of subject and viewpoint adopted.

Whilst it cannot be denied that Gilpin did much to promote the enjoyment of landscape and to popularize national tours, his view of nature was to prove too artificial for a nineteenth-century public increasingly enchanted by natural effect. Interest in picturesque theory soon flagged, but pictorially the picturesque was sustained. And as we have seen, the encapsulated landscape was its mode of survival (if somewhat transformed). The encapsulated landscape, where it survived in painting, often did so prettily. But it remained a relic of an eighteenth-century culture, a classical, rhetorical phrase which for the nineteenth century seemed curiously dated and irrelevant. Constable reflected the Romantic's concern when he rejected the artifice which the picturesque implied.

For Constable, landscape in art had to say something. Nature had to be invested with meaning, to be expressive of the artist's feelings about nature and about himself. This the picturesque landscape did not really do. Could not Constable have been thinking of the encapsulated landscape of the picturesque when he wrote:

> the old rubbish of art, the musty, commonplace, wretched pictures which gentlemen collect, hang up, and display to their friends [paintings which] may be compared to Shakespeare's "Beggarly account of empty boxes. Alligators stuffed" etc., — Nature is anything but this, either in poetry, painting, or in the fields.[28]

Gerald Finley

---

28. C. R. Leslie, *Memoirs of the Life of John Constable...*, p. 273.

The Hope for Moral Regeneration in French Educational Thought 1750-1789[1]

Despite a widespread feeling that they were living in an enlightened century, many eighteenth-century French observers lamented the sad moral state of their country. In his epoch-making *Essai d'éducation nationale*, which appeared in 1763, the high-court magistrate La Chalotais listed the moral ills which sometimes afflict great nations — widespread debauchery among youths, too extreme luxury, lack of affection for the motherland, neglect of duties, and so on — leaving the impression that he was thinking of his own country.[2] That same year Rivard, author of a series of memoranda on education, pointed to the increased number of crimes and scandals to justify his demand for reform.[3] The Academy of Marseilles sponsored an essay contest that decade on the best means of restoring morals in a society which had lost them.[4] During the seventies in an essay on education, De La Fare asserted that perhaps Europeans had sunk to the level of decadence which existed in Rome after it squandered the wealth of Asia.[5] And in the eighties the Comte de Thélis, an indefatigable advocate of various schemes for educational reform, expressed the fear that corruption would increase to the point where it would bring ruin to the nation.[6] One could multiply examples of

---

1. This paper is a by-product of a wider study tentatively entitled *Education for Citizenship: the Movement for Educational Reform in France 1750-1789*, to be followed later by a similar book on the Revolution.
2. L. R. Caradeuc de la Chalotais, *Essai d'éducation nationale, ou plan d'études pour la jeunesse*, s. 1., 1763, pp. 6-7.
3. D. F. Rivard, *Recueil de mémoires touchant l'éducation de la jeunesse, surtout par rapport aux études*, Paris, 1763, pp. 238-41.
4. N. M. de Fleury, *Essai sur les moyens de réformer l'éducation particulière et générale, destiné à l'instruction des pères et mères, et celle des directeurs des collèges et de tous les éducateurs...*, Paris, 1764, pp. 23-25 attempts to answer the question posed by the Academy.
5. De La Fare, *Le Gouverneur, ou Essai sur l'éducation*, Paris, 1768, pp. 82-83.
6. C. A. comte de Thélis *et al.*, *Mémoires concernant les écoles nationales*, Paris,

215

educational reformers and other authors who painted a similarly dark picture of existing moral conditions.

Others painted a gloomy picture, not only of the moral state of the country, but of man's place in the universe and his basic motives.[7] As a materialistic view of the universe developed in the wake of the scientific revolution, some authors saw man engulfed in a universe devoid of moral guideposts. "If the Divinity does not exist," argued Rousseau, "then only the evil man reasons, the good man is insane."[8] Of course Rousseau believed God *did* exist, but he foresaw accurately the moral crisis which would spring from his demise. Some saw man absorbed into a naturalistic world in a way which obliterated any moral qualities distinguishing him from his fellow creatures. Others depicted man caught in a deterministic system which deprived him of any autonomy. Still others portrayed him as impelled entirely by selfish motives, especially an obsessive drive for pleasure. Naturally there were all sorts of combinations of these views, but man seemed to relinquish any sure directives, to lose his freedom, to become a mere animal, driven by his passions.

Moreover, from Bayle onward, a succession of thinkers contended that man's pride and desire for domination even led him to enjoy the suffering of others. Evil appeared radical in man. Long before Sade, La Mettrie realized that in an amoral cosmos there was no reason to seek anything except self-gratification in any form one chose:

> Since the pleasures of the mind are the real source of happiness, it is perfectly clear that from the point of view of pleasure, good and evil are things quite indifferent in themselves, and he who obtains greater satisfaction from doing evil will be happier than the man who obtains less satisfaction from doing good. This explains why so many scoundrels are happy in this life and shows that there is a

1781-1789, 18 fasc. in 1 vol., I, pp. 6-7.

7. On the moral crisis caused by new conceptions of man's place in the universe see the invaluable study by L. G. Crocker, *The Age of Crisis, Man and World in Eighteenth Century French Thought*, Baltimore, 1963.

8. J. J. Rousseau, *Emile ou de l'Education*, first edition, La Haye, 1762; Nouvelle édition par F. et P. Richard, Paris, 1951, p. 356.

kind of individual felicity which is to be found, not merely independent from virtue, but even in crime itself.⁹

In view of the widespread belief in the lamentable moral condition of society, the gloomy picture of man's place in the cosmos, and the unfavourable portrayal of his motives, the optimism of most authors about the capacity of education to regenerate mankind was remarkable. La Chalotais contended that education could transform the morals of an entire nation within a few years. He suggested that one could develop a new race of men just as one could breed improved livestock.¹⁰ In his utopian novel depicting how the citizenry of France had been re-educated by the year 2440 Mercier argued in favour of the perfectibility of mankind.¹¹ In a section dealing with education in his memorandum to the king on municipal reform Turgot claimed that the country could be transformed beyond recognition within ten years.¹² Later in the series of proposals for national education compiled by the comte de Thélis, the duc de Charost wrote of the possibility of creating a completely new generation which would reshape the morals of the nation.¹³ And, to cite just one more example, the would-be educational reformer Vauréal claimed that the time was ripe for what he called *la refonte des moeurs* throughout the country.¹⁴

For some this hope for moral regeneration rested on rejecting the unfavourable view of human nature, on affirming the natural goodness of man. This view is usually associated with Rousseau, and certainly he supported it frequently. But Rousseau's picture of man as produced by society, that is by history rather than nature, was not very different from those who portrayed the baseness of human behaviour. Social man was a selfish, competi-

---

9. Julien Offrey de la Mettrie, *Anti-Sénèque, ou discours sur le Bonheur*, in *Oeuvres philosophiques*, 2 vols., Berlin, 1764, II, p. 166.
10. La Chalotais, *op. cit.*, p. 5.
11. L. S. Mercier, *L'An Deux Mille Quatre Cent Quarante. Rêve s'il en fût*, nouvelle édition, 3 vols., Amsterdam, 1786, II, p. 328.
12. A. R. J. Turgot, Mémoire au Roi sur les municipalités, *Oeuvres de M. Turgot*, 9 vols., Paris 1808-1811, VII, pp. 386-484, p. 399.
13. Thélis, *et al.*, *op. cit.*, V, pp. 6-7.
14. Le comte de Vauréal, *Plan ou essai d'éducation général et national, ou la meilleure éducation à donner aux hommes de toutes les nations*, Bouillon, 1783, pp. 59-60.

tive, vicious animal. That is why when depicting his ideal society in *Du Contrat social* Rousseau spoke of the need to annihilate man's original powers, to give him new ones alien to him, in short to change human nature.[15] Man would have to be remade for social life. In any case those who retained belief in the natural goodness of man probably constituted a distinct minority. Of course for them moral amelioration was simply a matter of protecting and encouraging man's innate impulses.

What produced optimism about the possibility of moral improvement was usually the belief in the malleability rather than the goodness of human nature. The assumptions of Lockian psychology were widespread among French educational thinkers. Locke had depicted the mind at birth empty, not only of knowledge, but of moral inclinations as well. By controlling what entered the mind one could shape human character.[16] Lockianism by no means prevailed in England – Fielding, Priestly, Shaftesbury, Hutcheson, Butler and others agreed that man was born with certain natural disinterested impulses. But in France Condillac and Helvétius carried Lockian psychology to an extreme conclusion. Condillac depicted even the intellectual operations of the mind as habits – he spoke of the habit of attending, the habit of recollecting, the habit of comparing, and so on.[17] And where Locke had claimed only that nine-tenths of the differences among men were the result of education, Helvétius made it ten-tenths. "Education can do everything," he declared.[18] His belief in the malleability of man was shared by scores of French educationalists. Even Diderot, who repudiated Helvétius' claim, conceded that education could do a great deal.[19]

Passmore has made the intriguing suggestion that Locke may

15. J. J. Rousseau, *Le Contrat social*, Amsterdam, 1762, ed., C. E. Vaughan, Manchester, 1918, p. 34.
16. J. Locke, *Some Thoughts Concerning Education*, London, 1963, esp. nos. 42, 66 and 216.
17. J. A. Condillac, *Traité des sensations*, Londres et Paris, 1754, Pt. 1, Ch. II, no. 39.
18. C. A. Helvétius, *De l'homme, de ses facultés intellectuelles et de son éducation*, 2 vols., London, 1772, in *Oeuvres complètes*, reproduction of the 14 vol. edition, Paris 1795, Hildesheim, 1967, vol. XII, section 10, ch. 1, p. 71.
19. D. Diderot, *Oeuvres complètes*, ed. J. Assézat, 20 vols., Paris, 1875-77, vol. II, p. 356.

have been influenced by certain seventeenth-century views of grace.[20] The orthodox view had been that men could not prepare themselves for grace without the help of grace. This seemed to leave man nothing which he could do by his own efforts. Consequently some theologians contended that men could prepare for grace. In France Pierre Charon, a writer widely read in England, certainly by Locke, had argued that in order to prepare the soul properly for the working of divine power we must denude it of all opinion and inclination, making it like a white sheet of paper. Whether or not Locke got his idea from such writers, this is precisely how he depicted the state in which we are born. Education could consequently work on the soul of man wholly prepared for grace. Education became the secular equivalent of grace in that it could create in us the will to be good. The educator now played the role of God, remaking the human heart. Even French educational reformers who wrote from an orthodox Christian standpoint usually affirmed this power of the educator to regenerate man.

The educator, unlike God, did not have supernatural powers. In fact he could only exploit the human tendency — man's one innate propensity — to avoid pain and pursue pleasure. But this did not reduce the confidence of Locke or his French disciples in the power of education. They believed that by calculated use of punishment and reward this tendency could be used to improve human behaviour. By constant association of socially desirable conduct with gratification and approval, and repeated connection of anti-social activity with misery and opprobrium, one could condition man to behave in a desirable way. Man's very pride and selfishness could be exploited for social advantages. Thus La Chalotais contended that the state could control morality by the way it distributed honour or blame, just as governments manipulated the monetary system.[21] In his scheme for educational reform in Sweden, Le Mercier de La Rivière proposed a whole series of devices designed to associate prestige and distinction with the

---

20. J. A. Passmore, "The Malleability of Man in Eighteenth-Century French Thought," *Aspects of the Eighteenth Century*, ed. E. R. Wasserman, Baltimore, 1965, pp. 21-46.

21. La Chalotais, *op. cit.*, pp. 6-7.

performance of social virtues.[22] And in his book on popular education Philipon de la Madeleine emphasized how pride could be utilized to encourage social morality. He suggested having a youth leader in each village preside over a tribunal which would chastise immorality and applaud virtue. In addition he wanted a journal in each village publicizing virtuous actions.[23]

Man's behaviour could thus be regenerated even though his motives would be base from an Augustinian viewpoint. Yet even Augustinians had conceded that man might act virtuously for the wrong reasons, that is, not for the love of God but out of concern for self. This distinction did not worry Locke or most French educational reformers. They were interested primarily in results. Their educational ideas coincided with a utilitarian theory of ethics. At first Rousseau did not like the idea of encouraging morality by appealing to man's selfishness. In *Emile* he protested against a passage in which Locke had advocated showing the child that the generous man, not only always enjoyed the most, but earned praise to boot. "That is to make the child apparently generous but really greedy," complained Rousseau. It would encourage a usurer's liberality.[24] But it was significant that when Rousseau later made his proposals for reforming the government of Poland, that is when he was concerned with moulding the citizen rather than with preserving the natural man, he too adopted the idea of exploiting the human desire for esteem by exposing the individual to social pressures from the earliest years onward.[25]

This hope of remoulding human behaviour was encouraged by certain inconsistencies and traditional assumptions in the thought of educational reformers. Many of them combined a strong belief in the complete malleability of the mind with the conviction that man did have some desirable inborn inclinations. "Experience,

22. [P. P. F. J. H. Le Mercier de La Rivière] *De l'Instruction publique; ou considérations morales et politiques sur la nécessité, la nature et la source de cette instruction*, Stockholm et Paris, 1775, pp. 22-34, 70-82.
23. Le Philipon de la Madeleine, *Vues patriotiques sur l'éducation du peuple tant des villes que de la compagne*, Lyon, 1783, pp. 221-25.
24. Rousseau, *op. cit.*, p. 97.
25. J. J. Rousseau, *Considérations sur le gouvernement de Pologne et sur sa réforme projetée*, Londres, 1782, in *Oeuvres*, ed. Massay Pathay, 20 vols., Paris, 1826-27, vol. V, pp. 297 ff.

against which one philosophizes in vain, teaches us that at birth we bring only an empty capacity which is filled up successively," declared La Chalotais,[26] but later in the same book he wrote of an eternal universal law engraved on human hearts and affirmed his belief in certain innate principles of justice and virtue.[27] Crevier, another educational reformer, ridiculed the robe magistrate for these contradictions at the time, but this did not prevent others from combining the same contradictory positions.[28] Such a combination allowed the educator to enjoy the best of two worlds. In shaping the human mind he could count on some inside support.

Yet another inner contradiction in the thought of many educational reformers bolstered their hope of creating a new man. They assumed that the universe, including the human world, was deterministic. Instead of producing fatalism, as one might initially expect, this determinism became the basis for confidence. It was the guarantee that habituation would have lasting results. Education could permanently shape character. "It is education alone which shapes man," claimed Philipon de la Madeleine. "He is never anything except what it wills him to be."[29] But these reformers assumed that somehow the educator himself could rise above his upbringing, could somehow escape from the closed world of cause and effect, and could thus introduce innovation. Again the educator appeared in a divine role. In some mysterious way he could intervene in the system to exercise his regenerative powers. God-like, he could use a deterministic universe without being bound by it.

But where would the educator get the values which he was going to impose on his fellow human beings? As we have seen, some eighteenth-century novelists and thinkers glimpsed a deep moral crisis resulting from man's cutting the traditional cosmic apron strings and setting out on his own in an amoral universe. Man seemed to have lost any sure basis for his values. However,

26. La Chalotais, *op. cit.*, p. 37.
27. *Ibid.*, p. 125.
28. J. B. L. Crevier, *Difficultés proposées à M. le Caradeuc de la Chalotais — sur le mémoire intitulé*, "Essai d'éducation nationale —" Paris, 1763, pp. 48-59.
29. Philipon de la Madeleine, *op. cit.*, p. 1.

most educational reformers seemed to have escaped this dilemma because they had not thoroughly de-mythologized their universe. Some still based their moral code on Christianity, although now most of them tended to justify it on the basis of social utility. Others advocated grounding ethics on a universal natural law, a concept largely derived from secularization of the ancient notion of a divine order. Still others assumed that in society there was an underlying harmony of interests if only men could be brought to realize it, again an assumption stemming from the old belief in a teleological universe. Reassured by such inherited habits of thought, most educational writers seemed cock-sure of their values. And none seemed disturbed by the possibility that the educator might play a satanic rather than a divine role.

The values which these reformers wished to inculcate were social and civic. They wanted to produce citizens concerned about the welfare of their families, interested in the well-being of society, obedient to the state, and warmly patriotic. For example Fleury called for a state educational program which would "... form good sons, good husbands, good fathers, good friends, in a word zealous defenders of the state and its laws."[30] The physiocrat Baudeau, writing on national education in the group's journal, underlined the importance of the virtue which he called *l'humanitisme*.[31] Even those who argued that Christian piety was the necessary basis for morality now mostly emphasized its social advantages. This preoccupation with social virtue was dramatized by the "Hommage à La Société" with which Lafargue introduced his *Poème sur l'éducation*:

> Douce Société, daigne, si je te sers
> En faveur de mon coeur, faire grâce à mes vers.
> C'est à toi qu'appartient l'Enfant qui vient de naître.
> Pour te servir un jour ta voix lui nomme un maître
> Fils, époux, père, ami, pour être citoyens
> Tu les attaches tous par les même liens.[32]

---

30. Fleury, *op. cit.*, pp. 42-43.
31. L'abbé Nicolas Baudeau, *Ephémérides du citoyen*, 15 Août 1766, vol. V, No. 13, p. 206.
32. Etienne de Lafargue, *Poème sur l'éducation...*, Paris, 1788, p. 1.

Most educationalists emphasized the inculcation of such values must begin early if it was to be effective. Even Rousseau, when he was considering public rather than natural education, stressed the importance of beginning at birth. "When first he opens his eyes an infant ought to see the fatherland, and up to the day of his death he ought never to see anything else," he wrote in *Considérations sur le gouvernement de Pologne*.[33] It was, however, difficult to see how the state could control indoctrination quite so early. For example Guyton de Morveau regretted that the legislation could not penetrate into the interior of private homes in order to enforce its moral code, but he hoped that once they had been reformed the colleges would be able to efface or at least reduce the evil consequences of preschool education. In time the products of these reformed colleges would become fathers carrying the new morality into their homes where they would communicate it to their children. The colleges would thus break the vicious circle of generation and give a new direction to public morality.[34] Some authors such as the abbé Coyer wanted state education to begin at four, but most reformers conceded that it was impractical to begin before six or seven, although parents might be provided guidance for the earlier years.[35]

In his article "Collège," in the third volume of the *Encyclopédie*, d'Alembert had complained that in the existing colleges not nearly enough attention was given to moral training.[36] A few authors denied this charge, but the vast majority of the scores who wrote about education in the following decades contended that ethics ought to be given a much larger place in the curriculum, even if this necessitated cutting down on the time devoted to the classics and other traditional subjects. Some wanted courses on ethics to run through the whole college program lasting six to eight years. Others wanted an entire year to be set aside to be devoted to studying ethics. Many proposed having a special chair in each college for a specialist in ethics.

33. Rousseau, *Considérations*, loc. cit., p. 298.
34. L. B. Guyton de Morveau, *Mémoire sur l'éducation publique avec les prospectus d'un collège suivant les principes de cet ouvrage*, s. 1., 1764, pp. 17-21.
35. L'abbé G. F. Coyer, *Plan d'éducation publique*, Paris, 1770, p. 5.
36. Jean le Rond d'Alembert, "Collège," *Encyclopédie...*, 17 vols., Paris, Neufchatel, etc., 1751-1765, vol. III, p. 635.

Daragon wanted an advanced course in ethics to be made a prerequisite for any public office.[37] Maubert de Gouvest thought that the course on logic should concentrate on practical questions of social morality.[38] All agreed that moral instruction had to be given a central position.

The pedagogical techniques advocated by these would-be educational reformers are very revealing. Many of them proposed what we would now call conditioning the child's behaviour. They were encouraged to believe in the effectiveness of such conditioning by the crude associational psychology common at the time which, assuming that men were attracted to what was pleasant and repelled by what was unpleasant, suggested that human behaviour could be directed by constantly associating civic virtue with social approval and antisocial conduct with public opprobrium — thus "reinforcing" desirable behaviour as the modern behaviourist would put it. Rivard proposed that teachers be trained in special institutions how to mould the child's heart.[39] Various other reformers suggested that social consciousness could be awakened by repeated direct experience, exposing the child to moving scenes, taking him on visits to hospitals or orphanages, or encouraging him to help needy families.[40] The student would in this way become habituated in the practice of various social acts. Civic virtue would become automatic.

It is not surprising that in the Age of Enlightenment many reformers proposed, not only conditioning and habituation, but appeal to the child's intellect. "No, man is not born wicked, since he is born rational, that is endowed with the capacity to distinguish the useful from the harmful," Perreau argued in a book on education for the people; "but it is true that we are all born surrounded by ignorance and error which, by blinding us about

---

37. J. B. Daragon, *Lettre de M^{xxx} à M l'Abbé^{xxx}, professeur de philosophie en l'Université de Paris, sur la nécessité et la manière de faire entrer un cours de morale dans l'éducation publique*, Paris, 1762, pp. 37-53.

38. J. H. Maubert de Gouvest, *Le Temps perdu, ou les écoles publiques. Considérations d'un patriote sur l'éducation de la première jeunesse en France avec l'idée d'un nouveau collège*, Amsterdam, 1765, pp. 8-29.

39. Rivard, *op. cit.*, pp. 81-86.

40. Coyer, *op. cit.*, pp. 236-40, l'abbé Athanase Auger, *Discours sur l'éducation, prononcés au collège royale de Rouen*, Rouen, 1775, pp. 140-48, and Vauréal, *op. cit.*, pp. 84-88.

our true interest, thus inevitably blinds us about our duties, which are simply this very interest clearly understood."[41] But on close examination this process of rational persuasion turns out to be a disguised form of conditioning. The teacher would manipulate the child's mind by pointing out repeatedly the positive repercussions of certain acts and the negative results of other acts. The reasons were nearly always consequences which would result from certain forms of behaviour. Reward and punishment were simply verbalized.

Moral training was not to be restricted to special programs but was to permeate the whole curriculum. History especially could produce a moral impact provided it was used carefully. La Chalotais, who called for history written from a philosophical viewpoint – he recommends reading Voltaire on the purpose of history, was one of a succession of educational writers who wanted history slanted toward a certain ethical viewpoint. He argued that children were well able to understand the basic moral conveyed by history, namely that it is wrong to harm individuals or people in general, and that wicked men deserve public execration. History properly selected could arouse the child's natural sense of justice "... which is quite lively in them, and would be likewise in all men, were it not stifled by prejudice and self-interest." Through concrete examples which would appeal to children, history could awaken sentiments of humanity, generosity, and beneficence. Children would learn morality almost without being aware of it. Above all history could provide what we now call behavioural models. La Chalotais called for a French Plutarch to glorify national heroes and suggested too that the lives of outstanding children would have a strong appeal.[42]

Other subjects also could be given a moral purpose. Lessons in grammar could be based on little didactic dialogues. Practice in translation could be based on extracts which conveyed a moral message. Vanière designed a whole *Cours de Latinité* in which all the passages from the classics were chosen to show the divine origins of the universe, moral duties with their happy results, and

---

41. J. A. Perreau, *Instruction du peuple divisée en trois parties. 1re partie: De la morale; 2e partie: Des affaires; 3e partie: De la santé*, Paris, 1786, p. v-vi.

42. La Chalotais, *op. cit.*, pp. 48-54 and pp. 92-101.

the dangers which sprang from certain passions.[43] Philipon de la Madeleine thought that biology could be used to drive home certain moral truths, especially the value of the work ethic which he wished to impress on the masses. For example, the life of the white ant could illustrate the advantages of hard work.[44] Vauréal thought that physics could be given a similar purpose. The new science could be used to emphasize the importance of order, the value of harmonious laws, and the interdependence of everything in the universe. Also physics could be employed to teach the child to accept the place in society which fate had allotted him.[45]

As though all this indoctrination would not suffice, Le More compiled a collection of *Maximes et pensées* for children which the teacher could quote as casually as possible at appropriate moments. He offered nearly six hundred adages culled from famous authors and classified as dealing with virtue, passions, wisdom, intellect, and society. Here are a few of these moral arrows, as he described them:

> Virtue is never unrewarded, because a fine deed is well repaid by the pleasure of having performed it.
>
> If goodness is the chief attribute of God, beneficence is the primary virtue of man.
>
> The happiness of men in this life does not consist of having no passions, but of being master of them.
>
> Wisdom is the only possession that men cannot take away from us.
>
> Prefer solid things to trifles, and always the useful to the pleasant.
>
> Man is obviously made to think, it is his whole dignity and his whole worth.
>
> We are born, we live for society.[46]

French educational reformers also had great confidence in the

---

43. M. Vanière, *Deuxième Discours sur l'éducation, dans lequel on expose tout le vicieux de l'institution scholastique et le moyen d'y remédier*, Paris, 1763, pp. 72-74.

44. Philipon de la Madeleine, *op. cit.*, pp. 211-12.

45. Vauréal, *op. cit.*, pp. 89-92 and pp. 111-12.

46. Abbé Le More, *Principes d'institution, ou de la manière d'élever les enfants des deux sexes par rapport au corps, à l'esprit et au coeur*, Paris, 1774, pp. 357-435.

power of the media at their disposal. Many of them believed that the printing press, with its capacity to turn out thousands of identical books, could be utilized for the state in order to impress a common ethical code on schoolchildren from one end of the country to the other. Print could shape a homogeneous citizenry. It was through specially designed texts approved by the state that La Chalotais hoped to transform the morals of the nation.[47] His fellow magistrate Rolland, who drew up a series of reports on education for the Paris *parlement* in the wake of closure of the Jesuit schools, likewise called for identical textbooks as a means of creating a common moral outlook throughout France.[48] And it was through a battery of elementary textbooks that Turgot hoped to teach a new generation their obligations to society and the crown.[49] Various other authors proposed moral catechisms, civic handbooks, and popular periodicals as instruments for mass indoctrination.

These eighteenth-century educationalists were also aware of the power of other media. Some of them wanted little didactic plays which would illustrate the morals which they wished to impress on the minds of children. Others wanted images of those heroes who were to serve as behavioural models to cover classroom walls or illustrate textbooks. Still others emphasized the potency of music as a potential medium for civic indoctrination. In his *Plan d'éducation publique* in 1770, the abbé Coyer asserted that music had a profound influence on the human mind, citing the use of songs in public instruction in ancient Israel, Athens and Rome. "If we had very simple, quite clear, well-draughted political laws, our pupils could sing about them, nourishing themselves on them," he wrote. "But lacking such laws, they will sing about the virtues — justice, beneficence, unselfishness, enthusiasm for work, affection for the fatherland — which are the aims of the laws. They will sing too about our illustrious men...."[50] In these various proposals we have the seeds of a modern multi-media approach.

47. La Chalotais, *op. cit.*, pp. 30-31.
48. B. G. Rolland d'Erceville, *Recueil de plusieurs ouvrages de M. le Président Rolland*, Paris, 1783, pp. 128-29, 184-85, 216-23, and 770-71.
49. Turgot, *op. cit.*, pp. 396-98.
50. Coyer, *op. cit.*, pp. 222-23.

Some of these French educationalists sketched plans for continuing indoctrination beyond the school years. For example, Philipon de la Madeleine wanted youth organizations in every village which would maintain young men in shape for work, would keep them out of taverns, would prepare them to rally in case of some emergency, and would train them for public works. In addition he proposed paramilitary units to furnish patrols for the streets at night, to provide firefighting squads, and to award insignia for outstanding service to the community. For all age groups he called for rural festivals in which common people would provide music, displays of produce, and communal meals at which outstanding husbandmen would be honoured. Continuing education would also include public lectures, collections of didactic proverbs, and publication of local examples of civic virtue, all devices designed to provide social controls, to reinforce the work ethic learned at school, and to encourage community service.[51]

The desire to mould a regenerate citizenry would seem to imply mass education, but many thinkers feared that too much schooling for the common people might depopulate the countryside and make manual workers discontented with their lot. The commonest solution to this dilemma was to advocate an educational system which was broad at the base but narrow at the top. The masses would be schooled in reading, writing, arithmetic and civic morality, but very few of them would be allowed access to higher learning. For example, in his series of articles on national education Baudeau advocated a hierarchy of schools beginning with *petites écoles* in every parish, *écoles de villes* in lesser urban centres to cater to the lower bourgeoisie, *collèges diocésains* in larger cities to train the upper bourgeoisie, *collèges des notables* for the aristocracy, and finally a *collège de la cour* for the royal family and great families. Such a system would allow for state indoctrination of the masses at the base without threatening the social order.[52]

---

51. Philipon de la Madeleine, *op. cit.*, pp. 243 ff.
52. Baudeau, *loc. cit.*, Vol. I, no. 7, 25 nov. 1765, pp. 97-112; vol. II, no. 5, 17 jan. 1766, pp. 65-80; vol. III, no. 2, 7 mars 1776, pp. 17-32; vol. IV, no. 4, 12 mai 1766, pp. 79-64; vol. V, nos. 10-13, 4 août-15 août 1776, pp. 145-208.

There are many attractive features in the proposals for educational reform in the three or four decades preceding the Revolution — the demand for a more varied curriculum, the emphasis on science, the repudiation of scholastic philosophy, and the vision of a regenerate citizenry. But from a modern vantage point some other elements appear pregnant with future dangers — the demand for strict state control, civic indoctrination from early childhood, careful manipulation of the child's emotions, standardization of training from one end of the country to the other, and the occasional call for social control through paramilitary organizations and popular demonstrations. In some of the suggestions for conditioning and habituation there are portents of Skinner's recent book with its disturbing title *Beyond Freedom and Dignity*. But once again this brings out the modernity of the eighteenth century. It raised the basic issues which concern us still.

James Leith

Ideological Immigrants in Revolutionary America

The ideological immigrants examined here were a small part of a larger and cohesive group of radical Englishmen who applauded the American Revolution and thought that the newly-created republic was "both by precept and example ... the best instructor in the only means of protecting ... liberties."[1] They belonged to an intellectual tradition, that of the Old Whigs or Commonwealthmen, which had preserved and developed the canon of political ideas of Harrington, Needham, Milton, Sidney, Neville and Locke. Because the Old Whigs knew that the same ideas which influenced them had crossed the ocean in the intellectual baggage of the settlers of the English colonies in America, there to find some realization in the Revolution, they tended to think of America as "the only great nursery of free men now left upon the face of the earth."[2] When the prospects for political reform seemed slight in England, particularly after the failure of the movements for dissenters' relief and during the political repressions of the 1790s, this ideological affinity between Americans and the English radicals naturally made the minds of the latter turn to thoughts of emigration. America represented for them the "asylum for the friends of liberty here...."[3] but in the event it was an asylum many contemplated but few sought. What did radicals expect and what in fact did they actually find when confronted with the reality of what they had considered to be the model republic? The answers to these questions illuminate details of both the character of revolutionary America and the state of contemporary English radicalism.

An examination of radical pamphlet literature and private

---

1. [John Cartwright], *A Letter to Edmund Burke, Esq...*, London, 1775, p. 16.
2. Jonathon Shipley, *Works*, London, 1792, II, pp. 191-92.
3. "The Price Letters," *Proceedings of the Massachusetts Historical Society*, 2nd series, XVII, 1903, pp. 278-79.

letters shows that the idea of America as an ideological haven was widespread. With the partial exception of the Puritan and Quaker settlements the appeal of the New World to Englishmen had been practical and economic. Handbooks promoting immigration both before and after the Revolution, reflected this, but the radicals considered emigration for quite different and unusual reasons. It was because they thought, in moments of despair, "that country ... will be free, and this country must go backwards, perhaps to its original state of barbarity,"[4] that they contemplated quitting England for the United States. Richard Price, the Dissenting theologian, predicted that "the time will probably come when a great part of Europe will be flocking to a country where, unmolested by spiritual and civil tyranny, they will be able to enjoy in safety the exercise of reason and the rights of man," and he was echoed in these sentiments by other pro-American radicals.[5]

Several leading radical figures in the later 1780s and the 1790s contemplated migration to America since their opinions were treated as crimes in England.[6] Numerous pamphlets and sermons, especially those directed to Dissenters, urged serious consideration of the move to the "asylum of suffering humanity."[7] The popular radical press, including John Thelwall's *Tribune* and the tracts of the London Corresponding Society pointed out the political attractions of America and urged large scale migration by labouring men "to the hospitable shores of America."[8] The

---

4. John Jebb, *Works*, London, 1789, I, p. 92.

5. William Morgan, *Memoirs of the Life of the Rev. Richard Price*, London, 1815, pp. 73-74; Thomas Day, *Reflections upon the Present State of England and the Independence of America*, 5th ed., London, 1783, pp. 105-7; [Samuel Heywood], *The Right of Protestant Dissenters to a Compleat Toleration Asserted*, 2nd ed., London, 1789, pp. 55-56, 60-63, 79; Joseph Priestley, *An Appeal to the Public on the Subject of the Riots in Birmingham*, Birmingham, 1791, pp. 100-4.

6. *The Diary of Sylvas Neville, 1767-1788*, ed. Basil Cozens Hardy, London, 1950, pp. 3, 31; *The Letters of Sir William Jones*, ed. Garland Cannon, Oxford, 1970, II, pp. 536-38; Thomas Hardy, *Memoir*, London, 1832, p. 58; *Memoirs and Trials of the Political Martyrs of Scotland*, Edinburgh, 1837, pp. 8-9, 16-17; Thomas Belsham, *Memoirs of Theophilus Lindsey*, London, 1812, p. 351.

7. Jebb, *Works*, III, p. 321: William Thom, *Works*, Glasgow, 1779, pp. 126, 147-48, 154-55, 202-5, 207-8; Heywood, *Protestant Dissenters*, pp. 60, 63, 79; *A Summary of the Duties of Citizenship*, London, 1792, p. 21.

8. *The Tribune*, ed. J. Thelwall, London, 1795-1796, I, pp. 3-4, II, p. 35, p. 43; [London Corresponding Society], *Address ... on the Subject of Parliamentary Reform*, London, 1792.

correspondence of Theophilus Lindsey, a Dissenting divine who was the centre of exchange for information and opinion among radical Dissenters, reveals how interest in America as an ideological refuge and projects for ministers to "transatlanticise" with their flocks were ubiquitous. Priestley's migration generated considerable interest and close attention.[9]

Religious liberty and its benefits, the absence of an oppressive establishment and the presence of a more natural piety and greater harmony, was one of the most frequently cited attractions of American life.[10] But it was not the only reason why its friends thought of revolutionary America as an ideological haven. These men, who held to a kind of cryptorepublicanism inherited from their seventeenth-century intellectual ancestors, were deeply impressed with the absence of hereditary political institutions in the new republic. Reforming literature commented frequently and favourably on this feature of the United States. It represented a purer form of government, a real republicanism. Therefore, America was esteemed as a retreat from oppression and a place where the greatest extent of natural liberties, improperly understood in Britain, might be enjoyed.

For example, Thomas Day's *Dialogue Between a Justice of the Peace and a Farmer* (1785) mentioned greater personal freedom, more democratic representative institutions, less expensive government and the absence of King, lords and bishops as features of the new United States which would attract potential immigrants.[11] Another Commonwealthman, Sylvas Neville, contemplating migration for himself, argued that the Americans were "much more virtuous and understand the nature of liberty better than the body of the people here." Another, Sir William Jones, thought that Truth, Justice, Reason, and Valour had flown to the purer soil and more congenial sky of America and that the sensible and rational ought to follow.[12] Joseph Gerrald, who had come to Britain from

9. Doctor Williams Library, London, Lindsey Correspondence, Ms. 12-57, fos. 6, 42; Letters to Turner, Ms. 12 44, fos. 57, 58, 59, 62, Millar Papers, Ms. 12-64, fos. 4, 21, 29.
10. See citations from Day, Heywood, Jebb and Shipley above; also Priestley *Familiar Letters . . . in Refutation of Several Charges Advanced Against the Dissenters*, Birmingham, 1780, pp. 34-35; Richard Price, *Two Tracts on Civil Liberty, The War with America, and the Debts and Finance of the Kingdom*, London, 1778, pp. ii-v, viii.
11. Thomas Day, *Dialogue. . .*, 3rd ed., London, 1786, pp. 11, 47-48, 99.
12. See citations from Neville and Jones above in n. 6 and Jones' poem, *The Muse*

a childhood in America and who was convicted for treason because of his radical activities, adumbrated the attractions which the new republic had for reformers. He claimed that in America

> ... that happy land of freedom and an equality of rights the blood of man is never shed to satiate the cruelty and ambition of crowned heads. America is without courts and therefore she is without wars.

Further, harmony and stability were preserved, because as every man had an interest in the state so no man had an interest in disturbing it. Americans were less rapacious and violent. Gerrald described the social order of the United States thus:

> In America, the Country which God and man have concurred to render the blissful habitation of abundance and of peace, the poor are not broken down by taxes to support the luxury of an insolent nobility. No lordly peer tramples down the corn of the husbandman, and no proud prelate wrings from him the tythe of his industry. They have neither chicanery in ermine nor hypocrisy in lawn. The community then is not divided into an oppressed peasantry and an overgrown aristocracy, the one of whom lives by the plunder of the state, while the others are compelled to be the objects of it. Plenty is the lot of all, superfluity of none.[13]

Here, the attack on hereditary institutions includes an idealized description of the social benefits of American republicanism. The tone and influence of Paine is present. The more popularly-based radicals, men like Thelwall and Thomas Hardy, also argued that the case of America demonstrated that improved social conditions were the result of what they interpreted to be democracy there. Popular tracts emphasized the social benefits which attended political reform in America. These would attract "the best sinews" of Britain.[14] Thus the theme of economic

Recalled, an Ode on the Nuptials of Lord Viscount Althorp and Miss Lavinia Bingham, London, 1780.

13. Joseph Gerrald, *A Convention the Only Means of Saving Us from Ruin...*, London, 1793, pp. 72-74.

14. See n. 8 above; also Hugh, Lord Sempill, *A Short Address to the Public*,

motives for immigration were specifically tied by popular radicals to America's political ideology and system. Not even revolutionary France, according to many reformers, was as attractive as America. Paine, looking for a refuge from political persecution, after ten years in France told a fellow English radical that "I know of no Republic in the world except America, which is the only country for such men as you or I."[15]

These examples of the image of revolutionary America in the eyes of its most sympathetic observers have been drawn only from those who specifically advocated emigration but it also can be found in the writings of those who were more sanguine of reform in England and thought of America as a model rather than a haven. To recapitulate, the radical argument was that the American republic was a model society which might fail to be imitated. It would therefore serve as an asylum for free men on a large scale. There true constitutional principles, known to some but violated in England, were maintained and formed the foundation of the republic. Popular sovereignty and limited government were not mere ideas but were embodied in American institutions and practices. America had demonstrated that hereditary institutions were not only otiose but pernicious. Real republicanism could only be realized without them. The American political order augmented personal freedom and dignity, civil and religious liberty, while they were contracting elsewhere. Further, it generated prosperity and a more egalitarian social order. The American Revolution, according to its ideological friends, was republican in a thoroughly radical way. They saw in it an assertion of democracy only implicit and undeveloped in their own inherited republican tradition, and a wholesale rejection of the values and purposes of the mixed constitution which obtained in Britain. At the same time it seemed to have avoided the excesses of the French Revolution. Virtue, it was argued, characterized the people and public life as well as ideas in America. There were, of course, the Loyalists, but all the patriots and revolutionaries were

---

London, 1793, p. 35; *One Pennyworth of Pig's Meat...*, ed. T. Spence, London, 1793-1795, II, pp. 283-84.

15. W. T. Sherwin, *Memoirs of the Life of Thomas Paine*, London, 1819, p. 191.

assumed to be equally faithful to the new principles, and distinctions were not made among them.

Obviously, many of these perceptions of the attractions of America were based on pre-conceptions of what a model republic should be. Like Western Marxists who were attracted by the sight of the Russian Revolution the English reformers knew revolutionary America's intellectual antecedents and had a decided notion of what a new republic would be like. But it is possible to check these notions against the observations and experiences of the few who actually went to America instead of reasoning why it should attract them.

Two, Catherine Macaulay, the radical historian, and William Hazlett, the father of the essayist, went almost immediately after the peace in 1783. Mrs. Macaulay visited John Adams at Boston and stayed with Washington at Mount Vernon in order to see how republican principles worked in practice. She reported fears that luxury was developing and detected deviations from true republicanism in discussions about strengthening the national government. She disapproved of the two-tiered legislatures which had appeared in several of the states and deplored the absence of some principle of rotation in office.[16] Hazlett migrated partly because of his unitarian opinions but he found that he was vilified for them and that a bigoted Calvinism obtained among American clergymen. He reported that it would be twenty years before the true spirit of toleration was realized. And although he asserted his fundamental support for the American republic he discovered that not all Americans were good republicans. He cautioned his English friends against Benjamin Rush, a Philadelphia psychiatrist who was being well received by pro-Americans in England. Hazlett warned that Rush was of the anti-democratic party which unfortunately existed in America.[17]

John Binns, who settled in America in 1798 after his narrow escape from a treason conviction, also found that political struggles had to be continued. He insisted that true liberty was not a grant, like that of Magna Carta, from above, but the result of the

16. Lucy Martin Donnelly, "The Celebrated Mrs. Macaulay," *William and Mary Quarterly*, 3rd series, VI, 1949, pp. 173-207.
17. "Price Letters," pp. 322-24, 334-36.

eternally sovereign people, working through congresses and conventions as in America, allowing limited power to their government. Once in America he became violently partisan for Jefferson, edited two Jeffersonian newspapers, and claimed to have invented the name "Democratic" for the Jeffersonian societies. The point was that he thought Jefferson's opponents were endangering the system he approved.[18] Similarly, Paine, after he returned to the United States, made distinctions among Americans and supported Jefferson against Adams and Washington. Adams while in England had been received as a wholly worthy representative of American republicanism. But Paine warned that the Federalists were trying to incorporate the forms and vicious practices of the British constitution in America and wished to subvert "the representative system of government, the pride and glory of America and the palladium of her liberties." He accused Adams of having conspired for a succession and the establishment of a dynasty. Only Jefferson and his supporters were genuine receptacles of the revolutionary tradition.[19]

Thomas Cooper, another ideological immigrant was forced by his actual experiences of the United States to qualify his original enthusiasm. Before he moved he had called for a political reform based on the explicitly democratic doctrine of the representation of persons, not property or interest. He explained at some length how America offered an example of the advantages of such a system which was "equal to the most sanguine expectations of her best wishers."[20] Yet, seeing few prospects for peaceful change in England he chose to quit it for a country whose politics he could approve. He visited the United States in 1793 and emigrated with his family the next year. His book, *Some Information Respecting America*, was addressed, he explained, to prospective immigrants of his own sort who were of modest fortune, who had political objections to the present government of England and who did not wish to suffer a "defalcation of political rights on account of

---

18. [John Binns], *Recollections*, Philadelphia, 1854, pp. 222-30.
19. Thomas Paine, *Writings*, ed. M. D. Conway, New York, 1894-1896, III, pp. 214-18, 388-91.
20. Thomas Cooper, *A Reply to Mr. Burke's Invective...*, London, 1792, pp. 24-27.

theological opinions." It reveals that combination of social and political interests characteristic of radical interest in America at this period.

America was a more advantageous place to live, he argued, because its principles rendered it free from the ill effects of inequality and civil oppression which plagued Europe. He described the absence of established religion, tithes, or religious strife, and the general prosperity, orderliness of government and equality of condition. Cultural life, it was conceded, was undeveloped, but America led the world in political theory. Not even revolutionary France, which Cooper had visited in 1792, was to be recommended above America. Cooper wanted to be able to differ from his neighbour in religion or politics and even hold erroneous opinions without "the orthodox intervention of the halter or the guillotine." He therefore urged men like him to come to America:

> There is no fault to find in the government of America, either in principle or practice: we have few taxes to pay, and those are of acknowledged necessity, and moderate in amount; we have no animosities about religion; it is a subject about which no questions are asked: we have few respecting political men or political measures.... The government is a government of the people, and *for* the people. There are no tythes nor game laws.... There are no men of great rank, not many of great riches. Nor have the rich there the power of oppressing the less rich, for poverty, such as in Great Britain, is almost unknown.

This rhapsodic account of the American republic is interesting for what it reveals about its author's perspective. Cooper's enthusiastic approval of the political system of the United States was like that of many other contemporary commentators, intimately connected with the fact that in a republic the poor could not be oppressed to support the luxury of insolent noblemen.[21]

Like other ideological immigrants Cooper knew, of course, that these were qualifications to the roseate picture he presented.

---

21. Cooper, *Some Information Respecting America*, London, 1794, pp. 3, 50-53, 56-57, 64-66, 70-73, 76, 78, 208-26.

Despite his panegyric on American religious liberty he also had occasion to complain about prejudices against unitarianism. He was attacked for his Jacobin principles and was threatened by the sedition laws of the Adams Administration as a subversive agent. He, too, warned against the Federalist party which, he said, was composed of the executive officers, most senators and great merchants. They leaned to British principles, wanted to extend the powers of government and were inclined to obtrude manufacturing into the arcadian republic. The popular party, which included most of the people and the majority of Congress, approved French theory but not practice, desired to keep the salaries, dignity and distance of public officers in an appropriately simple republican state, and wanted more frequent elections. Although he had observed that political divisions were less acute in America than Britain, Cooper himself was so virulent that he was imprisoned for six months in 1800 for libelling President Adams. Like other transplanted radicals he was firmly Jeffersonian.[22]

But of all the ideological settlers in America, Joseph Priestley, the scientist and theologian, was the most celebrated. His pro-Americanism, his conviction that true religion co-existed with true toleration in America, his judgement that a great revolution was taking place there which would win the applause of "the liberal, the rational and the virtuous part of the world" and attract large scale migration all featured in his polemical and historical writings.[23] After the destruction of his house and laboratory in the Church and King riots in Birmingham in 1792, Priestley began preparation for his eventual resettlement in Pennsylvania in 1794.

Priestley immediately announced upon his arrival his agreement with "the general principles and practices of a completely representative government, founded upon universal suffrage, and excluding hereditary principles. . . ."[24] The importance of this is that Priestley knew that his impressions and experience would be influential with his friends who were observing him and cherishing similar notions. Priestley's extensive correspondence with his

22. *Ibid.*, pp. 67-69.
23. Joseph Priestley, *Letters to the Right Honourable Edmund Burke*, Birmingham, 1791, pp. 39-40.
24. Priestley, *Memoirs*, London, 1904, pp. 108-9.

radical friends is preserved in Dr. Williams Library and in Warrington, the seat of a great Dissenting Academy. An examination of these letters illuminates the connection between English radicalism and America in this period and reveals what image the revolutionary republic projected. Moreover, since they record the impressions of a lively and profound mind, they are an important picture of the contemporary scene.

They reveal Priestley as at first full of wonder and approval. Just a few days after his arrival he wrote to Lindsey expressing his happiness and adumbrating the reasons why the United States gave him so much satisfaction. The letter is interesting both because it shows in what light America's English friends expected it to appear and because Priestley was later to be disappointed in many of the particulars he cited. He said that

> I feel as if I were in another world. I never before could conceive how satisfactory it is to have the feeling that I now have, from a sense of perfect security and liberty, all men having equal rights and privileges, and speaking and acting as if they were sensible of it. Here are no beggars to be seen, and families are easily maintained by any kind of labour, and whether it be the effect of general liberty, or some other cause I find many more clever men, men capable of conversing with propriety and fluency on all subjects relating to government, than I have met with anywhere in England.

In England, he said, he had been an object of aversion while in America people respected him. The Episcopalian church without the benefit of establishment had lost its tyrannizing spirit. He briefly described the two political parties and announced his judicious impartiality.[25] Clearly this letter, written before Priestley could have had a chance to gain much real knowledge of American affairs, was meant to reinforce a particular image of the American republic.

He continued to tell his English friends that universal representation and annual elections were the fundamental principles from which all other great advantages were derived. The result

---

25. Belsham, *Memoirs of Lindsey*, pp. 530-32.

was that there were no poor and no beggars in America. Crime was slight; the public debt and the burden of taxes were low; government was cheap; and the press was perfectly free. Although there was no church establishment and therefore no tithes, as much attention was paid to religion as in England. "I do not think," he wrote to George Dyer, the radical philanthropic reformer, "there ever was any country in the world in a state of such rapid improvement as this at present." Even the reduction of the inconveniences of travel and improvements in the conditions of inns and roads were seized by Priestley as an opportunity to praise a state of progress the like of which he believed was never known in the world before.[26] He rarely let down his defence of American institutions when writing to most of his English correspondents.

However, with his intimate and regular correspondents Priestley was more candid and revealed that there were disappointments. For one thing, his emigration was not treated with universal acclaim. William Cobbett, not yet converted to political radicalism, began a campaign of vituperation. Cobbett warned that Priestley's intention was to preach atheistical and seditious doctrines which would hurt America.[27] These attacks and the rising xenophobia which Priestley thought he discerned in the period which produced the Alien Act led him to plead the cause of ideological immigrants. They came because they were "unable to bear the encroachments that are continually making on their liberties, civil and religious," he argued, and had a moral claim on Americans who ought to assist the victims of persecution.[28]

Priestley's unitarianism had been the cause of much of Cobbett's vitriolic spleen. But it was the absence of unitarian sentiments, the scarcity of what he thought was true religion which Priestley lamented. After a year of settlement, when a more

---

26. Doctor Williams Library, Priestley Letters (hereinafter DWL), Ms. 12-13, fos. 37, 41; Warrington Public Library, Priestley Letters (hereinafter WPL), no. 44; *Life and Correspondence of Joseph Priestley*, ed. J. T. Rutt, London, 1831, II, pp. 355-57, 495-97.

27. [William Cobbett], *Observations on the Emigration of Dr. Joseph Priestley*, Philadelphia, 1794, pp. 60-62.

28. Priestley, *The Case of the Poor Emigrants Recommended*, Philadelphia, 1797, pp. 8-9, 15, 20-21.

balanced picture began to emerge in his correspondence, Priestly conceded that in parts of the United States there was very little practice of religion. He privately admitted that the "country abounds with unbelievers, more I think than England, and the young men in general, I believe, are more profligate. What religion there is is chiefly Calvinistic." His private hope was that rational religion would stem the tide of infidelity but he realized that unitarianism was little known or welcomed in America. It was some comfort that Jefferson, whom he at first suspected of irreligion, basically shared his opinions. But the knowledge that some of the states had preserved colonial laws against unitarianism and the hostility of most of the local preachers disquieted him.[29]

Priestley also became disabused of the notion that he could find more sympathetic and intelligent company in America than England. Six months after his first euphoric letter to Lindsey he confessed that much as he was pleased with America he considered himself in exile and longed for the presence of like-minded unitarian Christians. This lamentation he frequently reiterated in the years to follow. It was at its most intense during John Adams' administration when Priestley disapproved of the political tenor of the country, but it persisted until the very end of his life.[30]

The obvious solution to Priestley's isolation was to urge his friends to join him, but he hesitated to do so, for he encountered another check to his original illusions about America. Although it was a flourishing and promising country he had some difficulties adjusting to it. With some capital and enterprise and the right set of expectations large fortunes could be doubled because capital for investment was needed in America. Conversely, the high cost and scarcity of labour meant that working class immigrants would also prosper, and Priestley encouraged that class to migrate. But he did not encourage his friends who belonged to the middling classes of society to move. He explained that everything was the reverse of what it was in England and that he did not think there was ". . . an example in all history of any country being in so rapid a state of improvement as this is in at the present time. But in proportion

---

29. WPL, no 47; DWL, Ms. 12-13, p. 48, Ms. 12-45, p. 89.
30. DWL, Ms. 12-13, unnumbered fragment and fos. 70, 90.

as it is advantageous to the labourer, it is heavy on the man who must live on the labour of others. Living here is, I think, not less than twice as expensive as in any part of England...." This fact meant that one could not live on the income of a small fortune.[31] In this passage the essentially middle-class nature and expectations of Dissenting radicalism stand out in strong relief.

The radicals in England, it has already been noted, did not always appreciate the nuances of American politics. But closer acquaintance, as we have seen, led those who went to the United States to make distinctions among Americans. Priestley had begun with sanguine expectations and no partisan rancour. He was friendly with men of all parties, took no sides in politics and rarely commented on them. He was on good terms with Washington, who invited Priestley to visit him and favourably impressed him with his republican simplicity. He received marks of friendship from Adams and many other Federalists who were solicitous for his welfare so that he felt personally indebted to many of that party. Jefferson corresponded with Priestley about his proposed university and offered him a position there. Initially, then, he little concerned himself with politics and naively thought that all public men equally served what he took to be the cause of liberty. Despite his complaints in his early years his reaction when he contemplated events in England was that he rejoiced that he was in America.[32] When reporting Adams' election to Lindsey at the beginning of 1797 he still manifested this spirit. He wrote:

> I seldom trouble you with the *politics* of this country. Indeed, I think very little about them. But I must inform you that Mr. Adams is to be our next President, and Mr. Jefferson our Vice-President, and that there is no doubt they will act very harmoniously together, which will greatly abate the animosity of both parties. But such is the temper and habit of this country that if any thing be once decided, though by a single fair vote, all contention instantly ceases, and all will join the majority.[33]

31. DWL, Ms. 12-13, fragment, WPL, nos. 39, 42, 44, 46.
32. WPL, nos. 39, 42; Priestley, *Memoirs*, p. 112; *Corr. of Priestley*, II, pp. 373, 451.
33. *Corr. of Priestley*, II, pp. 369-371.

But these pleasant illusions were to last only a few months. By the spring Priestley was apprehensive about public affairs. To his friends he was candid about his fears and about the divisions and conservative dangers around him. The reaction in politics produced by the French Revolution meant that in certain quarters there was an aversion to anyone professing French principles, he told Lindsey. The common people did not share this new hostility but those who did were suspicious of immigrants from England who opposed the government there. Priestley, contradicting his assertion of a few months earlier, complained that "Party spirit runs very high in this country. Tho' I take no part whatever in Politics. I am now more grossly calumnated, as a supposed friend of France, in the Newspaper that has the greatest currency of any in this country, than I was in England." Priestley felt threatened by the Alien and Sedition Acts and was not comforted by a message from the President reassuring him of his welcome in America and yet cautioning him to be less controversial. He came to believe that all Federalists were in error. It seemed to Priestley as if the Tories of the Revolution were in power. Yet he insisted that the great body of farmers and common people and the back country were opposed to the government. Only the wealthy and those connected with the merchants were betraying the Revolution.[34] This was the dark night of Priestley's political soul. He bared his unhappiness and disappointments to his friends:

> ... it seems to be my fate to live in countries where the measures of government are such as I must condemn. Democratical & French principles, and Jacobinism, are, if possible, more reprobated here than they are with you.... Indeed I feel little interest in anything here, being too old to form new connections, or new objects of attention.[35]

The first ray of relief appeared near the beginning of 1799. In writing to another pro-American radical, Joshua Toulmin, Priestley, while still complaining about the state of politics and the rancourous abuse to which he was subject, noted that there was a

---

34. WPL, no. 52; *Memoirs*, pp. 109-12; DWL, Ms. 12-13, fos. 47, 48, 61.
35. DWL, Ms. 12-57, fo. 55.

solution. There was a party of good men who opposed the
government. In Kentucky, where Toulmin's son was secretary to
the state, most people were of it. Jefferson's campaign for the
presidency cheered Priestley and he was reminded that, bad as the
policies of the government were, the excellence of the constitution
provided a remedy. Yet he feared a Federalist victory in the next
national election for he thought that it represented "the true spirit
of Church and King" in America although under a different
name.[36]

Finally, with Jefferson's victory, Priestley's anguish and
doubts were over. The risk he thought he had been under of
deportation under the Alien Act was removed. And the revolutionary republic was saved. "You will rejoice," he wrote to a
friend in England, "with the friends of liberty in this country on
the election of Mr. Jefferson for our next President.... The
violence of the other party, and the extremes to which they were
prepared to go, are hardly credible."[37] Once more content,
Priestley ceased commenting on political matters. But very near
his death he pronounced himself satisfied with the United States,
"especially since the election of Mr. Jefferson whose administration is, indeed, excellent, highly favourable to the peace and
happiness of the country in all respects."[38]

These ideological immigrants, then, encountered some disappointments. Closer acquaintance made them realize that revolutionary America did not exactly fit the picture that their
ideological framework dictated. The religious situation, a major
attraction for many reformers, was not always what they had
hoped for. Political virtue was not universal and was threatened,
according to them, by a powerful unrepublican party against
which it was their duty to testify. Rancour and intolerance had
not disappeared.

But, although they had to alter its uncritical stance, those men
did not renounce their political allegiance to the model republic.
This reaction to the American scene, as well as their pre-
conceptions about it, emphasizes the radical character of the

36. *Corr. of Priestley*, II, pp. 412-15; DWL, Ms. 12-13, fos. 59, 60.
37. *Corr. of Priestley*, II, pp. 454-55.
38. DWL, Ms. 12-13, fo. 92.

Revolution. In their view it could only be represented by the Jeffersonian party. They did not think of the Revolution as a struggle over the preservation of traditional liberties acquired through prescriptive right, as some pro-Americans, like Burke, and some subsequent historians have. Rather, it was based on constitutional principles nowhere else embodied in practice. Therefore, it quite properly produced a radical, and even democratic, new order. So men like John Adams who tried to find some continuity with the old regime, some place for elements of a mixed constitution in American theory and institutions were rejected by the Revolution's ideological allies as outside the republican fold. Seen from their angle the Revolution was very revolutionary.

Also, their observation of revolutionary America illuminates their own radicalism. What they approved in America they also thought to be part of their own ideology. These English reformers saw the developments their own ideas had produced in America and then read those developments back into their own tradition. The Old Whigs had been neither democratic nor egalitarian throughout most of the eighteenth century. But it has not generally been noticed that in the last quarter of the century they were becoming so. This was partly the result of the symbiotic relationship between English radicalism and revolutionary America of which ideological immigration was a symbol and an agent.

Arthur Sheps

The Shadow of Edward Gibbon*

Whether we like it or not, our whole concept of the fall of Rome has been influenced by Edward Gibbon. He did not create the historical problem, but for the English-speaking world, he was largely responsible for its definition, and, perhaps because he wrote when he did, he made the problem relevant. Volume one of *The Decline and Fall* appeared in 1776, while Gibbon was member of Parliament for Liskeard, and a supporter of Lord North's government. The concluding volumes, four, five and six, were printed in 1788, on the eve of the French Revolution, which was to sweep away the Bourbon monarchy, and guillotine the king whom Gibbon had compared by innuendo to Arcadius and Honorius.[1] An age was coming to an end as *The Decline and Fall* progressed, and although Gibbon assured his contemporaries that the eighteenth century could not suffer a similar fall, nevertheless, society could not help but be affected by the message of Rome.

Roughly speaking, the elements of Gibbon's definition of the problem are these: First, the basic reasons for the fall of the Roman Empire were internal ones. In this, he agrees with a tradition going back to the humanists: before Gibbon, only Flavio Biondo had pointed to the barbarians, specifically Alaric and his Goths, as the cause of the Fall,[2] and after Gibbon, there has been a general reluctance to be nasty with the barbarians, even among those historians who have emphasized their role. Gibbon hesitated to suggest that the barbarians were guilty, in some way, of ushering in the middle ages. "The most civilized nations of modern Europe issued from the woods of Germany," wrote Gibbon in his ninth chapter, "and in the rude institutions of those barbarians,

---

* This paper was first given to a joint session of the Canadian Historical Association and the Classical Association of Canada at McGill University, 1972.

1. Ch. 3. In his *Autobiography*, Gibbon denied that the offending passage referred to Louis XVI, and claimed that it was written before his ascent to the throne. In the second edition, the passage was emended. (*Autobiography of Edward Gibbon*, "The World's Classics" London, 1950, pp. 196-97).

2. A. Momigliano, in *The Conflict between Paganism and Christianity in the Fourth Century*, Oxford, 1963, p. 3.

we may still distinguish the original principles of our present laws and manners." The cold climate of ancient Germany formed "the large and masculine limbs of the natives who were, in general, of a more lofty stature than the people of the South." This generally favourable picture is partly due to Tacitus, whose *Germania* Gibbon accepted without undue skepticism, but it was also because it would never do to have these "noble savages" perpetrating the Dark Ages. For that deed, persons more effete and servile must be found. This tenderness for the feelings of the barbarians has had a long life, and a small part of it may be due to the amount of research which the descendants of these barbarians have done in their several countries, in the history of Rome.

To be sure, Gibbon allows himself some purple prose when he describes the social customs of the early Germans. They had rude pleasures. "Strong beer . . ." he notes, "was sufficient for the gross pleasures of German debauchery." However, those who tasted Italian, and later Gallic wine, never forgot it, and afterwards preferred to get drunk on that. Gibbon does not seem to blame the Germans unduly for the increasing education of their palates. We should, perhaps, remember his own fondness for Madeira, and the fact that he died, apparently, of cirrhosis of the liver.[3]

The second element of Gibbon's definition was that the fall of Rome was essentially a problem to be seen in a western context. For Gibbon, the middle ages started in the third century, and their darkest period was the seventh to the eleventh centuries. The survival of the Empire in the east was no embarrassment, for it was simply a long death agony. Gibbon will allow the Byzantines no virtues in principle, although in practice, some few might provoke his admiration, like the last Palaeologos fighting to the death in the streets of Constantinople in 1453.[4] Byzantium represented the opposite of the "noble savage ideal: an overcivilized, effete polity, sunk in orientalism, servility and decay." Its survival could not be allowed to alter the course of historiography.

The equation of orientalism and inferiority was accepted

---

3. Sir Gavin de Beer, *Gibbon and his World*, London, 1968, pp. 129-31.
4. For Gibbon's prejudice against the Byzantines, see S. Vryonis, "Hellas Resurgent," in L. White, Jr., ed., *The Transformation of the Roman World. Gibbon's Problem after Two Centuries*, Berkeley and Los Angeles, 1966, pp. 92-118.

without question. In the eighteenth century, it seems to have been an axiomatic truth which no one considered worth questioning. Montesquieu, in his *Considérations sur la Grandeur et la Décâdence des Romains*, had remarked that in the series of civil wars from the third century on, those emperors with the support of European legions almost always vanquished those supported by Asian legions.⁵ Even a superficial review of the evidence for such a statement would leave one with grave doubts. Likewise Gibbon remarked, *à propos* the sons of Constantine I, that Constantius was "at the head of the effeminate troops of Asia" while "the martial nations of Europe" supported his brothers. In this particular instance in history, Constantius, backed by his "effeminate troops," emerged as the sole ruler of the Empire, while his brothers fell victim to defeat and assassination. Yet, the theory that orientalism meant decay and effeminacy was unimpaired thereby.

Behind all this is a very old model for the decay of empires, which owes something to Voltaire, to Montesquieu and to Machiavelli, but which ultimately goes back to ancient Greece. In the third book of Plato's *Laws*, where Plato digresses into history, he talks of the causes of decline. "But can a kingship be destroyed, or was any other form of government ever destroyed, by any but the rulers themselves?" he asks, and replies, "no, indeed, by Zeus."⁶ The Persian empire, which Plato took as an example, declined, first because the sons of royalty are naturally corrupted by their wealth, and this principle, operating over the generations, led to the decline of the Achaemenid dynasty. Second, the increasing despotism of the empire, and the loss of individual freedom meant that the people had no community of feeling with their rulers, and would not risk their lives for them.⁷

It is not a long step to the eighteenth chapter of Montesquieu's *Considérations*. The Romans had employed one set of principles in conquering all peoples, but when they succeeded in their goal, the republic could not last. The government had to be changed, and contrary principles adopted by the new government led Rome to

5. Ch. 16.
6. 683e. (Jowett's trans.)
7. 694a-698a.

collapse. There are general causes in every monarchy which make it great, maintain it, or overthrow it, and all accidents are governed by these causes. The Romans conquered the world not merely by warfare, but also prudence, constancy and wisdom, their love of glory, and of their country. These virtues evaporated under the emperors, and the Romans tried to maintain their empire by sheer militarism.[8]

For Gibbon, too, the decline was a natural phenomenon. The "principle of decay" was ripened by prosperity.[9] Gibbon puts the fall of Rome into a philosophic framework and makes it a comprehensible, rational development. The wonder was not that Rome fell, but that she lasted so long. Yet, it should be noted that he is never entirely clear about what the "principle of decay" is. We finish *The Decline and Fall* with an impression of causes rather than a well-argued thesis.[10] Gibbon does not say explicitly that Christianity caused the decline, though by innuendo he points the finger at it. In his *Autobiography*, he indicates that, had he realized that so many Englishmen were attached to what he calls "the name or shadow of Christianity," he would have softened his famous fifteenth and sixteenth chapters on the early church.[11] He does, however, in the conclusion of his third volume, blame the clergy for preaching passive obedience, and thus contributing to the servility of the age. At the same time, he pointed out that, "If the decline of the Roman Empire was hastened by the conversion of Constantine, his victorious religion broke the violence of the fall, and mollified the ferocious temper of the conquerors." In his last volume, we even find Gibbon protesting, in a footnote, against Voltaire's anti-Christian bias.[12]

In general, Gibbon's model for imperial decline contains the same elements as Plato's centuries before. Success and prosperity breed degeneracy and loss of freedom, and apparently effeminacy too: all attributes which, in the western tradition, have been

---

8. Cf. Sheila M. Mason, "Livy and Montesquieu," in T. A. Dorey, ed., *Livy*, London and Toronto, 1971, pp. 118-58.

9. Ch. 38.

10. In Ch. 71, Gibbon enumerates four reasons for the ruin of Rome, but these refer specifically to the destruction of the ancient monuments in the city itself.

11. *Autobiography*, p. 185.

12. Ch. 67, n. 15.

associated particularly with the orient. (It was not, perhaps, an accident that Plato chose Persia as his model for imperial decline.)

And so the conceptual model emerged. The empire reached its zenith at a certain definable point, which Gibbon dated to the Antonine period. Gibbon is not alone among his contemporaries in his admiration for the Antonines.[13] This was a period where the eighteenth-century Whig felt at home, or at least, *thought* he would have felt at home, which is not quite the same thing. From this point on, the Empire followed a kind of unsteady bell-curve downwards, with the conversion of Constantine providing the focal point for a sharp bend towards the vertical. In the east, the Empire took a long time dying, and one suspects that the bell-curve might have got out of hand, had not Gibbon managed partially to disguise the longevity of the Byzantine Empire by passing over its last centuries at break-neck speed, with the plea that his readers might otherwise find them tedious. The various causes of the decline are rational, and perfectly understandable. They can be picked out by shrewd historical minds, to say nothing of a host of amateurs. It will not do to say that the Roman Empire fell because it lost its last battles, and be done with the question. No one would believe us, and this in itself is a measure of the long shadow Gibbon still casts over the problem of the fall of Rome. Even now, if you tell the layman that the British Empire fell because of the National Health Plan, he will put you down for a crank, but if you tell him the Roman Empire fell because of bread and circuses, or some equivalent, he will take you seriously.

One reason for Gibbon's long shadow is that he based *The Decline and Fall* on very solid scholarship, which was not in the tradition of the *philosophe* who turned his hand to history. We do not find Montesquieu, much less Voltaire, figuring in the footnotes of modern books on ancient history, but we may still find respectful references to Edward Gibbon. As Professor Momigliano has already pointed out,[14] when it came to the use of sources, Gibbon was as much a child of the seventeenth century as

---

13. Sir Leslie Stephen, *A History of English Thought*, 3rd ed., London, 1902, I, p. 448.
14. A. Momigliano, "Gibbon's Contribution to Historical Method," *Historia* 2, 1954, pp. 450-63, reprinted in *Studies in Historiography*, New York, 1966, pp. 40-55.

of the eighteenth. The seventeenth century was a period of careful scholarship, which saw the publication of the Theodosian Code, with careful notes by Jacques Godefroy, the work of the Bollandists and the Maurists, and, most important for Gibbon, the *Mémoires écclesiastiques* and the *Histoire des Empereurs* of Lenain de Tillemont. One may suspect that the reason for Gibbon's thin treatment of the last years of the Byzantine Empire was not his proclaimed desire to avoid boring the reader so much as the fact that Tillemont's *Histoire des Empereurs* covered only the first six centuries of the Christian era. Erudition had been a hallmark of ecclesiastical history since Cardinal Baronius in the sixteenth century and perhaps even earlier: Eusebius of Caesarea, the father of ecclesiastical history, made a far greater display of erudition than did his classical counterparts. The *érudits* had fallen, to some extent, into contempt in the eighteenth century, and Gibbon did a great deal to restore respect to careful scholarship.

But Tillemont had been an annalist; Gibbon aimed to be more than that. When he reached the age of Constantine, for instance, he abandoned chronology and broke up the period into special subjects, thereby making it clear that this was an analysis of a set of problems he was writing, not a mere annalistic account.[15] Like the secular historians of the late Roman Empire whom he used, he was conscious of the gulf between ecclesiastical and classical history, and as was pointed out long ago by Suzanne Curchod, the lady whom Gibbon loved tepidly and abandoned dutifully, perhaps the historian who influenced him most was Tacitus. The secular historians of the late Empire were Gibbon's brothers under the skin. Long after paganism was a lost cause, they defended the classical traditions, which the eighteenth century recreated in its collective imagination after its own image. Therefore, in dealing with Constantine, Gibbon gave Zosimus far greater credit than he deserved, as he well knew. Procopius of Caesarea he greeted as a *philosophe* who had somehow survived into an age of darkness, and lacking any Switzerland nearby, had written his indictment of his own period in secret, and left it for a freer age to read.

Gibbon may have been wrong, but he could hardly help it. His

---

15. Cf. D. P. Jordan, "Gibbon's Age of Constantine and the Fall of Rome," *History and Theory* 8, 1967, pp. 71-96.

eighteenth-century background left him peculiarly unfitted to understand the thought-world of the late Empire, when free thinkers did not exist, and human nature and aspirations were very different from those of Gibbon's contemporaries: a possibility his century did not contemplate. Gibbon's Constantine, who is really an eighteenth-century politician looking out for his own interests, re-emerged, with a few changes, as Jacob Burckhardt's Constantine, and he remains a controversial figure.

I want to question the validity of Gibbon's model, but first let me remark on its extraordinary vitality. Gibbon did not found a school, but he has been followed by a gaggle of historians who have promoted various reasonable causes for Rome's fall. Almost all of them have, to some extent, followed Gibbon's model, which they have sought to emend, supplement, or in part, replace. Most of them accept the view that empires age, and that there is a principle of decay which proceeds from natural causes. Most of these causes which have been propounded for Rome's fall are not untrue, in the sense that some solid evidence can usually be found for them. Nevertheless, these historians reflect the intellectual *milieux* of their own times as much as Gibbon does. Nowadays, it is more a reflection of our technological society than the overwhelming nature of the evidence which leads us to speak seriously of lead poisoning[16] as a cause for Rome's fall, or the failure to use a rigid horse collar, or ignorance of the stirrup. The safety of the water drunk in most historical periods, including our own, has not been above question. But if lead poisoning is to be proved responsible for killing off the Roman upper classes, the first step is to induce scientists to agree that water carried in lead pipes does cause lead poisoning, and that they decline to do. As for the Roman horse collar, the inadequacy of which Commandant Lefebvre des Noëttes pointed out in 1931:[17] before we

16. Cf. C. Gilfillan, "Roman Culture and Dysgenic Lead Poisoning," *The Mankind Quarterly* 5, 1965, pp. 3-20, reprinted in M. Chambers, ed., *The Fall of Rome. Can it be Explained?*, 2nd ed., New York, 1970, pp. 55-59.

17. Richard Lefebvre des Noëttes, *L'attalage; le cheval de selle à travers les âges: contribution à l'histoire de l'esclavage*. 2 vols. Paris, 1931, I, pp. 83-88. For criticism, see P. Vigneron, *Le cheval dans l'Antiquite greco-romaine (Des guerres médiques aux grands invasions) Contribution a l'histoire des techniques*. Annales de l'Est. Mémoire 35. Nancy, 1968. Cf. J. Needham, in R. Dawson, ed., *The Legacy of China*, Oxford, 1964, pp. 268-74.

allow ourselves to be too greatly impressed, we should remember the nature of the archaeological evidence, and the extent to which it has increased over the last forty years. The breaststrap harness which should not appear in Europe until the eighth century, seems to me to be found on the arch of Septimius Severus at Lepcis Magna, and there is an example of a horse collar, albeit an ill-fitting one, on a Roman relief from Trier.[18] Nor did the offending Roman neck collar fade out with the decline of Rome; it was used by the German army as late as 1914. The situation is unclear. Yet, these technological theories are taken very seriously now, as any teacher of ancient history can testify, and far be it for me to slight fashionable history.

The first problem with Gibbon's model is that it saw Roman history in terms of a climax, defined as the Antonine period, followed by changes indicating decline from that climax. In so doing, it made no distinction between changes which indicated decay, and those which were simply a healthy effort to readjust to new circumstances. We cannot altogether blame Gibbon for this: apart from his eighteenth-century outlook, which did not teach him to appreciate change, he had the evidence of the Theodosian Code, which seemed to show a stalemated society, with status and occupation frozen by law. Actually, the opposite is closer to the truth. Social mobility was probably much greater in the late Empire than earlier under the principate. The laws intended to fix categories of persons and their descendants to their occupations reveal the volume of the movement they were designed — and failed — to check.[19] These laws were enforced only with the greatest difficulty, which is why they are repeated so often in the Code.

In fact, one could argue that the empire from the Severi to Justinian is the history of readjustment to rapidly changing circumstances. The eastern segment made it through. It found a new ideology. Christianity was harnessed. The empire became the imitation of Heaven, the emperor the viceregent of God and the

---

18. For illustrations, see: S. Perowne, *Caesars and Saints*, New York, 1963, Pl. 4b; E. Wightman, *Roman Trier and the Treveri*, London, 1970, Pl. 15a.

19. A. H. M. Jones, "The Caste System in the Later Roman Empire," *Eirene* 8, 1970, pp. 79-96.

friend of the Logos, and the holy men and ascetics, including the stylite saints whom Gibbon considered appalling, did not forget their duties to this world.[20] The extraordinary source of vitality which this new ideology supplied to Byzantium was something Gibbon was not fitted to understand.

We cannot say whether or not the western half of the empire could have followed the pattern of the east, for the age of the western fathers lasted hardly more than a generation. We should not underestimate the impact of the barbarian invasions on the church simply because it survived. In Africa, where the first Latin-speaking Christian community had emerged in the west, the Vandal king Huneric exiled a good portion of the bishops to Corsica to chop down timber for the Vandal fleet. No more Augustines came out of Africa. We can argue that the western Empire could never have followed the pattern of the east: that western Christianity always implied greater alienation from society than it did in the east,[21] or that the western economy was too weak, or manpower insufficient. It may be true that the fall was somehow inevitable. But there is no way now of demonstrating that what happened to the western Empire had to happen, and I greatly suspect that its period of readjustment was cut short because the political organization disintegrated under the impact of one battle too many lost to the barbarians.

The second problem with Gibbon's model is that, in its emphasis on rational, internal causes, it pays insufficient attention to the irrational, unquantifiable element. In the third century A.D., the empire was subject to suddenly increased pressure from the barbarians. This was a period of political and economic chaos, when one might have expected the Empire to fall apart, if it were following any reasonable pattern. But the political organization held together, and much changed, the Empire survived. From Diocletian to Valens, the Empire had a breathing space, before pressure mounted sharply once again. This time, the reason was the Black Huns, thrusting westwards from the steppe, and though

---

20. Cf. Peter Brown, "The Rise and Function of the Holy Men in Late Antiquity," *JRS* 61, 1971, pp. 80-101.
21. Cf. W. H. C. Frend, "Paulinus of Nola and the Last Century of the Western Empire," *JRS* 59, 1969, pp. 1-11.

I am sure there were reasonable causes for the Hun migration, I am equally sure they had nothing to do with what was going on inside the Roman Empire. To that extent, the Hun migration is an irrational factor.

Now, to give another example of the irrational: while the Empire faced its moment of truth, Sassanid Persia was seriously embarrassed by the White or Ephthalite Huns. Consequently, Persia was occupied defending itself, and left Rome's eastern frontier relatively peaceful until the reign of Justin I. Who knows what might have happened if Constantinople had faced pressure in the east as well as the Balkans? The government at Ravenna had no such good fortune. Not only did it have a long frontier to defend, but it encountered the proverbial last straw. Among its enemies was the one leader of genius whom the barbarians produced, Genseric, the Vandal king. Able, purposeful and intolerant of orthodox Christianity, Genseric gave the Asding Vandals an importance far greater than their numbers and strength warranted.

The loss of Africa to the Vandals meant not only the loss of a secure food supply, and a source of revenue for Ravenna, but also the loss of control of the sea. A century later, Belisarius' fleet, making its way to Africa from Sicily, was still terrified of the reputation of the Vandal fleet. Yet the story of the Vandal conquest provides a number of very nice examples of the irrational. Suppose the emperor Leo's expedition against the Vandals had been led by an abler man than Basiliscus? Or that Leo had not had to recall his second expedition for fear of Aspar at home? Neither at Ravenna nor Constantinople was there any failure to understand the importance of Africa, or what its loss meant, but an evil genius seemed to preside over all efforts to recover it until Justinian.

I am not the first to point out the importance of the Vandal seizure of Africa for the fall of Rome. Norman Baynes, in a review of Henri Pirenne's *Les Villes du Moyen Âge* in 1929,[22] argued that it was not the Arab fleet which ended the unity of the Mediterranean, as Pirenne had tried to demonstrate, but the

---

22. *JRS* 19, 1929, pp. 224-35.

Vandal pirate fleet based in Carthage. A few years ago, a New Zealand scholar, J. J. Saunders,[23] resurrected the thesis, and put forward the view that, but for the Vandal seizure of Africa, the western Empire would have weathered the storm. I should like to add that, had not the Vandals had leadership significantly superior to that of the other barbarian tribes who entered the Empire, it is unlikely they could have played the role they did.

To return to Edward Gibbon. I suppose we shall always accept his concepts about the decline and fall to some extent. He approached one of the great events in history with enormous confidence, rationalized it, made it very sensible and presented it all in stately prose. But one aspect of his model we should avoid. The Roman Empire did have to change, but it did not have to fall. The inevitability of the fall is a concept with a long respectable history: it owes something to Plato, who propounded a theory of the internal decay of empires, something to the prologue of Florus, who compared Rome's history to the aging of a man, but it owes much of its respectability and almost all its stateliness to Edward Gibbon. Yet, if we turn to the history of the fifth century, we find it full of unanswered and unanswerable questions: useless queries on a par with such items as "What if the battle of Waterloo had gone the other way?" or "What if the RAF had lost the Battle of Britain?" What if there had been no Genseric to lead the Vandals to Africa? Would it have saved the western empire, and destroyed the intellectual edifices of Spengler and Toynbee? Would Gibbon then have felt the same romantic urge to describe the fall of Rome, as he listened to the monks chant in Sta. Maria in Aracoeli on the Capitoline, which he erroneously believed was the Temple of Jupiter?

Allan Evans

---

23. "The Debate on the Fall of Rome," *History* 48, 1963, pp. 1-17.

A Genevan Reaction
to Diderot's Pensées philosophiques:
Jacques-François de Luc

Jacques-François de Luc was a proud citizen of eighteenth-century Geneva. That his name is not forgotten to-day is due largely to his friendship with another and more eminent "citoyen de Genève," Jean-Jacques Rousseau, and to the varied writings of his son Jacques-André who, with a much sounder and more extensive scientific knowledge than his father, made "un des plus honorables efforts qui aient été tentés au XVIIIe siècle pour combattre par les armes de la science, l'esprit d'incrédulité et les préjugés philosophiques du temps."[1] Not for these reasons did the elder de Luc probably expect to be remembered by posterity, but for a book whose aim, although not method, was similar to that attributed to his son's work in the passage just quoted: his *Observations sur les savants incrédules et sur quelques-uns de leurs écrits*, published in Geneva in 1762.

Its author is characterized by J. S. Spink in these terms: "Il était très pieux, très honnête, très patriotique et 'républicain,' très compassé et très ennuyeux. Il trouvait son plaisir dans les manoeuvres politiques et les fêtes patriotiques."[2] And, in fact, de Luc had been involved in the political life of his native city since the civil disturbances of the 1730s: "le parti des Représentants n'avait pas de chef plus actif que ce maître en horlogerie," states Sayous.[3] But what inspired him to write his *Observations sur les savants incrédules* was his profound religious convictions. This work reveals him as a sincere Protestant Christian, grieved by the inroads into Christian faith made by the unbelief expressed by so many contemporary writers. He does not use the term "philo-

---

1. A. Sayous, *Histoire de la littérature française à l'étranger. Le dix-huitième siècle*, 2 vols., Paris, 1861, I, p. 451.
2. John S. Spink, *Jean-Jacques Rousseau et Genève*, Paris, 1934, pp. 40-41.
3. *Op. cit.*, I, p. 443.

sophe" to refer to such authors — in his title or elsewhere — no doubt for reasons given in his "Discours préliminaire": "La Philosophie proprement ainsi nommée, étant l'amour de la Sagesse et l'Ecriture Sainte étant le Livre qui l'enseigne le plus parfaitement; tout Savant né Chrétien, à qui l'étude des Sciences humaines a fait perdre la Foi, pourra bien être Médecin éclairé, Géomètre profond, grand Physicien, Poète célèbre;... mais il ne sera jamais un vrai Philosophe."[4]

In the forty-two chapters of this book he touches on certain aspects of the work of Voltaire, Mandeville, Diderot, Toussaint, La Mettrie and others, refuting, in the light of his faith, particular points in their arguments. Its only unity is to be found in the author's Christian convictions and in his hostility to the "savants incrédules." His method is to take up a point made in one of their works, comment upon or refute it, then pass along to a more or less related point, not necessarily in the same work. Sometimes a lengthy discussion ensues, either dealing with the work being criticized or suggested by a point made in the work, the latter situation leading typically to an elaboration of his ideas concerning some aspect of Christianity.

Although he is most angered by atheism, de Luc's attitude is in general rather charitable towards the writers he criticizes; but so sure is he of possessing the Truth that inevitably there is a touch of condescension in the pity he expresses for them in their lack of faith. In the best Christian tradition, he sees them as victims of excessive pride and of a presumption which he describes as "un nuage qui dérobe à leurs yeux la plus essentielle de toutes les Sciences, celle du salut" (p. 26). It is on such a note that he concludes his book, quoting twenty-two lines of a poem by Jean-Baptiste Rousseau to emphasize his point that true humility of heart will allow the unbelievers to be persuaded of the truth of Christianity. This idea echoes as a *leitmotif* throughout this work and would appear to be for de Luc the supreme explanation of unbelief. Although this pride may have its source in learning, de Luc is not hostile to knowledge and learning in themselves, for if

---

4. Jacques-François de Luc, *Observations sur les savants incrédules et sur quelques-uns de leurs écrits*, Genève, 1762, pp. 10-11. All further references to this work are to this edition. Spelling has been modernized.

approached with humility, they enlighten the path to Salvation. The reader of the *Observations* can sense a genuine puzzlement on de Luc's part as to why these writers fail to be convinced by the Scriptures, and he twice uses the term "égarements étranges" in his chapter-titles to refer to what obviously seems to him a perversity, a blindness of which he can scarcely conceive. His typically Protestant faith in the Scriptures is untouched by the Biblical criticism of the previous hundred years; questions of textual accuracy, authenticity and the like[5] are irrelevant to this man for whom the Scriptures are self-justifying.

The engraving to be found on the title-page of the original edition of the *Observations* epitomizes this attitude, and illustrates very well the prestige de Luc attached to the Scriptures. Around the base of a short pedestal are such objects as sword, shield and helmet; on top of it, as on a lectern, a book labelled *Ste Bible* lies open, and from it rays of light emanate, penetrating the few dark clouds that lie in their path. Enlightenment, that central metaphor of the century, obviously does not have the same meaning for de Luc as for the *philosophes*, whose works might well be represented by the dark clouds threatening to cast a shadow on the source of all light. Certainly for de Luc their writings do not bring a freeing of man from the night of prejudice and superstition, but rather add to the human being's difficulties in his search for spiritual enlightenment.

Among the first writers to be criticized is "l'auteur des *Pensées philosophiques*." Never is Diderot named, for the anonymity which accompanied this work when it was published in 1746 apparently remained for de Luc as complete as ever in 1762.[6] Besides attacking this early work of Diderot, de Luc also deals briefly at various points with the translator and annotator of Shaftesbury's *Inquiry concerning Virtue or Merit*,[7] an anonymous individual whom he has no reason to associate with "l'auteur des *Pensées philosophiques*," but who, he realizes, has gone beyond a mere translation and has espoused Shaftesbury's ideas (p. 392). These are the only works of Diderot with which he deals.

5. See below, p. 277.
6. Such is also the case for Toussaint's *Les Moeurs*, 1748.
7. French version by Diderot: *Essai sur le mérite et la vertu*, 1745.

His concern is only with content. He is too profoundly involved in revealing the errors of his opponent to consider any literary qualities, to appreciate the concision and liveliness of style which undoubtedly contributed to the success of the *Pensées philosophiques*.[8] Only once does de Luc touch on such matters: in Chapter 2 he admits that it is "par des phrases bien tournées à la vérité" that the author expresses his ideas. This obliviousness to literary qualities is seen in de Luc's failure — in common with many contemporaries — to appreciate the structure of Diderot's work or to grasp the irony which occasionally elicits the reader's complicity.

Given de Luc's religious views, it is not to be wondered at that the first words of the *Pensées philosophiques*, "J'écris de Dieu," should arouse the critic's anger. How dare he say this, de Luc asks, "en fermant les yeux à l'éclatante lumière de la Révélation?" (p. 22). He points disgustedly to such a statement as "Il ne faut imaginer Dieu ni trop bon ni trop méchant" as a natural result of such perverseness. An author who talks in this way casts no little doubt on such statements as that he is "pénétré d'une vénération profonde pour cet Etre infiniment parfait" (pp. 22-24). Diderot's tendency to ignore Christian revelation comes in for indirect attack in de Luc's remarks on *Pensée* 25, which begins with the statement: "Qu'est-ce que Dieu? question qu'on fait aux enfants et à laquelle les Philosophes ont bien de la peine à répondre."[9] De Luc is here impressed with the wrongheadedness of Diderot's point. We are not asking for information, he says; this is merely a pedagogical device for teaching the child about what Scripture has revealed to us of God's perfections (pp. 36-38). Although the subject of Christian education is thus involved, de Luc makes no reference to the rest of this *Pensée*, which stresses the need to take the child's intellectual capacity into account by not telling him of God too early, and in the same breath, of telling him of ghosts, werewolves and the like: "On lui inculque une des plus im-

---

8. Other refuters were more aware of these qualities than de Luc. Cf. Robert Niklaus, "Baron de Gaufridi's Refutation of Diderot's *Pensées philosophiques*," *Romanic Review* 43, 1952, pp. 89-90.

9. Denis Diderot, *Pensées philosophiques*, ed. R. Niklaus, Genève, 1950, p. 20. All further references to this work are to this edition. Spelling has been modernized.

portantes vérités, d'une manière capable de la décrier un jour au tribunal de sa raison" (p. 20). But without specifically answering this charge, de Luc does devote several pages at this point to Christian education, rejecting Diderot's rationalistic assumptions by stressing the need for the child to be taught the Divine attributes early, and not waiting for reason to achieve a certain maturity, as recommended by an "auteur chrétien que je suis bien éloigné de confondre avec les auteurs incrédules," (p. 41) undoubtedly Jean-Jacques Rousseau.[10]

Much later in his book de Luc returns to our unbelievers' ignoring of revelation and questions the "religieux respect" for revelation professed by Diderot and Shaftesbury, since in fact they never fall back on its authority (p. 393). "Cependant, il ne peut y avoir d'autorité plus sûre ni plus respectable dans toutes les matières de ce genre," he adds after bemoaning the fact that "s'ils traitent du mérite, de la Vertu, de Dieu même; il leur suffit d'annoncer un Ouvrage philosophique, pour se croire en droit d'en exclure la Révélation" (p. 394). What a succinctly expressed reaction to that secularization of thought so characteristic of the Enlightenment!

Ironically, however, de Luc too shows traces of this secularization in certain of his ethical and religious ideas, to a consideration of which we shall now turn.

The first five of the *Pensées philosophiques* contain one of the many eighteenth-century apologia of the passions. Diderot resents their always being viewed unfavourably and insists that only great passions can lead to great things. "Sans elles," he proclaims in a very characteristic way, "plus de sublime, soit dans les moeurs, soit dans les ouvrages" (p. 4). Although insisting that "la contrainte anéantit la grandeur et l'énergie de la nature," (p. 4) he admits the need for establishing harmony among the passions and deplores the ascetic's attempt to destroy all passions (p. 5). De Luc has been sufficiently influenced by the optimistic moral systems of the previous half-century that he does not take exception to most of Diderot's remarks on this subject. He does not object to the enthusiasm with which, in these *Pensées*, the

---

10. Rousseau is referred to elsewhere (p. 275) as "un vrai chrétien philosophe."

passions are associated with forces of nature. Quite probably his un-philosophic mind does not perceive the incompatibility of Diderot's attitude with traditional ethics. But de Luc's common sense makes him admit that certain passions are useful, namely, "ces affections de l'âme qui lui ont été données par le Créateur" (p. 32). Using imagery that can be found in Fontenelle, Pope and Voltaire among others and which undoubtedly was a commonplace by 1762, de Luc says that such passions are "aussi nécessaires à l'homme que les vents aux navigateurs" (p. 32). As for excessive passions which lead to profligacy and vice, religion does indeed teach us to control and repress them. De Luc's chief objection concerns Diderot's attack on the "dévot qui se tourmente comme un forcené pour ne rien désirer, ne rien aimer, ne rien sentir" (p. 5). De Luc agrees that any such attempt to destroy the passions is wrong, but insists that this is not characteristic of the true Christian. Like many Genevan pastors of this period,[11] he rejects asceticism as a legitimate aspect of Christianity; such "dévots" are fanatics worthy of condemnation, since they reject the all-important social rôle of Christianity, upon which de Luc generally puts much emphasis: "le but de notre sainte Religion étant de porter les hommes à s'aimer, à se supporter, à se servir réciproquement, elle ne peut autoriser en aucune manière *Pacôme* ni *les Stilites*" (p. 34). Virtue is something to be practised within society and is not incompatible with "les Sciences et les innocentes douceurs de la vie" (p. 328). Human nature, though subject to weakness and corruption, is viewed quite optimistically by de Luc when he says, "L'homme est fait à l'Image de Dieu. C'est-à-dire, qu'il y a originairement dans l'homme un principe de toutes les Vertus morales, et tous les secours nécessaires pour conserver cette éminente prérogative" (p. 329). What a mellowing there has been of that stern Calvinist doctrine with its emphasis on original sin and predestination, which had dominated Geneva two centuries earlier! De Luc's is a gentler, more reasonable version of Christianity, in keeping with the change that came over the moral and religious tone in Geneva in the eighteenth century. "Le néo-calvinisme avait humanisé les caractères et levé le siège des

---

11. See Spink, *op. cit.*, p. 146.

consciences," as V. Rossel expresses it.[12] And J. S. Spink shows that Genevan pastors, "sous l'influence laïque," gave increasing importance in their thought to man's "conscience morale," even going so far as to believe in man's natural goodness.[13] The influence of French and English deists would appear to have penetrated the once-impregnable stronghold of Genevan Calvinism.

On the metaphysical level too, deistic influence probably accounts for de Luc's making no mention of *Pensées* 18, 19 and 20. In them, Diderot proclaims that the processes of nature, as revealed in the discoveries made by certain natural scientists of the previous one hundred years, constitute a far more decisive argument against atheists than do the "sublimes méditations" of rationalists like Descartes or Malebranche. That de Luc does not touch on these three *Pensées* suggests that these arguments − so prevalent in the early eighteenth century − for the existence of God based on the order of Nature had been absorbed into de Luc's Christianity, as they had been into that of many of his contemporaries.

And deistic influence pervades those pages in which de Luc distinguishes between natural and revealed religion and explains his view of the relationship between the two. This he feels impelled to do in connection with the last of the *Pensées philosophiques*, where Diderot, inspired by a line of questioning used by Cicero to determine the most courageous nation, imagines a dialogue in which devotees of each of several religions answer that after their own religion, "la religion naturelle" would be the one they preferred. He then returns to Cicero for the conclusion: "Or ceux à qui l'on accorde la seconde place d'un consentement unanime, et qui ne cèdent la première à personne, méritent incontestablement celle-ci" (p. 45). Is this Diderot's opinion? Most probably not, if we take into account his prefatory comment in this *Pensée* where he qualifies this line of reasoning as being "plus singulier peut-être que solide." Certainly this suggests an unwillingness to conclude one way or the other without fuller

12. Virgile Rossel, *Histoire littéraire de la Suisse romande*, 2 vols., Paris, 1889 & 1891, II, p. 72.
13. *Op. cit.*, p. 144.

examination than a work of this kind allows. The most obvious implication of this conclusion is the deistic notion that all religion can be reduced to a belief in a Supreme Being, a belief which makes revealed religions superfluous.[14]

De Luc rejects this reasoning, claiming to bring out its sophistry by distinguishing between two kinds of natural religions: "L'une du monde, introduite par l'ignorance et la corruption; l'autre de Dieu, conforme à la Révélation et que la Raison bien cultivée est capable de découvrir." Whence he can conclude that "l'argument de notre Auteur n'est donc fondé que sur un équivoque" (p. 222). His own argument is not clear and seems beside the point, nor is it rendered any clearer or more relevant by his going on to concede, as it were, that Christianity does differ from "la Religion naturelle corrompue," but that it is also destined to "rétablir la vraie Religion naturelle dans toute sa pureté." Without considering the claims of the other religions mentioned by Diderot, de Luc blithely concludes that "Le Christianisme doit donc avoir le premier rang, s'il n'est que le Naturalisme même porté à un plus haut degré de perfection" (p. 223).

De Luc devotes chapter XXIV to demonstrating that this last statement is true, but what it really demonstrates is the extent to which he has absorbed the deistic and rationalist assumptions of the age. Reason, he says, is the most excellent of the faculties with which the Creator has endowed man, and when "bien cultivée" can reveal God to man through contemplation of the universe. Natural religion, "qui vient de Dieu par la Raison, indépendamment de la Religion révélée," consists in paying homage to the Creator for his benefits and in following the Golden Rule, "le principe de la Justice" (p. 224). Such attitudes were prevalent in the eighteenth century and constituted the essential aspects of deism. But de Luc obviously has no intention of leaving the matter at this point. What of revelation? Why is it necessary? How is it related to natural religion? It was needed because of "le malheureux empire que la plupart des hommes ont laissé prendre

---

14. Cf. Voltaire's well-known dramatization of this idea in *Zadig*, chapter 12 ("Le Souper").

plus ou moins à leurs passions déréglées" which has corrupted and perverted reason. God revealed his will "en envoyant son Fils unique au monde, qui, par son exemple et ses enseignements a rétabli la Religion naturelle à un tel degré de clarté, que si la Raison est à cet égard un flambeau pour éclairer ceux qui la cultivaient d'une manière convenable, l'Evangile est un Soleil pour ceux qui l'étudient avec *humilité de coeur*" (p. 224).

Similar ideas were to be found in the sermons of Genevan pastors in the mid-eighteenth century[15] and were already current in England at the turn of the century among the "rational supernaturalists." The famous theologian Samuel Clarke, for example, held that men had lost their knowledge of natural religion, and that "there was plainly wanting a divine revelation to recover mankind out of their universal corruption and degeneracy." Ignorance and prejudices had obscured the bare light of reason, making necessary "some particular revelation to discover in what manner . . . God might acceptably be worshipped."[16] John Tillotson, Archbishop of Canterbury, in a very typical argument, insisted that revelation does not change natural religion but merely clarifies it. "Natural Religion is the foundation of all revealed religion and revelation is designed simply to establish its duties."[17]

De Luc wishes to show, in the tradition of the rational supernaturalists, that revelation is not inconsistent with rational religion, that if "la Religion Chrétienne . . . contient des choses qui surpassent en effet les lumières de la Saine Raison, elle n'en renferme aucune qui lui soit véritablement contraire" (p. 226). So, in pages bristling with quotations from the Bible, he proceeds to examine such doctrines as the Trinity and the Redemption. His discussion reveals a close knowledge of the New Testament in particular and a certain ingenuity in dealing with these thorny questions. Such pages no doubt inspired the rather cutting remarks of Charles Bonnet in a letter to Haller, where he remarks on "la liberté qu'il [de Luc] a prise de faire le théologien en traitant des

---

15. See Spink, *op. cit.*, pp. 128 ff.
16. Samuel Clarke, *Boyle Lectures*, 1705, as quoted at length in J. H. Randall, Jr., *The Career of Philosophy*, 2 vols., New York, 1962, I, p. 695.
17. John Tillotson, *Works* (ed. 1857), II, p. 133, as quoted in Randall, *op. cit.*, I, p. 694.

dogmes dont il eut mieux fait de ne point parler."[18] And his arguments are likely to remain unconvincing to any who do not accept the premise that "L'Ecriture sainte étant divinement inspirée ne peut rien enseigner de contraire à la saine Raison, qui est une émanation de la même source" (p. 236). Reason, then, for this eighteenth-century Christian is given a very honourable position and is closely associated with religious faith. No fideism here!

But, of course, it is not reason that has primacy in de Luc's thinking, but faith. In what would undoubtedly be for de Luc a central chapter in his book, "Essai sur la foi chrétienne," the author deals with the relationship between the two. But in speaking of the role of reason in faith, de Luc refers, not to men in general but to "savants chrétiens," that is, to those who already hold this faith. Reason acquaints them with the evidence of the proofs of the Scriptures' divinity, it makes them realize that God in his wisdom has not allowed us in this life to plumb the depths of religious truths; moreover, it is reason that teaches them that (quoting St. Luke) *"un coeur honnête et bon* est le plus sûr moyen de parvenir à la Foi Chrétienne" (p. 276). In short, for those possessed of humility, "la Foi Chrétienne est une aide sûre à la saine Raison pour lui faire entrevoir dans le vrai sens de l'Ecriture sainte, les merveilles de notre salut, au travers du voile sacré qui les enveloppe" (pp. 279-80). This chapter is an eloquent statement of the primacy of faith, viewed as a gift of God, never refused to the humble. Its eloquence, perhaps echoing the sermons of Genevan pastors, results from the strength of the author's convictions; it is a sort of "profession de foi." But de Luc never loses sight of the role of reason, and marvels at a statement that Voltaire, in his poetry, makes of Emperor Julian: "Infidèle à la Foi, fidèle à la Raison" (p. 280). Only ignorance of the true faith can account for such oppositions, thinks de Luc; so imbued is he with both the prestige of reason and the truth of Christianity that any such contradiction is simply unthinkable.

It is not, then, the rationalistic or deistic tendencies of "l'auteur des *Pensées philosophiques*" which arouse de Luc to

---

18. Rousseau, *Correspondance complète*, ed. R. A. Leigh, Genève, 1970, XI, p. 86.

anger, but rather any suggestion that atheism may not be, metaphysically and morally, an impossible position to defend. In *Pensée* 21, Diderot quotes a "professeur célèbre"[19] as granting that movement is essential to matter, but refusing to conclude that the world has resulted from the fortuitous play of atoms. "J'aimerais autant que vous me dissiez que l'Iliade d'Homère ou la Henriade de Voltaire est un résultat de jets fortuits de caractères," he is quoted as saying. Diderot declares that he would be careful not to reason this way with an atheist, who could proceed to take as his premise that "la difficulté de l'événement est compensée par la quantité de jets," and conclude that, given infinite time, any combination of matter is possible (pp. 16-18). What de Luc objects to here is Diderot's allowing doubt to be cast on the necessity of God's existence and for allowing the idea that movement is essential to matter to go unchallenged; he should have shown, says de Luc, that the atheists can never prove this (pp. 35-36). De Luc clearly does not understand the methods of a mind like that of Diderot, who in this work is deliberately exploring several points of view, creating an implicit dialogue. It is true that the atheist does seem to be given a great advantage and is allowed to go on at such length that René Etiemble is convinced that this represents Diderot's true opinion even in 1746.[20] Whether it was or not, his method does not call for explicit refutation of the atheist; rather it thrives on confrontation of divergent attitudes, as his later predilection for the dialogue form will indicate.

Elsewhere in his *Observations* de Luc finds a similar "étrange partialité" for atheism in "les auteurs de la *Philosophie morale*," i.e., in Shaftesbury and in his translator and annotator Diderot (pp. 403 ff.). Both say that "pour être convaincu qu'il y a du profit à être vertueux, il n'est pas nécessaire de croire en Dieu." Any such attempt to separate religion and morality de Luc considers deplorable enough, but he proceeds to point out that

---

19. Identified by R. Niklaus in his edition of *Pensées philosophiques* as probably D. F. Rivard, author of *Instruction pour la jeunesse sur la religion, et sur plusieurs sciences naturelles*.

20. René Etiemble, "Structure et sens des *Pensées philosophiques*," *Romanische Forschungen* 74, 1962, pp. 1-10.

"l'auteur français" goes further than his original by adding a note: "Hobbes était bon citoyen, bon parent, bon ami et ne croyait point en Dieu." De Luc is not vanquished nor even discouraged by such a statement; he simply refuses to believe it, declaring the opposite to be true and mentioning certain events in Hobbes' life which bring out the cowardliness and devotion to expediency of this "vil athée" (p. 406). There is no evidence that de Luc had any first-hand knowledge of Hobbes' work. Given his hatred of atheists, he is probably echoing the sentiments of many an anti-Hobbesian work and interpreting these events in the philosopher's life in the light of his own prejudices; but he nevertheless calls these events proofs of Hobbes' immoral behaviour. He accepts the time-worn assumption that atheism means immorality, presumably ignoring[21] Pierre Bayle's well-known defence of an atheistic society, a defence based on the inconsistency of human nature. De Luc quotes Diderot's echoing of Bayle: "Les hommes ne sont pas conséquents; on offense un Dieu dont on admet l'existence et on nie l'existence d'un Dieu dont on a bien mérité," (p. 407) only to dismiss it contemptuously, for Hobbes and other atheists are quite consistent: "ils prouvent la vérité de ces paroles de l'Ecriture Sainte: *L'insensé a dit en son coeur, il n'y a point de Dieu*," a favourite quotation of our author. Atheism produces a more emotional reaction in de Luc than any other subject (except possibly the "monstrous errors" of Mandeville!), and calls forth his most intemperate, least charitable language. But it is this discussion of atheism that reveals de Luc's hostility to the separation of religion and morality, a separation which has been shown to have been widely accepted in intellectual circles, at least in France, by 1740.[22] So de Luc, while accepting certain attitudes associated with the secularization of ethics, vigorously rejects the legitimacy of this separation in itself.

Such are de Luc's reactions to some of the more significant parts of Diderot's two earliest works touching on moral or metaphysical questions. But our Genevan Protestant also lavishes much attention on those *Pensées* which deal with the accuracy of

21. De Luc was acquainted with the work of Pierre Bayle, as can be seen from occasional references to it in the *Observations*.
22. See Pierre Hermand, *Les Idées morales de Diderot*, Paris, 1923, chapter I.

the Scriptures and with the early Christians and their pagan opponents, in particular Emperor Julian. This is probably the least original part of the *Pensées philosophiques*, but at the same time very typical of Enlightenment opinion on these subjects.

De Luc treats together the four *Pensées* 43 to 46 and, after quoting from them at some length, concludes that "toute personne judicieuse . . . reconnaîtra sans peine qu'elles forment un très dangereux mélange de bonnes et de mauvaises choses" (p. 54). Then he proceeds to separate these things into two lists, a method guaranteed to rob them of their significance by removing them from context. It also makes the irony of certain statements much less obvious, an irony which presumably the pedestrian mind of de Luc was incapable of perceiving. He can approve of such sentiments as: "Le Christianisme est la plus sainte et la plus douce des religions," without noticing that the lines which follow it in Diderot's text cast no little doubt on the author's sincerity (pp. 27-28). Diderot's description (through an edict of Emperor Julian) of the extent to which "les premiers enfants de l'Eglise sont sortis plus d'une fois de la modération et de la patience qui leur étaient prescrites" (p. 27) leaves one wondering why de Luc does not see through the *philosophe*'s irony. De Luc does realize that when Diderot refers to "l'humeur des zélés de son temps," he is using pejorative terms in reference to the Christians of the fourth century (p. 200). And in doing so, Diderot is contrasting them with the wisdom of Emperor Julian.

Julian (A.D. 331-363), traditionally referred to as "The Apostate," was a natural focus for controversy between believers and unbelievers in the eighteenth century.[23] The latter tried to show that Julian had been the victim of slander by generations of Christians, who hated him for his desertion of Christianity and attributed all sorts of evil actions to him. He now came to be thought of as a wise philosopher and proponent of tolerance. Voltaire sees him as a heroic figure, a sage equal to Marcus Aurclius: "Si vous le suivez dans sa maison, dans les camps, dans les batailles, dans ses moeurs, dans sa conduite, dans ses écrits,

---

23. See J. S. Spink, "The Reputation of Julian the 'Apostate' in the Enlightenment," in *Studies on Voltaire and the Eighteenth Century*, 72, 1967, pp. 1399-1415.

vous le trouvez partout égal à Marc-Aurèle."[24] In this rehabilitation of Julian, the *philosophes* tended to make him one of themselves, to overlook his attachment to pagan rites and myths. "Julian's religion was a mixture, common in that age, of philosophy, antiquarianism and superstition," writes A. H. M. Jones,[25] but the *philosophes* stressed only the first of these aspects, and Voltaire even adduces *raisons d'état* to account for Julian's seemingly incongruous concern for the forms of paganism.[26] On the other hand, this rehabilitation was a much-needed reaction to the particularly violent hostility towards Julian traditionally found in Christianity, more than against most pagans because Julian had supposedly been brought up a Christian and then betrayed his religion, an act viewed with a special horror by Christians. But had he, in fact, been an apostate to Christianity? This is the approach that Voltaire takes,[27] it is the approach that we find in the *Pensées philosophiques* where, after quoting an edict of toleration issued by Julian, Diderot concludes, echoing Shaftesbury's *Miscellaneous Reflections*: "Tels étaient les sentiments de ce Prince, à qui l'on peut reprocher le paganisme, mais non l'apostasie: il passa les premières années de sa vie sous différents maîtres et dans différentes écoles, et fit dans un âge plus avancé un choix infortuné; il se décida malheureusement pour le culte de ses aïeux et les Dieux de son pays" (p. 29). De Luc fails to comment on the irony in this statement, in which the terms used to describe the choice made by Julian contradict the judgement of them as expressed in such words as "infortuné" and "malheureusement." De Luc is so imbued with the desirability of Christianity and wickedness of paganism that it is quite probable that he was oblivious to the irony here and simply nodded his head approvingly. Certainly he has no doubts about Julian's apostasy. In the list of bad things to be found in these pages of Diderot is the fact that the author "extenue artificieusement l'Apostasie de Julien" (p. 55).

But the main part of de Luc's criticism is the use to which

24. Voltaire, *Oeuvres complètes*, ed. Louis Moland, Paris, 1877-82, XIX, p. 542.
25. *Decline of the Ancient World*, London, 1966, p. 59.
26. *Op. cit.*, XXVI, p. 288.
27. *Op. cit.*, XXVIII, p. 6; XXIX, p. 246.

Diderot puts a long quotation from an edict of Julian, "fragments choisis et rapportés à dessein de faire passer Julien pour Philosophe," as de Luc quite rightly says. He will try to show that these words of Julian are "au contraire une preuve évidente de la perversité de son coeur" (p. 58). Firstly (p. 59) he quotes a paragraph of the edict omitted by Diderot which shows Julian inciting the Bosreans to drive out their bishop who speaks ill of them. Secondly, (p. 61) he quotes from the historian Ammianus Marcellinus (the chief contemporary pagan source for this period) a passage that states that Julian's real purpose in encouraging Christian bishops to express their ideas was essentially to divide and conquer, "rien n'étant plus capable d'augmenter leurs divisions, que la pleine liberté qu'il leur donnait." It is indicative of de Luc's mentality that he finds this to be more unflattering to Julian than to the Christians! It does counteract Diderot's tendency to idealize Julian, and suggest that political cunning based upon assessment of actual circumstances was as much a motivation as sweet reasonableness. Finally (pp. 62 ff.), after bringing out Julian's monumental hypocrisy in certain matters, de Luc describes, by long quotations from two eighteenth-century French historians, the underhanded way in which Julian went about destroying the Christian religion and his complicity in occasional acts of violence against Christians or those who would defend them. The refutation concludes with the charitable supposition that the author of the *Pensées philosophiques* was unaware of these facts when quoting fragments of the edict in question favourable to Julian; "car s'il s'était rappelé dans quelle oppression cet Empereur tint ceux de ses Officiers qui voulurent exécuter son Edit à la lettre, tandis qu'il prit hautement la défense des infracteurs de cet Edit; comment aurait-il pû se résoudre à faire honneur à Julien d'une perfidie aussi marquée?" (pp. 74-75). Since Diderot's knowledge of the Edict would appear to be limited to what Shaftesbury reports in his *Miscellaneous Reflections*,[28] he was probably not in fact aware of all the unflattering details of Julian's policies. For both thinkers, Julian was a philosopher whose pagan virtues deserved a better press than they had received

---

28. See Franco Venturi, *Jeunesse de Diderot*, Paris, 1939, pp. 361-62.

at the hands of prejudiced Christian writers through the centuries, and they tended to underplay his faults.

For de Luc, Julian could do no right. Here was a man who had been taught the Scriptures in his youth, yet failed to appreciate their divine character, the sublimity of the ideas concerning God to be found therein. "Aucune considération ne devait être capable de lui faire embrasser le Polythéisme" (p. 89). De Luc, a prominent Genevan bourgeois, was no scholar familiar with the writings of the later Roman Empire and especially with those competing with the Christian Scriptures for attention. He was blinded by his exclusive concern with Christianity and lacked the ability to take an unbiased view of fourth-century history, by which he might have assessed Julian with less prejudice.

In fact, de Luc even condemns "les Auteurs chrétiens qui, sans y prendre garde, pallient les mauvaises qualités de Julian l'Apostat" (p. 88). Attempts made by the abbé de la Bletterie in his *Vie de l'Empereur Julien* (1735) to present a less biased account of Julian, free from at least the blatant slander, meet with criticism from de Luc who, in the unconscious arrogance of his certainty, attributes this to carelessness: "sans y prendre garde." No wonder then that the unbelieving author of the *Pensées philosophiques* should arouse his hostility!

The historical emphasis of Christianity has frequently encouraged arguments based on the literal truth of certain events, especially miraculous ones, in the life of Christ, and their relationship to Old Testament prophecy. Such evidence was adduced by the rational supernaturalists of which we have spoken, and de Luc takes this approach; but he does not dwell on miracles, possibly because he realizes their weaknesses as proofs in themselves when dealing with unbelievers who could, and did, adduce miracles claimed by other religions. This means that no mention is made of Diderot's sceptical commentary on the *convulsionnaires* found in *Pensées* 53 to 55. Moreover, being Protestant, de Luc could not appeal to the tradition of the Church to "validate" the miracles, as Catholic apologists often ended up by doing.[29] It is rather by an appeal to the prophecies recorded by

---

29. E.g., Abbé G. Gauchat in *Lettres critiques*, Paris, 1755-63, cited in R. R.

Scripture that de Luc goes about answering the comment of Diderot in *Pensée* 45 that "la Divinité des Ecritures n'est point un caractère si clairement empreint en elles, que l'autorité des Historiens sacrés soit absolument indépendante des Auteurs profanes" (p. 30). De Luc disagrees radically with the first clause, adducing as evidence of the Scripture's divine origin "la sublimité des idées qu'elle nous donne de Dieu et ses adorables perfections," as well as "la pureté de son Culte et la sainteté de ses Dogmes et sa Morale," (p. 202) without appreciating to what extent the content of such words as "sublimité," "pureté" and "sainteté" varies with the individual and the culture, and presupposes a prior acceptance of the religious context. But apart from these characteristics, de Luc proclaims that Old Testament prophecies concerning the birth, death and resurrection of Christ provide overwhelming evidence of the truth of Christianity. Like many another apologist, he fails to realize that since those who wrote of Christ knew of these prophecies, they could scarcely help but be influenced by them in their accounts of events. The attitude which dominates the several pages devoted to this subject is seen in the following declaration, very characteristic of the tone and style of the *Observations*: "Tout savant, dis-je, qui né Chrétien, est néanmoins tombé dans l'incrédulité et qui voudra faire de généreux efforts pour vaincre les obstacles qui l'empèchent de méditer sur l'accomplissement exact de toutes ces prophéties; pourra-t-il resister à des preuves aussi évidentes de la divinité de notre Sainte Religion?" (p. 204).

The question really at issue here is what constitutes credibility in these matters. The appeal to historical fact, hoping to meet the doubter on ground he would accept, was a common method of defending Christianity in the eighteenth century. Genevan apologetics were concerned with establishing the historical reality of Christ's mission, from which the divinity of his doctrine could be argued. But Diderot, like others of the *philosophes*, was not satisfied by this approach and refused battle on these historical terms. In *Pensée* 46 he enunciates the general principle: "moins un

---

Palmer, *Catholics and Unbelievers in Eighteenth-Century France*, Princeton, N.J., 1939, p. 63 and passim.

fait a de vraisemblance, plus le témoignage de l'Histoire perd de son poids." There is then a difference of opinion as to what kind of facts are possible. Diderot is convinced that his reason is capable of telling him what is not possible: "Grâce à l'extrême confiance que j'ai en ma raison, ma foi n'est pas à la merci du premier saltimbanque" (p. 36). And he ends an apostrophe discreetly addressed to the "Pontife de Mahomet" with the advice: "Veux-tu que je devienne ton Prosélyte; laisse tous ces prestiges et raisonnons." The basis for this attitude? "Je suis plus sûr de mon jugement que de mes yeux" (p. 36). De Luc has nothing to say concerning this militant rationalism of Diderot (perhaps for reasons already suggested) and yet he reacts vigorously to a consequence of it, which he feels endangers a cornerstone of Christian belief. Diderot followed up his general principle of historical evidence (mentioned above) by saying: "Je croirais sans peine un seul honnête homme qui m'annoncerait *que Sa Majesté vient de remporter une victoire complète* sur les Alliés; mais tout Paris m'assurerait qu'un mort vient de ressusciter à Passy, que je n'en croirais rien" (p. 32). De Luc realizes that the very fact of Christ's resurrection is at stake in such an attitude, but all he can do is appeal to history and attempt to demonstrate the reliability of the evidence; therefore he proceeds to show, with little psychological insight, that the honesty and common sense of the witnesses to Christ's resurrection are beyond reproach, and to refer the reader for more details to the work of certain "vertueux et savants Anglais," "Mrs. Homfroi Ditton et Sherlock," (p. 213) whose arguments are, in de Luc's opinion, strong enough to overcome all but the most inveterate unbelief.[30]

And, of course, credibility does depend on the trustworthiness of the document that reports the evidence. The Biblical criticism of the late seventeenth and early eighteenth century became a powerful dissolver of faith, an element in that "crise de conscience" of which Paul Hazard wrote. In *Pensée* 60 a series of questions brings out exactly those criteria used to determine the authenticity of any text, but intended here to bear upon the

---

30. Bibliographical data on the chief works of Ditton and Sherlock may be found in the Bibliography of J. S. Spink, *Jean-Jacques Rousseau et Genève*, pp. 307, 309.

Scriptures. Has the collection of writings always been the same? If it has changed, what criteria of selection were used to add or subtract passages? If, as you have to admit, says Diderot, ignorant copyists or malicious heretics have mutilated the text, it must be restored to its "état naturel" before its divinity can be proven. And the Church can hardly fulfill this function until its infallibility is proven by the divinity of the Scriptures, a statement which dismisses the validity of certain Catholic apologists' conclusions,[31] but which has no relevance for the Protestant de Luc and elicits no reaction. Diderot concludes: "On ne répond à cette difficulté, qu'en avouant que les premiers fondements de la foi sont purement humains; que le choix entre les manuscrits, que la restitution des passages, enfin que la collection s'est faite par les règles de critique; et je ne refuse point d'ajouter à la divinité des livres sacrés, un degré de foi proportionné à la certitude de ces règles" (p. 43). In view of the lack of "certitude" in the critical criteria mentioned, this statement well expresses that scepticism characterizing a number of the *Pensées*. When Diderot touches on the fact that some esthetically inferior Church paintings have been said to be divinely inspired, and asks the disarming question: "Quelle application ne ferais-je point de ces tableaux aux Saintes Ecritures, si je ne savais combien il importe peu que ce qu'elles contiennent soit bien ou mal dit?" (p. 31), de Luc recognizes the technique sometimes used by the *philosophes* to disseminate their ideas with a modicum of safety, and refers to the "indirecte et maligne application" Diderot makes of his remarks on Church paintings (p. 55-56). However, de Luc the Protestant is able to agree with Diderot the freethinker to the extent of finding the latter's other remarks on these paintings "judicieuses."

But all that de Luc seems to see in this matter of Biblical exegesis is a certain petulance which emphasizes "les fautes que peuvent y avoir glissées les Copistes et les Traducteurs" (p. 214). That he does not appreciate the significance of the whole question is suggested by his choice of words: the modal auxiliary "peuvent," and especially the verb "glisser," both of which imply a certain fortuitousness and lack of real importance to be

---

31. See R. R. Palmer, *op. cit.*, chapter IV.

attributed to these "fautes." De Luc feels that overemphasis on such errors shows a frame of mind inimical to "une sérieuse et sincère étude de ce Livre divin," (p. 214) which alone — and not the testimony of pagan authors — can lead us to recognize the hand of God in the Scriptures. De Luc is convinced that the essentials come through unscathed. This whole critical enterprise would seem for him to be evidence of a certain perversity of heart: "C'est bien moins l'esprit que le coeur, qui suggèrent ces moyens illusoires de résister à l'évidence des caractères de divinité que l'Ecriture Sainte renferme" (p. 215). Would not this also be de Luc's attitude to Diderot's statement in Pensée 61: "C'est en cherchant des preuves que j'ai trouvé des difficultés. Les livres qui contiennent les motifs de ma croyance, m'offrent en même temps les raisons de l'incrédulité"? Certainly, this typically deistic sentiment is left unrefuted by de Luc, quite possibly because the heart and will, rather than the intelligence, are involved.

And it is to this kind of argument that de Luc ultimately returns in his conclusion. To *philosophes*, who claim they have difficulty believing in the Christian message, he quotes from the Epistle of St. James where, because God resists the proud and spares the humble, men are urged to humble themselves before the Lord. To this de Luc adds: "Tels sont les sentiments qu'il faut revêtir pour obtenir le précieux don de la Foi, et qui nous le procurent infailliblement" (p. 417).

Would such unbelievers as "l'auteur des *Pensées philosophiques*" be for de Luc among those likely to find salvation in this way? He is obviously not in the same category as those perverse fellows Mandeville and La Mettrie, who are explicitly referred to as "ces savants corrompus" (p. 11). Admittedly, for de Luc, Diderot's pride of knowledge has lead him to grievous errors in matters of religion, but nowhere is he referred to in the violent terms reserved for the real villains of eighteenth-century unbelief. If one judges by the moderation with which de Luc speaks of Diderot, occasionally even finding himself in agreement with him, it is very probable that he would be a leading candidate in de Luc's mind for that change of heart which would make him see the truth of the Christian faith and use his literary talents "à faire triompher cette Foi du libertinage et de la superstition" (p. 13). Had he known the identity of the author and been familiar with the *Lettre sur les aveugles*, his attitude would presumably have been less charitable!

In any case, his objections to Diderot are generally of a very unphilosophical nature, both in approach and content. He tends to react to specific consequences of an idea or attitude without going beyond them to the general notion. His remarks do not reveal any extensive knowledge of philosophical problems, although it is obvious that he was familiar with the ideas of certain deists, who seem to have had some influence on his thought. We find a much more philosophical and systematic approach in the refutations written by Formey, Polier de Bottens and Allemand, which appeared in the five years following the publication of the *Pensées philosophiques*.[32] De Luc's belated reaction was rather that of a Protestant Christian layman with considerable knowledge of his religion and of its Scriptures, but lacking the ability and intellectual background to give a reasoned refutation of his opponent's thought. He was obliged to fall back on statements which proclaim a "truth," either historical or doctrinal. These statements form the basis for his objections, yet most often they are too subjective to compel assent, or are based on premises accepted by de Luc as part of his Christian faith. To this extent, de Luc in his observations on Diderot is not a skilled polemicist, but a believer reduced to calling out: "How can you fail to see the Truth?"

Yet undoubtedly these very aspects of de Luc's work, although detracting from its literary and polemical value, make it more representative of a typical Protestant reaction to the thought of the *philosophes* than we could find in a learned theologian or professor of philosophy or Hebrew. From a serious-minded Genevan bourgeois without great learning we would not expect quotations from erudite works of religious apologetics. He *was* familiar with certain widely-read Protestant works, such as those of Jacques Abbadie and William Sherlock, but for the most part, he fell back on the Scriptures, accepted as the Divine Word of God. Equally typical of many of his compatriots were those

32. See F. Venturi, *op. cit.*, p. 94 ff.

rationalistic tendencies we have observed in de Luc, that more humane version of Calvinism, more open to worldly pleasures and pursuits and taking a more optimistic view of human nature and destiny. It is highly likely then that in these remarks inspired by Diderot's earliest works, de Luc was voicing the sentiments of many another sincere Calvinist of his time.

Douglas G. Creighton

Varieties of Infernal Experience: Pope's Dunciad & Dante's Inferno

Offhand remarks of a number of readers of Pope show that his *Dunciad* has brought the *Inferno* to their minds. Austin Warren says that Pope's poem "is not without reminders of the *Inferno* with its moral categories, its wry jokes, and its smoky lighting."[1] For Matthew Hodgart, "the *Dunciad*, which like T. S. Eliot's *Waste Land* presents contemporary London as an image of hell, ... is a comic Inferno."[2] Patricia Meyer Spacks draws a parallel between Dante's sinners, "the images of [whose] damnation objectify their interior states," and Pope's dunces, whose "satiric, degrading imagery, action, and setting ... project interior states of dullness."[3] G. Wilson Knight is a bit more persistent, he compares the *Inferno* and the *Dunciad* on several occasions, but most of his comparisons seem to me of dubious relevance.[4] In all these remarks, and several others, the *Inferno* appears merely as one term of a momentary metaphor, but it appears often enough to suggest that a more extended comparison might illuminate both poems.[5]

To orient ourselves, we may recall that the *Inferno* recounts

---

1. "Pope," in *Essential Articles for the Study of Alexander Pope*, ed. Maynard Mack, Hamden, Conn., 1964, p. 95.
2. *Satire*, World University Library, New York, 1969, p. 233.
3. *An Argument of Images: The Poetry of Alexander Pope*, Cambridge, Mass., 1971, p. 92.
4. *Laureate of Peace: On the Genius of Alexander Pope*, London, 1955, pp. 3, 7, 37, 57, 62, 92, 152, 180-81.
5. My aim is what might be called "pure comparison," since as far as is known Pope was unacquainted with Dante. The *Dunciad* is quoted in the 1743 (B) version, from the *Twickenham Edition of the Poems of Alexander Pope*, vol. 5, ed. James Sutherland, 3rd ed., London, 1963. The *Inferno* is quoted from the translation of John Ciardi, New York, 1963. I have also consulted the commentary and prose translation of Charles S. Singleton, Princeton, 1970, but I have avoided referring to controversies such as the one over the authenticity of the letter to Can Grande. Since I am only a tenderfoot in the dark wood of Dante scholarship, my reasons for choosing one position rather than another would encumber the paper to no purpose. Like all students of the *Dunciad*, I am greatly indebted to Aubrey Williams' fine monograph, *Pope's Dunciad: A Study of its Meaning*, London, 1955.

Dante's journey through hell under the guidance of Virgil. Hell is a funnel-shaped cavern reaching to the centre of the earth, elaborately subdivided so as to provide separate places of punishment for many different kinds of sin. After reaching the bottom of hell, Dante and Virgil climb up to the surface of the earth at the antipodes of their starting point. In the *Purgatorio* and *Paradiso*, Virgil escorts Dante up the Mount of Purgatory to the Earthly Paradise at the summit, where Beatrice takes over and guides him on through heaven. Dante tells us in his letter to Can Grande that on the literal level his poem is a representation of "the state of souls after death" and that other levels of meaning are communicated through the four-level system of allegory used in biblical exegesis.[6]

Generically, both the *Dunciad* and the *Inferno* of course have close affinities with the epic, though neither one is precisely "an epic" by most definitions. These affinities stand out, though, if we take the central feature of the epic to be a plot which allows the hero to practise in an eminent degree the virtues that his culture considers the most important. The *Inferno* is clearly epic by this standard, and what makes the *Dunciad* a mock-epic is that its hero's virtues are those of an anarchic counter-culture that is undermining the poet's culture. The *Inferno* is profoundly democratic in that all Christians, not just a few adepts, are called on to follow Dante in his journey. The *Dunciad*, on the other hand, leans toward the aristocratic; the counter-culture results from the misguided attempts of a mob of poetasters to follow in the footsteps of ancient heroic poets. Both poems present themselves as human analogues of sacred scripture. Dante asserts this by announcing that his poem is to be interpreted by the methods of scriptural exegesis; Pope produces a mock-scripture by constant ironic allusions to the Bible and to Logos theology. This feature contributes to the epic quality of the poems because the early epics played the role of sacred scripture in their culture. The encyclopedism of both poems, their attempt to include every facet of the authors' culture and to present a complete epitome of their worlds, as rich and multifarious as reality itself, is another

6. "Dante's Letter to Can Grande," tr. Nancy Howe, in *Essays on Dante*, ed. Mark Musa, Bloomington, Ind., 1964, paragraphs 6-8, pp. 36-38.

characteristic of both epic and scripture. Dante's allegorical method invites the kind of elaborate and exhaustive but neverending commentary that is usually lavished only on epic and scripture, and, needless to say, his invitation has not gone unheeded. The tradition of allegorical composition and interpretation of epic continued into Pope's day, and while the *Dunciad* is hardly a formal allegory (despite Scriblerus's prefatory statement, p. 50), the dark conceit of the invocation to Book 4 reveals a tendency in that direction: "Of darkness visible so much be lent, As half to shew, half veil the deep Intent." For this and other reasons, especially the example provided by Pope's own elaborate counter-commentary, the *Dunciad* has also inspired a voluminous exegetical tradition, though of course nothing like that of the *Commedia*.

If satire is an attack carried on by means of a fiction, then the *Inferno* is satirical through and through, ranging from the harshest and most abusive personal satire to a more generalized kind of medieval "satire against mankind." Yet no one would call the poem "a satire." Its emphasis on the intellectual, moral, and spiritual development of its hero, its didactic concern that its readers develop along with the hero, and its position as the first part of a comic trilogy show clearly that the satire it contains is subordinate to other purposes. It is prominent enough and personal enough, however, to have left Dante open to two charges often levelled against Pope: that his poem is merely a versified grudge, a vehicle for pure spite or vengefulness, and that its poetry often disappears behind the mass of topical details. One can imagine a friend of Dante's writing from Bologna, as Swift wrote Pope from Dublin, to complain that many of the allusions were incomprehensible twenty miles outside of Florence.[7]

Both Pope and Dante have been defended by the same kinds of arguments, of which two varieties are the most important. One asserts that the poets have reached beyond their own private motivations and the specific identities of their victims to achieve an enduring and universal significance. The moral and literary categories, the striking and memorable images bestowed on all the

---

7. Letter of 16 July 1728, *Correspondence of Alexander Pope*, ed. George Sherburn, Oxford, 1956, 2.504.

sad variety of sin and dullness, are fundamental; the individuals concerned are secondary, and as they become less important, so does the original motivation of the poet. Pope claimed that "the Poem was not made for these Authors, but these Authors for the Poem" (p. 205). I think Dante would have agreed in principle, though the importance of some of his victims might require certain qualifications. In any case, everyone can think of plenty of present-day candidates for both poems.

The other kind of defense justifies the personal attacks, on either aesthetic or ethical grounds. The aesthetic defense has perhaps been most clearly formulated by John L. McKenzie in a discussion of the bloodthirstiness of some of the poetry of the Old Testament.[8] Theologians and ordinary Christians can and should learn to hate the sin and love the sinner, but such a distinction is difficult for a poet to maintain in practice, since he works best when dealing with concrete particulars. The distinction is especially difficult for the satirist: he can denounce sin in the abstract, but he cannot punish it that way; he has to punish sinners. Pope himself, on the other hand, usually defended personal satire on ethical grounds — "if some are hung up, or pilloryed, it may prevent others"[9] — a position which Dante obviously shared. The two kinds of defense outlined here do not contradict each other, but anyone who maintains either of them, I think, must acknowledge that both the *Inferno* and the *Dunciad* are extreme test cases for the amount of topicality a long poem can attempt to absorb without succumbing entirely to the impermanence of its materials.

Another illuminating perspective on the satire of the two poems appears in Earl Miner's recent suggestion that the image of the falling city (derived ultimately from Juvenal's third satire) embraces the central concerns of the genre. Not only does most satire employ urban settings; it also evokes the myths of the great cities of the past that have symbolized civilization: Troy, Jerusalem, Athens, Rome. From one point of view, Miner's image

---

8. *The Two-Edged Sword: An Interpretation of the Old Testament*, London, 1959, pp. 281-85.

9. Letter of 2 August [1734]; *Correspondence*, 3.423. See also 26 July, pp. 418-20.

shows how the *Inferno* goes beyond satire. All of lower hell is enclosed within the red-hot iron walls of an infernal city, Dis (Cantos 8-9). This city is not falling: it has fallen, irredeemably. But the cities of Dante's Italy, especially Rome and his native Florence, are constantly falling (quite literally, in terms of the poem's fiction); one after another, crowds of their citizens tumble down into the infernal gulfs (see also the opening of Canto 26, quoted below, p. 286). And beyond the confines of hell loom the heavenly Jerusalem and the ideal Rome on which Dante modelled his political philosophy. The involvement of the *Dunciad* in the falling city is too obvious to need elaboration: architecturally, politically, poetically, theologically, London is sliding down into the profound embrace of Dulness.

Joseph Warton dropped a valuable hint for us when, in the course of his rambling *Essay on Pope*, he called the *Commedia* "a sublime and original poem, . . . a kind of satirical epic."[10] Warton was one of the earliest eighteenth-century English readers of Dante, and his description shows that he was convinced of the value of the *Inferno* but uncertain how to account for it. The expression he arrived at, "a sublime satirical epic," must have had for him the force of an oxymoron, considering how consistently he maintained throughout his essay that didactic and satiric poetry such as Pope wrote belongs to a poetic order inferior in kind to the sublimity of Milton and other poets of the first rank. He may have felt that the epic qualities of the *Inferno* endow the satire with worth and dignity, or conversely, that the profound moral values that underlie Dante's satire and the setting of eternity in which it is pronounced are enough to raise satire itself to the dignity of epic. In any case, the epic and satiric aspects of the poem must have formed some kind of synthesis in his mind. In the *Dunciad*, of course, these aspects are related quite differently; the epic manner clashes with the satiric matter, and the resultant mock-heroic sharpens the satire.

Another perspective on this mixture of styles appears in Canto

10. *An Essay on the Writings and Genius of Pope*, I, 1756, p. 190. As particular examples of the sublime Warton cites the inscription on the gate of hell at the beginning of Canto 3 and Dante's recovery at the beginning of Canto 6 from the swoon caused by pity for Paolo and Francesca.

26 of the *Inferno*, where the false counsellors walk their round, each one enveloped in a sheet of flame, and Dante carries on his celebrated interview with Ulysses. Harvey Goldstein has argued persuasively that this episode is primarily concerned with literature: by the end of it Dante has clarified his attitude toward the stylistic canons of the classical epic and has finally overcome the temptation to pursue eloquence for its own sake.[11] Dante's admiration for the classic authors he knew and his great debt to them are obvious: in limbo, he gladly assumed the place offered him among Homer, Horace, Ovid, Lucan, and Virgil (4.100-2). When Virgil first appeared to him, Dante addressed him as

> ... my true master and first author,
> the sole maker from whom I drew the breath
> of that sweet style whose measures have brought me honor.
> (1.82-84)

Twice in the *Inferno* Virgil characterizes his own poem, as a "high tragedy" (20.113) and as "high verses" (26.79). In his letter to Can Grande, on the other hand, Dante characterized his own poem in quite different terms; it is a comedy, because it ends prosperously, and it is written in a style appropriate to comedy: "the manner of speech ... is lowly and humble because it is vulgar speech which even simple women use" (par. 10, p. 39). However great Dante's admiration for Virgil may be, it is clear that he himself is following a different path.

Here in Canto 26, though, epic devices are particularly prominent. The opening apostrophe to Florence is written in the grandest of styles:

> Joy to you, Florence, that your banners swell,
>   beating their proud wings over land and sea,
>   and that your name expands through all of Hell!

A few lines further on, the glimmering flames of the false counsellors are compared to fireflies in a long epic simile, and

---

11. "*Enea e Paolo*: A Reading of the 26th Canto of Dante's *Inferno*," *Symposium* 19, 1965, pp. 316-27. Goldstein's approach derives in part from Renato Poggioli, "Tragedy or Romance? A Reading of the Paolo and Francesca Episode in Dante's *Inferno*," *PMLA* 72, 1957, pp. 313-58.

Elijah's ascent to heaven in a fiery chariot is put to the same use. The epic associations of Ulysses and Diomedes are obvious. Between the beginning of the canto and these epic devices, however, Dante has told us how

> I mourned among those rocks, and I mourn again
>   when memory returns to what I saw:
>   and more than usually I curb the strain
> of my genius, lest it stray from Virtue's course.
>
> (19-22)

The cause of this grief and fear soon appears, as Dante, captivated by the strange sight of the false counsellors, leans over their trench so far that only a handhold prevents him from plunging down among them; he is poised, as it were, between Virgil and Ulysses.

To summarize the implications of this episode quite baldly: Virgil, who will guide Dante as far as he can before being replaced by Beatrice, suggests the limited but real worth of pagan eloquence. Ulysses, the enemy of Aeneas and Troy and therefore of Dante's beloved *romanitas*, embodies false counsel, the use of language to mislead, the most relevant aspect of which for Dante would have been misuse of his poetic talents. Ulysses' exploration, which has the appearance of a true epic voyage, is in reality a fool's errand, for it leads nowhere, as opposed to that of Aeneas, which led to the founding of Rome. In distinguishing his own low comedy from Virgil's high tragedy, Dante, like Milton, is implying that where his poem differs from the classics it is "not less, but more heroic." When Dante does use an obviously high style, as in this canto, he usually has a precise end in view. The effect of the grand apostrophe to the vice and infamy of Florence is virtually mock-heroic. By applying to false counsellors an unmistakable epic topos, based on Homer's and Virgil's treatment of military campfires, the firefly simile emphasizes the danger inherent in the epic attitude to both style and life.

The *Inferno*, then, like the *Dunciad*, is an offspring of farce and epic, a deliberate mixture of styles, but for a quite different purpose. Pope doesn't reject or criticize the epic or its style; within the *Dunciad*, it shares the normative status of scripture and "Nature." It is Cibber, not a real epic hero, who goes fool's errands. (The *Dunciad* in this respect differs from *The Rape of the Lock*, which I think does imply that the disparity between ancient warriors and modern ladies is smaller than might appear at first glance.) Fundamental as it is, though, the different purposes behind the mixture of styles in the *Dunciad* and the *Inferno* should not be allowed to obscure the striking similarity of the means.

Beyond these generic and stylistic relationships, a great number of themes and techniques invite examination. Many of these are aspects of the infernal setting common to both poems. In the *Dunciad*, there are actually three different underworlds. There is the one presented in Book 3, to which Cibber descends in direct imitation of Aeneas's descent to the classical underworld. There is the underworld of Fleet Ditch, scene of the diving contest in Book 2. Finally, there is the metaphoric hell which encompasses the whole world of the poem; this is created primarily by means of allusions to *Paradise Lost* and the Bible, and reveals Cibber and his dunces as servants, witting or unwitting, of an uncreating word that is ultimately the language of Satan. This last variety of infernal experience establishes the moral perspective of the poem and shadows forth its profoundest meanings, reinforces the generic relationship between the two poems if we recall that in Northrop Frye's literary geography hell is the proper habitat of satire, and thus provides the strongest justification for this paper.

The two poems vary greatly in their presentation of hell. The *Inferno* is narrated in the first person; its hero recounts his own journey, he acts and suffers, shivers with fear and screams with rage. Once Virgil has to cover his eyes to prevent him from glimpsing the Medusa and turning to stone (9.49-60). But there is a radical distinction between Dante the pilgrim, journeying through hell, and Dante the poet, who has already seen heaven before he begins his tale. The poet is saved, the pilgrim is still working out his salvation in fear and trembling. Thus an important aspect of the autobiographical allegory is the presentation of an earlier state of the poet's soul, the constant tension between the two states, and the development of one into the other. For example, the poet's memory, which preserves his infernal experiences so as to prevent him from backsliding in the future, also enables him to become the pilgrim again, that is, to share the condition of his readers, uncertain of their salvation, and to present his experiences in all their immediacy:

> How shall I say
> what wood that was! I never saw so drear,
> so rank, so arduous a wilderness!
> Its very memory gives a shape to fear.
>   (1.3-6)

For most modern readers the aesthetic vividness is the main *raison d'être* of the poem, but of course for Dante it was only a means to the end of leading his readers to undergo their own conversion. Pope, on the other hand, is quite detached from the world of his poem, except for his admission in the invocation to Book 4 that Dulness will ultimately overwhelm him too and "take at once the poet and the song." The only process in the poem is the gradual triumph of Dulness. Pope, like Dante the poet, does not change. Neither does Cibber, who unlike Dante the pilgrim is a denizen of hell, not a visitor. Pope's readers are of course invited to learn from the poem and to do what they can to delay the ultimate triumph of Dulness, but they too look at the scene from outside; there is no one corresponding to Dante the pilgrim to share and guide their experience.

Both poems include the commonly accepted furnishings of hell — monsters, darkness, cacophany, stench, flames, and so on. Their topography is also similar. The *Dunciad* lacks the schematic and hierarchic divisions of the *Inferno*, but the different methods of ditch-diving in Book 2 suggest different varieties of bad writing. Book 4 makes some attempt to distinguish different kinds of dunces, and the disposition of the whole into prefaces, text, notes, and appendices is another step toward classification. Pat Rogers has in fact recently suggested a greater similarity between the two poems from this point of view: he compares Dante's layout of hell to Pope's use of the connotations of the different areas of London to create a kind of symbolic moral geography as one element of the poem's structure (*Grub Street: Studies in a Subculture*, 1972, pp. 2-3). The arrangement of bad poets as turtles, eels, ostriches, parrots, and so on in *Peri Bathous* (Chapter 6) might also be seen as a whimsical analogue of Dante's moral categories. Corresponding to the funnel-shape of Dante's hell, the *Dunciad* is characterized by an eddying, vortex-like movement, a sort of slow-motion maelstrom of sludge. Here again the imagery of *Peri Bathous* is close to that of the *Inferno*. In view of the lack of a guide for poetasters, Pope declares, "I have undertaken this arduous but necessary Task, to lead them as it were by the hand, and step by step, the gentle downhill way to the *Bathos*; the Bottom, the End, the Central point, the *non plus ultra* of true Modern Poesie!" (Chap. 1). As Dante approaches the bottom of hell, references to weight and gravity occur more and more frequently, until he arrives at the final circle, "which bears the weight of all the steeps of hell" and indeed the weight of all the earth (32.3-8). Weight is even more prominent in the *Dunciad*. Arnall, one of the Fleet Ditch divers, is distinguished for "weight of skull" and is blessed "with all the might of gravitation" (2.315, 318). At the convocation in Book 4, none of the dunces needs a guide, "by the sure Attraction led, And strong impulsive gravity of Head" (75-76). Here gravitation draws men to Dulness in a parody of the physico-theological metaphors that used it as an image of the love of God. Thomas R. Edwards has suggested that the action of the *Dunciad* is analogous to the physicist's concept of entropy — the gradual running down of the universe caused by the dissipation of heat energy — and in a strikingly similar metaphor someone else has characterized the ninth circle of hell, where everything is frozen immobile except Satan's wings, as "a kind of theological absolute zero." In terms closer to Dante's own, the devil approaches as close to non-being as possible, and at the end of the *Dunciad* everything becomes nothing as non-being takes over the universe.

The underworld has traditionally been regarded as a place to encounter and recognize the self, especially in its less attractive aspects. For those condemned to the underworld, this is the end of the story. Dante's sinners, like Virgil's, learn the true nature of their sins, but there is no escape for them. They still will their sins, and thus, paradoxically but unavoidably, they will their punishments too, because the punishment is the essence of the sin. Or in other words, they can't escape the self which they have created by their sins, and thus they "yearn for what they fear" (3.123). For the hero who visits the underworld and returns, however, the journey provides self-knowledge that can lead to a life of greater virtue. Dante thus learns the true nature of all the sins he has committed or is capable of committing. By these discoveries he learns to avoid the sins and hopes to teach his readers to do likewise. In St. Paul's terms (*Colossians*, 3.9-10), the descent underground symbolizes the burial of the old man, enslaved to sin, and the return to earth is the birth of the new man.

Pope's three varieties of hell provide different types of self-recognition, or perhaps more accurately, self-encounter, since the dunces do not know themselves accurately. In the Virgilian underworld of Book 3, Settle informs Cibber:

> "Son; what thou seek'st is in thee! Look, and find
> Each Monster meets his likeness in thy mind."
> (251-52)

Cibber's monster-breeding mind is a parody of the mind of God, stocked with the Divine Ideas that form the patterns of the created world, and it produces the "new world" of Dulness. Or if we emphasize epistemology rather than creativity, Cibber's mind is perfectly equipped to represent the world he inhabits: both world and mind are chaotic. Like Marlowe's Faustus, the dunces carry their own hell around within them. The underworld of Fleet Ditch is highly erotic:

> First he relates, how sinking to the chin,
> Smit with his mien, the Mud-nymphs suck'd him in:
> How young Luteria, softer than the down,
> Nigrina black, and Merdemante brown,
> Vy'd for his love in jetty bow'rs below,
> As Hylas fair was ravish'd long ago.
> (2.331-36)

Smedley loves mud and *merde*, and it is of course himself that he encounters in what he loves. These encounters set in relief an important aspect of Pope's hell that we are apt to minimize if we concentrate too exclusively on the demonic implications of his allusions: for the dunces, it is not at all a place of punishment, but rather a kind of infantile holiday-world freed from adult restraints.[12] Smedley dabbles in the mud like any small boy, and here is Cibber's reaction to Settle's underworld revelations: "Joy fills his soul, joy innocent of thought" (3.249). Nevertheless these self-encounters are fundamental to Pope's aesthetic condemnation of the dunces, because they write exclusively out of themselves, like the spider in Swift's *Battle of the Books*. The only materials of their art are their own egos. They are the image of their god, "wrapt up in Self, a God without a Thought" (4.485). Thus their selves and their literary productions reflect each other like empty mirrors in an eternally closed system.

As any reader of Milton would expect, both hells are parodies of heaven, and the actions of their inhabitants parodies of religious actions. The religious parodies of the two poems are in fact strikingly similar. In the *Dunciad*, we have the manifold Antichrist aspects of Cibber and Dulness. Dulness baptizes Cibber as John the Baptist did Jesus:

> The Goddess then, o'er his anointed head,
> With mystic words, the sacred Opium shed.
> And lo! her bird, (a monster of a fowl,
> Something betwixt a Heideggre and owl,)
> Perch'd on his crown.
>
> (1.287-91)

There is the rather obscure parody of both the Annunciation and the Eucharist in Book 4, where Mummius recounts how Annius

> ...taught by Hermes, and divinely bold,
> Down his own throat . . . risqu'd the Grecian gold;
> Receiv'd each Demi-God, with pious care,
> Deep in his Entrails — I rever'd them there,
> I bought them, shrouded in that living shrine,
> And, at their second birth, they issue mine.
>
> (381-86)

---

12. See Emrys Jones, "Pope and Dulness," *Proceedings of the British Academy* 54, 1968, pp. 231-63. If, as Jones suggests (pp. 240-41, 253-54), Pope felt a certain attraction toward this kind of disinhibition and communicated it to his readers, my statement about the detachment of both Pope and the reader from the world of the *Dunciad* (above, p. 289) would have to be qualified to some degree.

Further on, there is the clearer parody of transubstantiation in the work of the cook whose "specious miracles" turn pigeons into toads and reduce "three essential Partridges" to one (549-62). At the very bottom of Dante's hell, we find the most overwhelming parody of all. Satan's three heads ape the divine Trinity. Frozen immobile in the ice except for his wings, which circulate the icy winds of lower hell, he parodies God as unmoved mover. In Canto 19 we find the simoniacs stuffed head-first into vertical cylinders that Dante very deliberately compares to baptismal founts.[13] Instead of the water that is poured over the head of the infant being baptized, fire plays over the soles of these sinners' feet. In Canto 26, Virgil addresses the double flame that enwraps Ulysses and Diomedes, and

> As if it fought the wind, the greater prong
>   of the ancient flame began to quiver and hum;
>   then moving its tip as if it were the tongue
> that spoke, gave out a voice above the roar.
>
>   (82-85)

The allusion to the Pentecostal tongues of fire is unmistakable. Besides emphasizing the moral and religious aspects of Ulysses' use of language, this image brings out the implications of earlier flame images, such as the one just cited: water on the forehead is the sign of the Holy Spirit, flames on the feet are the opposite. These flaming parodies of the Holy Spirit relate Dante's central religious concerns to his concerns for language and art, and enable him to show how sin distorts the sinner's language. Pope's parodies of

---

13. This heels-over-head image appears also in Swift's "On Poetry: A Rhapsody":

> For Instance: When you rashly think,
> No Rhymer can like *Welsted* sink,
> His Merits ballanc'd you shall find,
> The Laureat leaves him far behind.
> *Concannen*, more aspiring Bard,
> Climbs downwards, deeper by a Yard;
> Smart *Jemmy Moor* with Vigor drops,
> The Rest pursue as thick as Hops:
> With Heads to Points the Gulph they enter,
> Linkt perpendicular to the Centre:
> And as their Heels elated rise,
> Their Heads attempt the nether Skies.
>   (393-404)

course work in the opposite direction; they enable him to extend the significance of his poem beyond its basic concern for art and language by showing the ultimately religious consequences of every misuse of language.

Language and art are involved more directly in many of the sins that Dante distinguishes: violence against God, Nature, and Art (respectively blasphemy, sodomy, and usury) and falsification, such as counterfeiting or alchemy. At the end of Canto 11, Virgil tells Dante

> how all of Nature, — her laws, her fruits, her seasons, —
> springs from the Ultimate Intellect and Its art:
>
> . . . .
>
> [and] that Art strives after by imitation,
>   as the disciple imitates the master;
>   Art, as it were, is the Grandchild of Creation.
>
> (99-105)

Pope would probably have assented to this formulation, though God is less prominent in his aesthetic theory than in Dante's. (Indeed, it has been said that Nature is the god — and a jealous god — of Pope's art.) According to the doctrine of the medieval church, simplified and extrapolated a little, usurers sin against art (and for that matter against nature as well) because instead of exercising their art on nature in order to grow or manufacture something new, they merely manipulate money in order to produce more of the same. Moreover, since money is not a thing in itself but merely a medium of exchange, it is not a proper matter on which to exercise art. In other words, the usurers try to make both art and money out of nothing, which is exactly what Pope's hired hacks do.[14]

In twentieth-century terms, though, it is the falsifiers who most obviously sin against art and nature. There is no fundamental difference between this view and Dante's, for he makes Capocchio boast "how good an ape I was of Nature's ways!" (29.140). The *Dunciad* is a whole menagerie of apes like this: they falsify nature

---

14. It is worth noting that Ezra Pound has found the medieval concept of usury a source of powerful metaphors; see especially Canto 51.

by distorting it, giving flowers to Zembla and showers to Egypt; by concocting a sham poet for the book-sellers to chase after; by disguising food as we have noted above. These miracles, of course, are worked by their uncreating word. This word does not stop with effects like those just mentioned, though: Circe-like, it transforms the nature of the world. Prose swells into verse, verse loiters into prose (1.274). Schoolmasters "petrify a Genius to a Dunce" (4.264). "Crowds turn coxcombs as they gaze" at Cibber (2.8). Here the closest analogue in the *Inferno* is the circle where thieves are punished by being changed back and forth from reptile to human form (Canto 25).

To return to the violent against nature and God, full-fledged sodomy does not occur in the *Dunciad*, but for Dante masturbation was a variety of it. I would suggest that masturbation is a fitting image for the sterile and excretory art of the dunces and that it perhaps underlies the celebrated urinating contest in Book 2. The situation of the violent against God is more complex and, according to one view, more directly relevant to the *Dunciad*. In a four-hundred-page commentary on Canto 15, André Pézard has argued that Dante placed Brunetto Latini not among the sodomites, as the traditional interpretation has it, but among the violent against God, the blasphemers.[15] His blasphemy was to forsake his native vernacular, in Dante's view the direct gift of God, for another language, French — not merely to write in French, but to exalt it at the expense of Italian. Thus the rain of fire in this canto recalls not only Sodom and Gomorrah but also, as elsewhere, the Pentecostal tongues of fire which bestowed the gift of tongues on the apostles. Latini's offence may strike us as tenuous grounds for eternal damnation, and we may attribute the latter to Dante's vehement nationalism, but its underlying rationale, the participation of human words in the divine Word, is traditional enough and very similar to that of the *Dunciad*.

Pope would also have welcomed Latini's companions as Pézard sees them. Priscien sinned against "grammar," i.e. Latin, as Latini had sinned against the vernacular. Since for Dante Latin was a language codified by human art, Priscien and Latini also sin against

---

15. *Dante sous la Pluie de Feu (Enfer, Chant XV)*, Paris, 1950.

art and nature respectively. Francesco d'Accorso was a true ancestor of Scriblerus: he not only wrote a voluminous and befuddling commentary on the *Institutes* of Justinian, who had codified the laws precisely in order to rescue them from glosses, but also denied that lawyers needed to study philosophy or theology, since everything is contained in their own specialty, the *Corpus Juris*. Andrea de' Mozzi is damned for indulging in blasphemy while preaching, in order to gain glory and/or money. Among his memorable utterances from the pulpit is this one: "The grace of God is like goat-droppings; it falls down from above, rolling and scattering itself everywhere" (Pézard, p. 214 — my translation). Not only would this effusion have earned de' Mozzi a place in *Peri Bathous*; by using such language a preacher runs the risk that his congregation may not realize where scripture ends and buffoonery begins. In effect, he thrusts his own words into the Bible as Bentley thrust his into *Paradise Lost*.

We may turn now to two larger motifs. One is the image of the journey, which on both literal and metaphorical levels permeates both poems. Behind Dante's journey through hell to heaven lie three earlier journeys. In his letter to Can Grande, he cites the Exodus of the Jews from Egypt as a common-place symbol of the conversion of the individual from sin to grace. Early in the second canto, wondering why Virgil should have come to him, Dante recalls how Aeneas journeyed from Troy to Italy to found the Roman Empire as a preparation for the later voyage of St. Paul, who planted Christianity in it, and then asks

> But I — how should I dare? By whose permission?
> *I* am not Aeneas. *I* am not Paul.
> Who could believe me worthy of the vision?
>   (31-33)

But in fact, in the course of the poem, he does recapitulate both these journeys. Besides their relation to Dante as an individual, Aeneas and Paul together represent the kind of partnership between Church and State (or grace and nature) which Dante had worked so hard and so vainly to establish because he felt that it was an essential foundation for the Christian life of his fellow Italians. And this of course is one reason for his choice of Virgil, the poet of *romanitas*, as his guide. In the *Dunciad*, as Aubrey Williams has shown, the opening characterization of Cibber as one who "brings the Smithfield Muses to the ear of Kings" is acted out in the first two books by reference to a Lord Mayor's procession from the commercial "City" to the seat of government in Westminster and by a series of allusions to the early books of the *Aeneid*. The poet whom Dante follows serves as a guide that Cibber steadfastly ignores or misinterprets. In the third book, Settle shows Cibber the world-wide progress of Dulness, which closely follows the *translatio studii*, the traditional notion of the westward passage of the arts and sciences from their birthplace in Babylon to Egypt, Israel, Greece, Rome, and then, after the Dark Ages, north to France, Holland, and England. It may not be amiss here to remark that toward the end of his life Pope was contemplating a political epic based on the legend that London had been founded by Brutus, Aeneas's grandson, and was thus, like Rome, a New Troy. His purpose, like Dante's, would have been to show his country the way back to sound politics. The main difference between the *Inferno* and the *Dunciad* is that Pope does not make a journey himself and that all the journeys in his poem are away from light and order; the main similarity is the way the journey motif supports the political dimension of the two poems.

The manifold relationships among these various journeys prompt a cautious and diffident look at a second general motif, biblical typology, which is central for the *Commedia* and which may illuminate the *Dunciad* as well. To illustrate the way his poem should be interpreted, Dante outlines to Can Grande the figurative senses of the Exodus: "our redemption through Christ; . . . the turning of the soul from the sorrow and misery of sin to a state of grace; . . . the passage of the blessed soul from the slavery of this corruption to the freedom of eternal glory" (par. 7, p. 37). The technical names for these senses need not concern us here, but we should note that the first refers to the New Testament, the second to the present life of any Christian, and the third to the future life after death. In other terms, typology is the exegetical method of a philosophy of history according to which history does not just happen but is both guided and propelled toward a fulfillment by divine providence and energy. The individual is thus taken up into a dynamic process, two stages of which he can see in the Old and New Testaments.

Such a method of interpretation could, and did, lead to results far more grotesque than anything in the *Inferno* or the *Dunciad*, but it has one very important feature. As a method of composition, unlike the personification-allegory of the *Roman de la Rose*, *The Faerie Queene*, or *The Pilgrim's Progress*, it does not involve endowing an abstract quality like pride or chastity with a human form which will allow it to act. Nor, unlike the allegorical exegeses of Homer and Ovid or other methods, like Origen's, of reading scripture, does it extract a cosmological, moral, or theological proposition from a narrative text. Rather, it looks for analogies between concrete, historical actions and persons in the Old Testament and the New Testament, and then tries to relate the analogies to the lives of contemporary Christians.[16] One consequence of this method is that the Old Testament "type," such as the sacrifice of Isaac, does not have its full meaning until it is completed or fulfilled by the more important New Testament "anti-type," in this case the sacrifice of Jesus, and that neither event means much to the Christian until he has tried to conform his own life to it. Biblical events are thus both realities in themselves and signs of other realities.

It is easy to see how this perspective pulls together many of the aspects of the *Commedia* that we have already examined. It reinforces the analogy between Dante's poem and the Bible in that both are trying to conduct the reader into the proper typological relation to a series of texts. Dante's sinners are in hell because they have refused to play their proper part in the typological scheme of scripture. Its emphasis on relations between real events and

---

16. Erich Auerbach was the first to emphasize this aspect of biblical typology and to apply it to Dante; see his "Figura," *Scenes from the Drama of European Literature*, tr. R. Manheim, New York, 1959, pp. 11-76, 229-37. For a useful analysis of Auerbach's approach and the later contributions of Charles S. Singleton, Robert Hollander, and A. C. Charity, see Jean Pépin, *Dante et la tradition de l'allégorie*, Montreal and Paris, 1970, pp. 31-45. See also Elizabeth Salter, "Medieval Poetry and the Figural View of Reality," *Proceedings of the British Academy* 54, 1968, pp. 73-92, and Paul J. Korshin, "Figural Change and the Survival of Tradition in the Later Seventeenth Century," in *Studies in Change and Revolution: Aspects of English Intellectual History 1640-1800*, ed. Korshin, Menston, Yorkshire: Scolar Press, 1972, esp. pp. 118-20.

persons provides another justification for Dante's insistence on filling his poem with so much concrete historical detail. Dante's contemporaries had metaphorically extended typology beyond scripture in order to show that profane history was also under God's providence. Thus Aeneas could be called a "type" of St. Paul, because his voyage prepared the way for the spread of Christianity, and Dante is trying to continue Paul's work as well as he can. The attitudes that Dante expressed in the Ulysses episode and his final parting from Virgil at the top of the Mount of Purgatory become clearer when we see that Virgil's relation to Dante is very like that of an Old Testament type to its New Testament fulfillment.

Pope certainly knew about typology, though there is no specific record of what he thought about it. If not elsewhere, he would have encountered it in the religious polemics from the reign of James II that he read so assiduously in his youth. He saw it operating in Dryden's *Mac Flecknoe* and *Absalom and Achitophel*, and less explicitly but perhaps more imaginatively in Milton. He probably knew the rather idiosyncratic version of it expounded by his friend and editor William Warburton.[17] The way he made his career as a satirist and country gentleman into an *imitatio Horatii*, as Reuben Brower has felicitously put it, but made his own satires more pointed and Juvenalian than Horace's, is strongly reminiscent of Dante's relation to Virgil.

One justification for extending typology beyond its strict boundaries is that as a method of reading the Old Testament so as to relate it to the New, typology involves the same kind of critical activity as relating the sub-plot of *King Lear* to the main plot or the card-game to the rest of *The Rape of the Lock*, and, as Aristotle remarked, the ability to perceive analogies is one of the surest marks of genius. The main justification for looking at the *Dunciad* itself typologically, though, is the biblical history that underlies it. Along with other kinds of religious allusions and the events mentioned above (p. 292), the poem alludes with varying degrees of clarity to the creation, Noah's rainbow (2.173-74),

17. Pope read the proof-sheets of Warburton's voluminous *Divine Legation of Moses* (*Correspondence*, 4.341), but he may not have persevered to the very last chapter, which contains the discussion of typology.

Moses' view of the promised land ("Argument" to Book 3), Jesus among the doctors (1.203-4), the first Pentecost (1.8 — cf. *Acts* 2.17-18), and of course the apocalypse. It also embodies its own version of the overall typological pattern: Book 4 fulfills Book 3 as the New Testament fulfills the Old. But it is the "force inertly strong" of Dulness, not the providence and power of God, which controls this fulfillment. The biblical apocalypse is the end of history, but the beginning of a new kind of life; the apocalypse in the *Dunciad* is not a climax but a cosmic anticlimax. The effect of the typological perspective, I think, is to deepen the tragic implications of the mock-heroic aspect of the poem. The *Aeneid* and the other classics to which Pope alludes do not have the built-in drive toward the present and future that the Bible has, but the biblical context of the *Dunciad* is strong enough to encourage us to assimilate them to it. Thus it becomes tragic, not merely unfortunate, that Aeneas as well as Jesus should be "fulfilled" by Cibber, and similarly with all the other modern anti-types of classical types that swarm through the poem. From this point of view the action of the *Dunciad* is the thwarting of the divine plan for history. A typological perspective also shows more clearly the status of the dunces as signs of other realities beyond themselves, which is another way of saying that "the Poem was not made for these Authors, but these Authors for the Poem."

Such metaphors as "the *Dunciad* is Pope's *Inferno*," I would suggest, epitomize one method of comparative literature. To the extent that a study like this one is successful, the two terms under discussion will interact in such a way as to illuminate each other, as the two terms of a metaphor do. (In such interactions, the differences between the terms are of course as important as the similarities.) Our metaphor follows the traditional method of using the better-known term to elucidate the lesser-known, and, since it takes as one term an acknowledged masterpiece that Pope did not know, it implicitly claims for the *Dunciad* a kind of universality which other recent critics have defended in other ways. But it also has wider implications. A metaphorical assertion such as "Bossuet is an eagle" is primarily a statement about Bossuet, not about eagles, as our metaphor is primarily a statement about the *Dunciad*; but to say that Bossuet is an eagle directs our attention to those qualities of the eagle that make the comparison possible and perhaps makes us more keenly aware of them. In the same way I hope I have stimulated some thought about the *Inferno* and about Dante's religious and artistic outlook. In other words, our metaphor contains a subordinate assertion: the *Inferno* is also Dante's *Dunciad*.

William Kinsley